Children *of the* Doomed Voyage

Janet Menzies

WILEY

Published in 2005 by   John Wiley & Sons, Ltd, The Atrium, Southern Gate
Chichester, West Sussex, PO19 8SQ, England
Phone   (+44) 1243 779777

Email (for orders and customer service enquires): cs-books@wiley.co.uk
Visit our Home Page on www.wiley.co.uk or www.wiley.com

Other Wiley Editorial Offices

John Wiley & Sons, Inc. 111 River Street, Hoboken, NJ 07030, USA

Jossey-Bass, 989 Market Street, San Francisco, CA 94103-1741, USA

Wiley-VCH Verlag GmbH, Pappellaee 3, D-69469 Weinheim, Germany

John Wiley & Sons Australia, Ltd, 33 Park Road, Milton, Queensland, 4064, Australia

John Wiley & Sons (Asia) Pte Ltd, 2 Clementi Loop #02-01, Jin Xing Distripark, Singapore
129809

John Wiley & Sons Canada Ltd, 22 Worcester Road, Etobicoke, Ontario, Canada, M9W 1L1

Library of Congress Cataloging-in-Publication Data

(to follow)

British Library Cataloguing in Publication Data

A catalogue record for this book is available from the British Library

ISBN-13   978-0-470-01887-3 (HB)
ISBN-10   0-470-01887-9 (HB)

Typeset in $11\frac{1}{2}$/14pt Garamond by MCS Publishing Services Ltd, Salisbury, Wiltshire.
Printed and bound in Great Britain by T.J. International Ltd, Padstow, Cornwall.
This book is printed on acid-free paper responsibly manufactured from sustainable forestry in which
at least two trees are planted for each one used for paper production.

10 9 8 7 6 5 4 3 2 1

Please return / renew by date shown.
You can renew at:
norlink.norfolk.gov.uk
or by telephone: 0844 800 8006
Please have your library card & PIN ready.

NORFOLK LIBRARY
AND INFORMATION SERVICE

Children *of the* Doomed Voyage

Contents

For those *in* peril *on the* sea

The Second World War tragedy of the SS *City of Benares* remains to this day the worst ever sea disaster involving British children. More than half of all those on board the evacuee ship were lost after it was torpedoed by a German U-boat. Of 90 'seavacuee' children voyaging to safety in Canada, 77 died. This book tells the story of the survivors in their own words for the first time – but it is dedicated to the memory of the 258 people who did not survive.

CHAPTER ONE

Children
of the Blitz

From the top of Bess Walder's house in Kentish Town you could see a long way across the rooftops and streets of north London. Since the bombing raids, the view was even better. The familiar roofscape of tiles, chimney pots, gutters and garden walls was now gap-toothed. Brick dust rose and swirled in twisting eddies and then settled again, lying thick on random hills of rubble and masonry that spilled across pavements. Where half a terrace had gone, it looked like a giant doll's house with the front removed. Wallpapered walls, pictures still hanging and bedroom doors open – but with no bedroom, no floor, simply the drop of 20 feet or so onto a junk pile of brick, soaking carpet shreds and broken furniture.

Across the way from Bess's look-out spot was a house that had been hit at the very beginning of the bombings. Now it was laid bare, revealing different colours and patterns of wallpaper in the kitchen, the sitting room, the bedrooms and a baby's nursery. For a long time there was even a little green vase, miraculously unbroken, perched on the tiled mantelpiece of a bedroom fireplace that seemed stuck there in the middle of nothing. The vase must have been shaken off in the end, in some recent bombing, because it was no more to be seen. Instead the bombed-out site was beginning to be decorated by fireweed: bright purple-pink flowers of rosebay willow herb that had even grown through the remnants of a wardrobe in what was once the backyard.

But that morning in the late summer of 1940, Bess and her brother Louis weren't looking at the bomb sites. Instead 15-year-old Bess was concentratedly watching the gaps to see if she could get a glimpse of the postman as he began his round, two or three streets away. Yes, there he was, postbag and gas-mask carrier banging awkwardly together as he picked his way across broken paving slabs, a wad of letters already in his hand. He disappeared from Bess's sight for a while and then reappeared at the end of her street. Bess craned forward out of the window to get a better view, while Louis, who was 10 years old, tugged impatiently on her cardigan. And the postman was waving. He was definitely waving, and what he was waving was a large, brown manila envelope that Bess knew perfectly well would have On His Majesty's Service stamped on it.

'We just flung ourselves down the stairs and into the street,' remembers Bess, 'and we were almost tearing the envelope apart in our keenness to get hold of it. You see, every morning my brother and I would run up to the top of the house and look over the housetops across the bomb damage, to see if we could see the postman arriving. And I had made a bet with the postman. I said, "Look, if you've got a letter that says On His Majesty's Service and it's addressed to my mother and father, will you wave it at me as you come down the street?" and he said, "You wicked girl. I'm not supposed to do things like that."

'However, he did, and there he was, waving the letter. I took it in to my mother and she was busy cooking breakfast, so she just quickly stuffed it into her apron pocket. We were sitting down to breakfast as people did in those days, round the table, not on a breakfast bar, sitting at a big table on which there was toast, marmalade, a soup spoon for your porridge, and cornflakes if you like, and then followed by egg and bacon. Most doctors today would say, "Oh my God!" My mother had a big iron-brown teapot and that was the breakfast teapot into which tea went – not teabags, tea leaves – and then she had a silver strainer and she would pour the tea into the cup, so all the tea leaves got left in the tea strainer. I wonder how many people use that now? Anyway, she was in the process of making the tea when we said, "What did the letter say, Mum?" and she said, "Wait til' I've finished."

'Obviously we couldn't, so in the end she said, "Oh, all right. Yes, this is it, yes. You're going." Well, we exploded into laughter and we threw our hands up in the air and said "Hooray, hooray!" Looking at it now I think to myself, if I'd been my mother, I would have felt a bit put out about how easily we could leave her. But we weren't thinking about her, we were just thinking about us. She said, "Sit down and eat your breakfast." Which of course we didn't. So that was the beginning.'

It was the news Bess and Louis had been waiting for ever since their parents had applied for them to have places on the Government-run Children's Overseas Reception Board (CORB). This was the scheme launched in June of 1940 to evacuate children by sea to safe havens in the Commonwealth countries (then known as Dominions) of Canada and South Africa especially, and also possibly to the United States. In the Commonwealth countries, one of the first responses to the outbreak of Second World War had been for people to write home to family members still living in Britain and offer refuge to various young nephews, nieces and cousins. Those with relatives who had emigrated to the States received the same invitations, and at an official level, so did the British Government. As the threat of invasion grew, a formal plan was developed to take children aged under 16 from areas most at risk of bombing – especially London, Liverpool, Southampton and Newcastle – and evacuate several shiploads, with Canada as the main destination. The scheme was to be organised through the children's schools. Notes went home to parents, and when the CORB office officially opened on 20 June, there were already more than 3,000 parents queuing up to apply for their children to become 'seavacuees'.

At 15, Bess Walder was just young enough to qualify for the scheme, and the moment she heard about it, she made up her mind that she was going: 'Actually, for me the idea had really started a very long time ago, before the war ever broke out. I had a teacher called Miss Mitchell. She had taken a long summer holiday in Canada, and she came back to school after the holidays and explained to us girls where she'd been. She told us all the most wonderful stories about the Rockies and how those magnificent trains used to go through the forests and over the bridges of the lakes and through the mountains. I thought that must be heaven; if ever I wanted to go anywhere, I would like to go to Canada. Well, you can imagine, when I heard about this scheme for evacuating children to all these wonderful places, they were our Dominions – Canada, Australia, New Zealand, South Africa ... And there were people who were waiting to have us, who would welcome us into their homes and treat us as their own children, just for the war. Of course the word Canada lit me with a furious excitement, because I remembered Miss Mitchell and her tales of what a wonderful country it was.

'And then – almost magically – here was an opportunity for me, of all people, to go there. Well, that was too good to miss. I thought, that's for me. So I really set to work on my mother. I said all sorts of things. I said, "You know if you want me to go to school and be really clever – and not have to wait until all the schools start back in London again – why don't you let me go to Canada?" I was going on, "Look Mum, if you want me to grow up to be a really good, clever girl, send me to Canada, please." I was bribing her of course, and she knew it. She said, "Oh you are a wicked thing." But then she said, "I'll have to talk to your father." So they had a long conversation and in the end they decided that if it was possible, both I and my brother should go to Canada. My mother had friends there who said they would look after us. They were people that she could trust, so everything was set in motion, and eventually of course it led to us going on the CORB scheme.

'But to begin with we had a long wait. My mother and father had to sign a big paper to say that we would be acceptable to go, and that we were healthy and fit. And then of course we had to wait for a reply. Waiting for that reply was like having a tooth pulled.'

Up in Liverpool, Beth Cummings and her mother had been going through the same thought processes: 'It wasn't an easy decision to make. My mother was very worried about it. We both knew – by this time I was nearly 15 – and we both knew that the north Atlantic was a dangerous place. It was as simple as that. We mightn't have had television. We mightn't have had all the instant things we have in today's world, but we had newspapers and the radio, which gave us quite a lot of information. So we knew exactly what was going on in the Atlantic.'

And yet, in common with thousands of other families in Britain's urban areas and ports, they still wanted to go. Why was it that by that mid-summer of 1940, so many parents were willing to send their children across the north Atlantic, one of the most dangerous of all war zones? And why were the children themselves so desperate to go?

One of the main factors weighing with both parents and children was the Government's first abortive evacuation scheme to the countryside, which had begun nearly 12 months before. In the space of just three days at the end of August 1939, nearly one and a half million children under the age of 15 had been herded off to rural areas and assigned new homes. The evacuation was insensitively code-named Operation Pied Piper – and it turned out to be about as popular as the original Pied Piper of Hamelin's activities.

Beth Cummings explains: 'Well, in theory the mass evacuation was going to work, but in practice it simply couldn't. I don't think it would ever have been very satisfactory. This was partly because the war hadn't really arrived, and although we had blackouts and air-raid warnings, all we were thinking was that it wasn't nice to be dragged from home when we didn't have to be. And also, really, when you think about it, you open your door to a billeting officer and he presents you with two strange girls and you're going to have to look after them – feed them and more or less keep an eye on them – all for eight shillings each a week. It wasn't everybody's cup of tea, you know. How welcome you were was a bit chancy really. It depended on the people you were billeted with. They all varied. My friend Thelma and I were quite lucky, but some of us were billeted with rather grumpy old couples. It was just one of those things – some didn't quite understand young people, and so it wasn't that easy.

'It happened three days before the war broke out. My brother Jeff, who was in the Territorial Army, was called up and I was evacuated with my school to Chester. Chester of all places – it is only 17 miles from Liverpool. But at that time the Liverpool secondary schools were evacuated all together with their teachers to places in Cheshire, North Wales and Shropshire. It was all very odd really because they went by what school you were at, so we ended up separated from our local friends who lived near us but who happened to be at a different school. We only had our school friends.

'The day we were evacuated we went from Liverpool Central Station, which doesn't exist now. There we all were with our labels on, and all we knew was the school was being evacuated. Our mothers all came to see us off. My mother was very sensible. She wasn't crying or anything. She was just worried, that was the only thing. Then for some reason it took us all day to get to Chester, and why I honestly don't know. It was quite weird really. But when we eventually arrived in Chester we were met by the Boy Scouts with bars of chocolate and crisps in paper carrier bags. Then we were allocated to different houses, two each to a house. Thelma and I were put in Sealand Road – and the odd thing is that it wasn't far at all from Sealand Aerodrome, which did seem to defeat the purpose a bit. But we were billeted with a very nice couple. Our school was put in with Queen's School, Chester, which meant that we only had half a day teaching. We had our lessons in the afternoon, and the Queen's School girls had theirs in the morning. Then the rest of the time we would be busy playing games – hockey and so on – and so it wasn't really very satisfactory. I don't really think we were altogether welcomed.

'But the evacuation was meant to be a voluntary thing. You didn't have to go, though of course, if your school went, most of the children went with their schools. But all the same quite a lot of the children actually left school and stayed on at home in Liverpool, going to other schools that hadn't been evacuated. As I said, in theory the evacuation sounded a wonderful idea, but in practice it just didn't work. Later on what used to happen was that we would dive into General Station in Chester and get a train home for the weekend! We had had enough of it really, and we'd go home for the weekend and come back on the Monday.

'The train started out in Holyhead and went through to Liverpool Lime Street via Chester, so we'd meet the boys who'd been evacuated up to Holyhead and who were on their way back to Liverpool too. We weren't supposed to do this but we did it! It was a form of playing truant really, and we loved that bit – and actually our mothers didn't really mind either. The war hadn't arrived, you see. There was nothing going on, so we all thought it was a bit of a waste of time to be perfectly honest. In the end we were all very relieved to get home again that Christmas.'

Down in London, Bess Walder had been equally unimpressed with her evacuation experience: 'My school was Parliament Hill Girls' Grammar School. It was thought to be in direct line of fire, because a lot of the girls there came from Jewish families – and they were frightened. Many of their parents had asked, "When can our girls move away from London?" Also by this time raids had begun. Not huge ones, but there had been the odd bomb dropped. So when we were all told that we could evacuate to a school that had kindly offered its premises, the parents were pleased. My mother thought it was a great idea.

'We didn't know where we were going at first, then we discovered it was St Albans. In those days St Albans was way outside London. So we all got onto a bus – I think they were Green Line buses – and shot off with some luggage away to St Albans. My family didn't do tearful farewells, it wasn't Dad's style. He used to clap us on the shoulder and say "come on". That's how we were. And my mother said, "Be a good girl. Don't do anything naughty." And off I went.

'We congregated in the girls' grammar school hall, and we were told that there was a list of people who would be willing to take us.

We would be taken to one of the houses on the list. If the lady of the household liked the look of us, we would stay with her for the war. And lo and behold, I was whisked off to a very nice family called Stevenson. The father was a big, hefty bloke – a builder – and the mother was dainty and very sweet. She had two quite grown-up daughters, well, older than I was. They were really rather spoilt, because they had all sorts of people looking after them, doing odd jobs for them. I suppose you would call them servants. And I came from a family that didn't have anybody doing jobs for us; we all did them for ourselves.

'So I wasn't used to servants. We all did our own thing at home. If we wanted a bed made, either we did it ourselves or my mother did it, but nobody else would be doing it, and certainly not my Pa! It took a bit of getting used to. So I made my own bed quite cheerfully. I would wash up. I would feed the cat, I would even clean up after the cat. And these were absolutely unheard-of things in the Stevenson household. When my teacher came round to find out how I was getting on, Mrs Stevenson said, "She does all sorts of things for herself", which she thought was absolutely crazy. So I came out of one environment into another and it took a bit of getting used to.

'But they were very kind and I had access to their beautiful rooms, which I'd never had before. At home we didn't have anything that was luxurious. And there was a beautiful garden. So I suppose I had a very happy time. St Albans was a lovely town, and we had access to the lovely fields around St Albans. Really, we had a very pleasant environment to live in – but I didn't want to leave London. I liked London. I liked the noise, I liked the sound of trams, and St Albans didn't have trams.

'One day I just thought, oh I want to go – I'm fed up with this. As it was I used to go home every weekend and take my washing – and that was something else they disapproved of, you see, because they had the maid to do it and I didn't want the maid to do it! So every weekend I used to trundle home, on this Green Line bus, and my mother would do the washing for me and send me back. Really, the whole point was lost because there were no air raids. It was this phoney war. It was hardly conducive to leaving your home behind. So I came away from St Albans, back to my home and, I thought, to school – but of course, as my mother had told me, the schools had all closed down.

'There was a bit of a row because I wanted to come home and didn't care whether there was a school for me or not. But that made things very difficult. Both my mother and my father were very keen on education, and they wanted their girl to have the very best education she could find under the circumstances. But I had made up my mind that I didn't want to stay in St Albans any longer. I didn't like the idea of the two schools sharing. In any case Louis, my younger brother, was still at home. So I told my mother, "I'm coming home." She said, "You can't come home." I said, "I can." She said, "I shall go and visit your teachers." I said, "I don't care." And my father said, "Oh, let her come home if she wants to. You can teach her just as well as some of those teachers I know." That was when my mother gave in and said, "Well, if she's made up her mind to stay, there's nothing I can do." Mother was a very clever woman and she did have a degree, which was quite special for a woman in 1940. So that was that.

'Then I started having great fun because the school next door to where we lived had been turned into an auxiliary fire service station. In place of the playground things that used to go on there, there were taxi drivers and their taxis, who'd offered to give their services to the auxiliary fire service to pull their pumps. And very successful they were. They were also some very interesting things for me as a girl growing up. I used to go into the big hall where the men had their lunches and I used to play the piano for them. I played all the favourite songs, and I became a star turn. And there was this nice young man that I liked very much, and we had quite interesting conversations, which my father disapproved of strongly.'

The evacuation experiences of Beth and Bess were typical of those happening all over the country, so it was natural for parents to begin looking for their own solutions to the problem of how to protect their children without making the whole family utterly miserable. For those with relatives who had already emigrated to the Commonwealth countries, it seemed logical to send the children to family members across the Atlantic. When Beth Cummings came back from her abortive evacuation to Chester, it wasn't surprising that her mother began to think of their cousins in Canada. Beth remembers: 'My mother had just then received a letter from an aunt in Canada, saying would she like to send me over there for the duration of the war. The Canadians were very, very concerned about our welfare. Many Canadians had emigrated there after the First World War, and so they had plenty of relatives and friends in this country. Everybody was all doing the same thing – offering their relatives and their friends to send their children to Canada to them until the war was over.

'But we all knew what was going on in the north Atlantic, so this was one of the problems for my mother, and then, as she was thinking about it, the Government brought out a scheme called the Children's Overseas Reception Board. This scheme meant that you could send children to the Dominions overseas. They could go to Canada, South Africa, even Australia or New Zealand, and in some cases to the United States. The idea was they could go to relatives or friends who would sponsor them as foster parents. Well, this seemed to make my mother feel it must be the right thing to do. If the Government have brought a scheme out it must be right, it must be correct. So she applied for me to go – and in fact she even decided to try and book a passage with the Canadian Pacific steamships in case I was rejected from the CORB scheme.'

Bess Walder also noticed that her mother too felt this Government-organised scheme would offer extra security: 'I think one of the things that helped my mother was that it was planned that the Royal Navy would be protecting us en route to Canada,' she recalls. By the mid-summer of 1940 an additional factor heavy on parents' minds was the increased severity of the bombing raids, not only in London but in the various northern dock cities like Liverpool and Newcastle. In Liverpool, Beth Cummings remembers: 'The scheme really got going round the end of July 1940 and by that time we were getting very bad air raids. That swayed my mother to realise that she had made the right decision. We all thought she had, because it was very frightening. During August the raids really got very, very bad. At that time I think most mothers were worried about their children. I think that was the main thing, they were worried and a little bit frightened about what might happen to their children.'

But not all those earmarked for the CORB scheme were like Bess and Beth, children from close families whose mothers only reluctantly let them go in the face of the even greater dangers at home. Unhappy families don't miraculously become normal just because there is a war on. When the stepmother of Kenneth Sparks, from Wembley in north-west London, heard about the CORB scheme and realised that her relatives already living in Canada would make Kenneth eligible for it, she seized the opportunity. With the Government's blessing, she finally had a chance to get her stepson out of her way, and it would probably be best for the boy in any case.

Kenneth admits: 'I think that was probably a godsend for her, that Canadian scheme. Yeah, I'm sure it was. Any scheme where I could be got out of the way was a good scheme – but to go to Canada meant I might not be back for a long time, and that would mean she could let my room out. We were not a loving family whatsoever. My stepmother was not particularly fond of children. Not only did she make my life a misery, but she wasn't even that loving to her own children. I mean, she did bring me up – fed me, give her her due, and clothed me – which I suppose in those days was something. Pre-war times were difficult because Dad was out of work quite a bit. My stepmother seemed not to want children around at all – I couldn't have any friends in the house to play with, that was never allowed.

'At the time of the CORB scheme I think they were already trying one way or another to get me to leave home so that they could use the room for my stepsister to live in. I'm not sure how aware I was of it at the time, because in those days it was different from now – you were a child and you did as you were told, and if you didn't do as you were told you got a good hiding. And, you know, in some ways I was no worse off than a lot of other children whose fathers were out of work. In fact, if you go by central London, I was better off than a lot. At least I'd got somewhere to live and I was getting food.

'All the same, I think my stepmother was awfully glad to see me go because it meant she'd got that annexe to put my stepsister in, so she could then let a room out to make more money. Me going gave her that extra space and, of course, the extra money. I've got a vague idea in a way that money was one of her gods, perhaps because of not having had a lot, so I imagine that she was glad of anything she could make. I don't suppose she really wanted me to come back. I think she hoped I would stay in Canada permanently, because when I eventually came back, she'd got a lodger in. I think she would have really liked to have been able to let the room long term, but I spoilt all their plans 'cos I kept coming back! Mind you, they succeeded one way or another because later, after I went into the Navy, I hadn't been gone very long and she had let the room out within a matter of a few weeks.'

A few miles away from Kenneth, in Southall, the Baker family had a very different approach to the CORB evacuation scheme. The Bakers had applied for places for both their two sons, Bobby, who was nearly 13, and his younger brother John, aged 7. Like most of the families involved in the scheme the Bakers had links to Canada, as John explains: 'We had aunts and uncles who had moved to Canada, so I think that's why Bobby and I got places. I suppose the first that I knew about it was that it was put to us as being a holiday. We were going to go and see cousins and aunts and uncles that lived in Canada, probably for the duration of the war. But my parents wouldn't have kept anything from us. They were very truthful in all in their dealings with us. I'm sure they were very apprehensive about letting us go. It must have been a huge persuasion by the family as whole for them to say well, okay, they will be all right going to family – because it was my mother's sister who was in Canada, so we weren't going to just anybody. I think that made them feel that we would be all right once we got there. And of course I know they would have said to Bobby that I needed to be looked after because I was the younger one, and it was his responsibility to look after me, which he did very well, because I'm here to tell the tale.'

Though John and Bobby were no nicer to each other than most young brothers, the family was a close one. John remembers a typical incident: 'We were in Townsend Road – our house, 90 Townsend Road, Southall. We had what we called the scullery out at the back. It had a stone floor, and in it was the copper, where we boiled the water to put the clothes in to wash, and then you would put them through the mangle and all the rest of it. And we used to have baths out there as well. We had this big bath – a galvanised bath – and the two of us boys were there waiting for a bath. Mum was getting things ready, and obviously tired, but Bobby was playing up and being very naughty. So Mum whacked him on the shoulder with a hairbrush – broke the hairbrush. Bobby came out in floods of tears, I went and rushed in to help Bobby. Mum was so distraught at having hit Bobby and hurt him that she was in tears too and somehow we stepped on the edge of the bath, which all tipped over. There we were, all sat in the middle of the floor of the scullery crying our eyes out, soaked with water all over the place. That was a memory that I have of Bobby, bless him.'

Another loving family going through agonies over the decision to send their sons on the scheme were the Capels in Hanworth, Middlesex, not far from where Heathrow Airport now stands. Derek Capel, then aged 12, remembers: 'It was hard because we were a very close-knit family. But it was 1940, Dunkirk had just happened. We had no troops, the Germans were lining up invasion barges. That was the news – invasion and everything like that. And my family in the past had German Jewish connections. My mother realised what was happening to anybody with a Jewish link in Germany, that they just literally threw 'em out. I don't think at that time there was so much news of concentration camps in the way we finally found out. But all the same I know my mother was worried, so when the opportunity came for my brother and myself to go to Canada, my parents put in an application. It took them a lot of heartache – a lot of thought, a lot of soul-searching. But they did it in the end and at that time they didn't regret it, I don't think, because we were going to be safe. To their eyes, at least some of the family were going to be safe. My baby sister was only two, far too young to go, so they decided to stick it out with her there and just the two of us, Alan and me, we went.'

Fred Steels, then aged 11 and living in Eastleigh, near Southampton, sums up the parents' dilemma: 'Mum was terribly undecided, but I think in the end she thought it was the lesser of two evils. You go over there and have a chance of safety for the war, or stay here and take the chance of being bombed, killed or whatever, you know. So she did decide to let me go, though there were quite a few tears, I will admit. I was over the moon though, I thought it would be a brilliant idea. But my Mum was always a bit superstitious about the sea, 'cos of us living at a seafaring port, with family in the Navy and so on. And then you know, your Mum realises that you're going and she doesn't know when you're gonna come back, if you're ever gonna come back. We did have a rather tearful parting and she kept hanging on to me. It was like trying to get away from an octopus. But eventually she realised that I did want to go and I think she knew she had to let go. My Dad was a bit more staid, but even he had a few tears in his eyes I think. But as for me, I think I was more excited with going than anything else. I couldn't wait to get there.'

Fred's attitude was pretty much the norm among the children on the CORB scheme, nearly all of whom thought the evacuation overseas was the adventure of a lifetime. John Baker says: 'It was put that it was going to go for a holiday and, well, holidays are always fun. In those days also holidays weren't something you did, so going on holiday was an adventure in any case.'

Adding to the excitement for the children was the general air of secrecy and mystery about the whole seavacuation operation. For Beth Cummings it was the official documents – arriving in the big, brown envelope On His Majesty's Service – that added a lot to the adventure: 'When it eventually arrived, the letter itself was rather interesting. There was a lot in it that sounded very dramatic. It said things like they didn't know when a ship would be available and that it would be unpredictable. But then there was a bit about how any ship taking children overseas to Canada or to any of the other Dominions would be in a convoy escorted by the Royal Navy — that is, it would have the support and protection of no less than the Royal Navy. And in addition, there was this section saying you must not tell your neighbours that your daughter is going, or your friends. This must be something you keep to yourself and to your close family. Your daughter must not tell her friends or her school friends that she's going. Oh it was terribly secret, and rather — well you know, by the standards of a 14-year-old — it was intriguing!

'Though actually, I think it was only such a big mystery simply because of the need to keep all movement of shipping secret from possible spies. But all that makes you feel very important. It was such an adventure, and I thought, this is just the job. I was very, very excited. It didn't really bother me too much about the dangers of the Atlantic. All we teenagers at that time were rather taken with the armed forces, and there was a bit of "Ooh, it's the Royal Navy" — all this sort of thing. It all seemed a bit romantic in those days. So obviously that was what I was set on. I didn't think about — and this is sad really — I didn't think how sad my Mum would feel. She must have felt it terribly, me leaving her, because since my father had died the two of us were great friends, great chums.

'The other really interesting thing in this letter was this list of things I should take. I was allowed a small suitcase — one that wasn't too big for me to carry myself — a small haversack and a gas mask, of course. Also there was a list of all the things to go in the case — it was quite detailed. To this day I've got the original list and you can see where my mother's ticked off the things as she got them. And this was all to be ready, so that it could be available at very short notice.'

So everything was got ready for Beth up in Liverpool. But down in London, at Bess Walder's home, the long-awaited letter and its contents caused predictable ructions in her extrovert and often outspoken household. Bess confesses: 'Well, of course, when the letter finally came, then there was an argument as to what we should take with us! My father had done quite a bit of travelling in the past, and upstairs in our loft there were two cabin trunks that had belonged to my father when he was in his travelling days. They were covered with all sorts of exotic labels, which had always fascinated me, and I thought now's the chance, I'm going to get a maple leaf on mine. So when we first knew we were going on the scheme, these old things were taken down, not without problems because the loft was a bit narrow, and my father wasn't good on ladders. Anyway, eventually we got them downstairs and then we chose which one we wanted. Naturally my little brother claimed the big one, because he wanted to take his Hornby train set with him and it had to go in its entirety or he would not go. That was a threat not to be taken lightly, so I said, "Okay, I don't need the big one" and ended up with the little one on the grounds that all my clothes were small and sort of soft – and there was nothing hard like railway engines inside!

'We had received a list of clothes to be taken on the voyage by the evacuees. Along with things like towels, the girls' list included a sewing kit, which I hadn't got – and my brother's list had no sign of a sewing kit whatsoever. I said to my mother, "Why don't the boys have sewing kits?" And she said, "Oh, that's because the girls are all going to sew for them." I was a bit cross about that.

'But we went on packing and my mother looked at the green dressing gown that I wanted to take and said, "No, you can't take that, it's disgusting." Well, this was a particular thick, heavy green dressing gown that had passed down through various female members of the family over several generations. It was Jaeger. And as you know, once upon a time anyway, Jaeger clothes never wore out. But my mother went out, and with her precious clothing coupons (which we all had in those days) she bought me a very nice, very silky dressing gown and said, "Now dear, this is for you." Well, Dear said "Don't want it, I want my green dressing gown, it's got big pockets in and I like it and it's warm and I'm going to a cold country." What an ungrateful, ungrateful girl I was! Mum just shrugged her shoulders and said, "All right." What happened to the silk dressing gown, I don't know, but the green dressing gown got packed, with all the other kit – and who would have known how important it was going to be!'

Bess and Louis went ahead with filling up the trunks with things they considered to be the bare essentials: favourite books, the train set, clothes and so on, only to discover that they would have to re-pack with barely anything at all. Bess remembers: 'Another letter came saying because of the space available on board, it would be necessary for all the children to have reduced luggage. We would be provided with adequate clothing when we arrived, so there would be no need to take big supplies of clothes. Therefore, it said, none of the children will need huge cases, in fact they can use attaché cases. And they actually gave the sizes. I can't remember what the sizes were now, but that was what we had to have – so of course my brother went berserk because of fitting his Hornby train set in.'

Not owning a Hornby train set, Kenneth Sparks over in Wembley was not facing the same packing dilemmas as Louis Walder, but his imagination was fired by the prospect of the sea voyage: 'I was so excited. To be going away, especially on a boat, was the most exciting idea. I didn't at all know what to expect when I got there. I had a small suitcase with a spare set of clothes in, and of course you had your little gas-mask box. And a label tied to my lapel with my name on. My father didn't see me off because he was at work. My stepmother took me as far as Euston station on the underground from Wembley. They had two lots of railway lines at Wembley, but one was the normal underground and the other was electric trains that went direct to Euston. So she took me there, waved me goodbye and that was it, I was there with all the other people that were going to catch the train up to Liverpool.

'It was all a little bit frightening in a way 'cos I was still quite youngish. But on the other hand it was also something I'd been looking forward to, and I was lucky in as much as one of my friends was with me, from Wembley, and there was a little group of us and we were all chattering to each other.'

For Beth Cummings, already living in Liverpool, there was no lengthy journey to get to the ship, so her notice that she would be travelling came at the last minute: 'It wasn't until Monday the 9th of September that my mother was told that a lady would call for me the next morning at 11 o'clock and that I must have everything ready to go with her immediately. There was no mention of where, or what was happening or anything. Anyway, the next morning this lady called, and it was just a question of a quick hug and a kiss for my mother and off I went down the road, in my school uniform. The lady carried my case for me and we went down to the bottom of the road. We turned right at the bottom and I waved to my mother just like I always did if I was going to school, and away we walked.'

A lot of the seavacuees describe the actual moment of parting from their families as coming rather suddenly after the long build-up of all the preparations. Some found it almost an anti-climax finally to be setting out on their journey. Derek Capel remembers: 'My father had to go to work as normal because he was an engine driver. So he just said cheerio to Alan and me before he went on to work about five o'clock in the morning. Then my mother came with us by train across London and eventually we got a taxi to the station. My mother gave us a big cuddle, and before we could do anything else, someone just took hold of us and we were gone. And so we found ourselves alone. I hung on to me brother and we finished up in this railway carriage with an older woman sitting with us, an escort I suppose. And off we went. We didn't know where we were going or anything like that. As we went along gradually the train blacked out. We still didn't know where we were going until we finished up in Liverpool.'

And so from all over the country, the seavacuee children converged on Liverpool. There were 90 of them, with ages ranging from 4 to 15, and they had no idea what they were letting themselves in for.

CHAPTER TWO

Dodging
Bombs

N ot all the children who eventually set sail from Liverpool
on the voyage to Canada were seavacuees. There were a few
private fee-paying passengers who had booked a passage
on board the seavacuee ship, the SS *City of Benares*. Most of these
were either VIPs on Government-related business or émigrés
continuing their harrowing flight from Nazi-occupied Europe to
the safety of the Americas. But there was also a handful of mothers
taking their children to relatives in Canada, leaving husbands
behind to continue the war effort.

Among these was American citizen Florence Croasdaile, 38,
whose British husband was a prisoner of war in Germany. For
her there was little point in staying in England, so she was on her
way back home to her mother, along with her two children
Patricia, 9, and Lawrence, who was only 2. Alice Bulmer from
Wallasey was travelling to Canada with her 14-year-old daughter
Pat. Letitia Quinton, 41, whose English naval officer husband had
died, was returning to her native Canada with her son, Anthony,
later to become Lord Quinton. Also boarding the *Benares* at
Liverpool were the Choat family. Frank Choat was an Australian
who had been severely wounded at Gallipoli, and was now taking
his wife Sylvia and their three children back to his homeland. Colin
Ryder Richardson, 11, was travelling alone on his way to stay with
family friends in the States.

The most noticeable of the children travelling privately were the Bechs. Their mother, Marguerite, was on her way to Canada to spend the war with old family connections, leaving her Danish husband back in England — he was the managing director of the Royal Danish Porcelain Company. Marguerite had her three children with her: Barbara, 14, Sonia, 11, and 9-year-old Derek. Barbara remembers how the children formed up into a little gang: 'Colin Ryder Richardson tagged along with us because he and Sonia were pretty much the same age and he didn't really have anyone with him. Then there was Anthony, who I think must have been 16. The other children were pretty young, so it was natural for us to club together. Sonia and Colin got along particularly well, so we pretty soon made firm friends.'

The Bech family hadn't had the same luggage restrictions imposed on them as the seavacuee children, so for them packing was a rather more enjoyable process — though no less complicated, as Derek explains: 'We packed up all our treasures. I had all these souvenirs of the Battle of Britain in a suitcase and I had my toys. I had some very nice German cars that were my pride and joy, and those went in the suitcase. Sonia had a china doll which was her favourite and that went too. We took all this with us because we were going away to a new home, we didn't know for how long, so we didn't want to leave anything behind. I had all these little, sort of war mementos which I thought would be interesting for the people over in Canada to look at. They were just little things, like spent machine-gun bullets. And I remember I had a sort of rack which was actually a machine gun mounting — mind you, that was quite a big one so I might have had to leave that behind. But I had bits of bomb shrapnel. I also had the clips from machine-gun belts, those are the bits that fall off as the bullets fire. Oh, and I had some bits of canvas with that swastika thing on them, which had come from a Messerschmidt 109, or so I told people. But people were actually interested in these things. Anyway, they all went in a suitcase and off we went to Liverpool to catch the boat.

'We had to go by train from Bognor to Victoria, because we were living in Sussex at the time. Then we had to go across London by taxi to go to, I think it was either King's Cross or Euston. I remember being in the taxi and trying to get down Baker Street and we kept being diverted through other roads because a whole lot of the buildings had been bombed the previous night and the roads were blocked.'

His older sister, Barbara, remembers the whole period as being a time of great uncertainty: 'We really didn't know quite what was going to happen from day to day. Down on the Sussex coast where we lived they were having dog fights over our heads and bombers crashing on the beach. So the whole idea of going to Canada just seemed like one more thing. You know, when it's such a total upheaval you can hardly take it in. By then really one's whole world had collapsed round one anyhow. So in a way there was no lifestyle to be leaving behind you – that had all disappeared during the course of the year from war breaking out to us leaving for Canada.'

For Marguerite Bech there was a particularly compelling reason to take the major step of leaving the country. Her younger daughter, Sonia, explains: 'My mother had experienced Zeppelin raids in the First World War and they'd completely scared her stiff. So when we started having air raids again, she was really much more frightened than we were. I have to admit we children just assumed they would never want to bomb a little place like Bognor. Yes, the big bombers were going over our heads, but they were going to find London and Birmingham and Liverpool. Even at the age of 11 I knew that they wouldn't be stopping for us.'

But though her children couldn't imagine what the future of the war would hold for Britain, Marguerite knew full well that things were only likely to get worse, and so the family found themselves on their way to Liverpool. Derek says: 'We caught the train from Platform 13 – which obviously wasn't significant at the time, but I couldn't forget it now. We were booked in at a hotel – the Adelphi Hotel in Liverpool – for the night before we boarded the ship. At that stage we didn't know when it was due to sail, I don't think we had even been told the name of the ship. So we had a pretty straightforward train journey and we arrived at the Adelphi, and we were shown to our rooms – two beautiful rooms, because the Adelphi was a nice hotel.'

His sisters, sharing a suite, were equally impressed by the luxurious Adelphi, which was at the time Liverpool's premier hotel. Sonia was particularly struck by having more than just one room: 'We had an en-suite bathroom which we'd never seen in our lives before. And the rooms were beautiful, the size, and a sitting room with a chaise longue! But we had just got into our lovely beds when we were told to go down to the Turkish baths in the basement of the hotel where we had to sleep for the night because there was an air raid coming – so we didn't see much of that beautiful suite!'

Derek says: 'Yes, we had just gone to bed and there was a knock at the door, "Madam, the air-raid siren has sounded, would you please go down to the basement." And so we all had to pack up and go down to the basement of the hotel which was the old Turkish baths. And we slept the night on wooden benches and not in our luxurious rooms.'

Barbara remembers how bizarre it felt to be sitting in the tiled mosaic surroundings of a Turkish *hammam* while Liverpool was pounded by bombs: 'Well, I suppose it was as good as an air-raid shelter, but it wasn't as nice as our lovely rooms. We sat there with all the bangs and crashes outside. At least we were well down out of the way in the basement. It was terribly noisy, but fortunately I don't think any bombs fell very near us. By dawn we went back up and had a little sleep – but only a couple of hours, because then it was time to get a quick breakfast and leave for the docks.'

Surprisingly the children don't remember their mother, Marguerite, being particularly scared that night, despite her fear of bombing. Sonia thinks it was because the family were all preoccupied with the following day's journey: 'I think by this stage we were all so hyped up to get onto this boat that we just didn't focus on the air raid. My mother had so much on her mind – the three of us to think about, all our luggage, and all the things she had to organise on her own without my father to help. At that time too, bombing was becoming pretty standard. There was a raid every night in Liverpool, it was very, very bad.'

The bombing on the night of 11 September − the eve of the planned sailing of the *Benares* − was one of the worst night's bombings for Liverpool. Yet the children seem to have taken it quite matter-of-factly. Derek agrees: 'You just took it as a matter of course in those days. I mean, fear was with you all the time then − whether you were in the Turkish bath or walking down the street, I suppose you were always conscious that something could happen, so you didn't think any more than that of it.'

By that September, with the Battle of Britain being waged over the Bechs' heads down on the south coast and German bombing raids all over the country, Britain's youngsters had become a tough and resilient band. And children who lived in central London, like Colin Ryder Richardson, were pretty much 'Blitz kids' by this stage. When the very first air-raid warning sounded, Colin, who lived in St John's Wood, London, was down in Lingfield, Surrey, spending the day with his grandfather: 'We were digging an air-raid shelter in my grandfather's garden. We'd heard on, I think it must have been the 11 o'clock news, that war had been declared, and in no time at all the first air-raid siren went off − so we jumped into the half-dug air-raid shelter!

'It's amusing to remember it now, but then we hadn't a clue as to what was going to happen. We thought about poison gas and all sorts of frightful things. I remember digging in deep, heavy clay to get this air-raid shelter built and us taking refuge in it thinking all the bombers were already coming over. But that time it was a false alarm. Then, when the real thing began in London, you would hear the aeroplanes coming. They had what are called desynchronised engines to confuse the anti-aircraft batteries. So you would hear this whirr, gap, whirr, gap, whirr, which was somehow very frightening.

'We lived in St John's Wood, and they had anti-aircraft guns on Primrose Hill, which was very near. Whenever the guns went off the tiles came off our roof − and the blast, it's incredible. The air-raid sirens would usually happen in the night. So we would go down to the air-raid shelter next door. It was a horrible place to go, like a tomb, and running with water. You jumped up on the bed and tried to keep yourself as dry as possible. Then the all-clear would sound and you'd get back into bed, and almost immediately the sirens would go a second time. So you ended up thinking you might as well stay the night down in the shelter – at least my parents did – or otherwise you were up and down all the time. It got to the point where you would hear the siren and then you think well, is this a real raid? Is it going to be near us, or is it somebody else is getting it?

'And then you hear planes and you think, well, maybe they're our boys or maybe it's the bombers. Then the whole thing sort of gets worse and worse, and if you're in the area where they're actually dropping the bombs – and St Johns Wood was pretty much in the thick of it – suddenly all mayhem breaks lose. Guns start firing, bombs start dropping. You just don't know what to think or say or do, or which way to go. You've taken the best cover you can, and you just pray and hope that it's going to go away. It certainly isn't very good for your nerves.

'While the raids were on you would see men with tin hats all over the place. They'd be standing at barriers, saying "unexploded bomb", which usually wasn't true. The problem was that a lot of the time, if there was a bomb crater they didn't necessarily know whether there was a live bomb still in it or not. And again there were incendiaries dropping here, there and everywhere. Of course you were always worried that they were landing on the roof of your house – there could be one in the attic and you wouldn't know. We had baths full of water and buckets and sand and stirrup pumps and everything else. You'd only to look out of the window to see roads burning where the tarmac caught fire when an incendiary had landed. My parents were both air-raid wardens, they would be helping control crowds and doing whatever was necessary for a warden to do at that time.

'Quite often if we felt we were in the middle of a series of bad raids we would go to the nearest underground, which was St John's Wood tube station, and take refuge in there. It was relatively safe because you're quite deep underground. But you could never be sure that bombs wouldn't come down the escalator well, or even hit the top level of the station and bury you. The underground was a dirty place, and there were always masses of people on the platforms. You watched the last few trains coming in and there was a white line on the platform and you mustn't put your bedding anywhere beyond the white line, so that people could get off the trains. Then, when the last train had been through, sometimes you even slept between the tracks. Later they started putting up steel bunks, which made things a little more comfortable. But there were people of all ages and all backgrounds down there, a total mix. Some people were hysterical and causing problems. Other people would be trying to have parties – playing accordions or whatever.

'The wardens tried to get everybody relatively quiet by 11 o'clock at night so you could have a chance to sleep. But when the raids were on you couldn't really sleep. If you were at home and the siren went, your decision was whether to get out of bed or stay in bed. But if you stayed, you'd be awake listening for the anti-aircraft guns opening up. When they got going and the bombs started falling, that was your cue to shift. Eventually a bomb dropped very near our house – there was earth covering everything, clay everywhere, and shrapnel. The following day I went back to school at Charterhouse, but I ended up in the school sickbay. I couldn't eat anything, then I turned yellow – I'd got jaundice. I think it was pretty clear to my parents that it was a result of the shock of the bombing.'

At the same time as Colin was enduring nightly bombing in the heart of London, the Bechs down in Sussex were equally in the thick of the war – but it was another aspect of the war, and for the Bechs a very different, almost surreal experience. In London, bombs actually fell to earth. Those on the ground were as much at risk of death as the British and German pilots themselves – the Blitz was in no way a spectator sport. But the Battle of Britain was a different matter. Those living on the south coast at the time have vivid memories of watching the war in the air, which took place over their heads that hot Indian summer of 1940. Lying sunbathing on their backs on the short turf of the South Downs, Sonia and Derek Bech could watch the deadly ballet of fighter planes taking place hundreds of feet above them.

Derek remembers: 'In Sussex the Battle of Britain was all around us. Selsea Peninsula had three of the four front-line fighter stations – of which Tangmere is probably the best known. As a 9-year-old boy I was constantly running out of doors when I heard a plane go over. Of course I was in the spotting club, and I knew all the German planes. They used to come low. They came in across the coast and we used to hear the rattle of machine-gun fire. Well, many of these planes were shot down and you're out watching, you had a front-line view. I used to see where they were crashing and I got on my bicycle and pedalled away like anything – many a time I was one of the first to arrive on these crash sites. I saw one horrible sight just down by Pagham Harbour. There was a German bomber that had crash-landed and caught fire and I remember seeing the crew. I don't know whether they were dead or not, but they were all ... their bodies were burning. All around the plane was all in an awful mess with the debris. I can't remember any more detail about it, but my mother said I was white as a sheet when I came home. I'd never seen a dead body before then and I suppose it was my first contact with death.

'But I still went out to see these crash sites. One day I saw two Spitfires – they were coming out of a low cloud base, and one cut the other one in two. I went to the crash – I was pretty well the first on the scene – and the head of one of the pilots had been decapitated, sliced off. What can you do? You just accepted it and that was it. Then somebody arrived with a tarpaulin and covered up the body. Another time they were bombing Tangmere and we had a Junkers 87, the old Stuka, came down. I have a photograph of myself looking at the wreck. I had many souvenirs off that plane. There was one day when I actually brought home a bomb – much to the surprise of my mother. She said, "Where did you get that?" I'd just found it lying around, and within a very short time she'd called the Home Guard and it disappeared. But these things happened, and you didn't turn a hair at it really.

'Mind you, there wasn't a lot of point in my mother trying to put a halt to my activities, because it's very difficult to stop somebody who's ahead of the game! I was out looking for these crashes and I got there pretty quickly. It was something all we boys did. Most of us were out collecting souvenirs and shrapnel and getting bits of guns. A friend of mine, he had the diving brakes of that Stuka which crashed, and he was going home with it on a bicycle when he passed the policeman coming the other way – but he got away with it, and after the war he gave it to the Tangmere Military Museum. Because obviously it was frowned upon at the time. Whenever there was a crash site it was always guarded, either by the Home Guard or a soldier or a policeman, so people wouldn't take stuff away. But we used to talk to the policeman and one of us would go round the back and rip a piece off. It was done so universally that they just turned a blind eye at it. It didn't feel like breaking the law really, but I suppose I did have quite a good collection!

'The routine was, you would hear the dog fight – a burst of machine-gun fire it would be – and you'd look up and usually one plane got shot down as a result of the fight. You'd see the plane spiralling down to earth and you knew roughly whereabouts it had come down, so I would be on my bike and, knowing the terrain fairly well, I knew all the shortcuts to get there quickly. You'd be standing there, just surveying the scene, but of course a lot of the planes came down with their bombs still there in the bomb-bays, unexploded. It must have been pretty dangerous I suppose, but we never thought of it at the time. The police never really used to tell us off, they were quiet friendly.

'But we were terrors really. They had these old tanks drawn up on the shingle on Pagham Beach which the Typhoons used to fly over and strafe for firing practice – but we boys used to play in them and once or twice the children were actually caught in the tanks when they were strafed by rockets. But nobody got killed. It was just all part of the game.

'To be honest, for me it was a very exciting time. It was dramatic to see these low-flying planes. They used to come in straight from the sea, flying at about 100 or 200 feet. But quite often in Bognor they used to machine gun people in the street. They had these tip-and-run raids, so you had to be constantly alert. Even at school we had our lessons in the air-raid shelter because of the risk of being bombed in the classroom. We would be there the whole day sometimes, just as if it was a normal classroom. We had to have our recreation there as well because it wasn't safe out on the playing fields – I can remember learning to play chess. But it was an exciting time. I look back now and there was always a buzz around. I had friends at school and we used to talk about it – did you hear about the raid last night? Did you hear those bombs in Portsmouth? The bombers used to fly right over us on the Portsmouth raids and if they hadn't got their bombs away there, they would jettison them along on the coast where we were as they turned back to go to France. So we were very much in the front line. And that's what my mother was trying to escape from.'

Only a few miles westwards along the coast, Fred Steels' home at Eastleigh, on the outskirts of Southampton, was feeling the effects of being near an important port that was an obvious target for the bombers. Without one of the small Anderson shelters used by many families, the Steels family took refuge at a local factory: 'We were living in Blenheim Road at the time and there was a big shelter at the Aldi locknuts plant, in the factory cellars. We had one close call when the Germans hit the cog-making building, but luckily the bomb didn't go off – it just decided to skid down the stairs and wound up at the front door. The air-raid warden told us to get out just in case it did go off, but in the end they managed to get it out and defuse it.

'One night, though, I was out in the garden when another raid started. We saw this shadow and looked up and there's this damn great land mine coming down, straight on top of Pirelli's. But there again, at least it was going the other way! If it had been coming over our way I would have been terrified. But mostly they were aiming for Southampton. At the time most of us kids thought of the whole thing as more excitement than anything, so I can't in all honesty say that I was that frightened. It was all just a vast new experience really.

'It was only later, when things were getting a little more serious, that I started taking a bit more notice. When Hitler gets this bright idea of invading us, then in preparation for that, the German bombers and fighters were coming over in hordes trying to wipe out the RAF. We had about 600 planes I think it was to their 2,000, so we were slightly outnumbered. And at the time, with things as they were, well, it was a bit of a toss-up really, whether we thought we'd win or we wouldn't. Because things were getting very hectic. We used to spend most of the time outside watching the dog fights. The sky was absolutely covered in vapour trails. We'd see one would get hit and come down, but you never knew whose it was, not until you got reports afterwards.

'Then it was in the middle of all this I suppose that we got the call to go on up to Liverpool to get the ship. We were met at Liverpool and they took us to a local children's home and school – they were called the Fazakerley Cottage Homes. And even when we were waiting there a couple of nights for embarkation, we were still getting bombed.'

The Capels were another family who didn't have an Anderson shelter, but as the war began, like many in their close-knit community on the outskirts of west London, they were frantically digging. Derek Capel, then aged 12, remembers: 'We were all sitting at home – my mother, father, my brother, my sister and me all sitting there – and the announcement came at 11 o'clock: declaration of war. We sat there and damn me if after about two minutes, the siren sounded. So the whole family just ran around the house looking – where do we hide, where do we shelter? We had nothing. And so we finished up under the kitchen table. But we had this field up the top of our road, which was like our recreation field. Well, the second the all-clear sounds, everybody's out their houses and up there like a shot, and there were more trenches dug in that field in that day than anywhere else! Even when we knew it was a false alarm, they still carried on digging trenches! That later became our allotments, that top field, but that day it was just a mass of trenches. Everybody – women, children – everybody digging holes.

'We found out later that it was a British plane that had triggered the warning, but that afternoon – without anybody saying anything – everybody just went up to the field and started digging shelter trenches. After three or four days the trenches got so full up with water that we all gave up and decided the kitchen table was best. We never had an Anderson shelter. They did build these upright shelters behind our estate, but they got so messy and smelly nobody used them. So we just stayed indoors. We ended up with this sort of a system where if anything happened you'd roll out of bed and get underneath it and grab the springs so you'd be out of the way of flying glass or anything.

'There was one raid I particularly remember – I think it was just before we left to go up to catch the ship – when they hit the Port of London. That was a night raid and they hit the port with incendiaries and everything. And that night there was low cloud and there was this terrific red reflection in the sky off the under-surface of the cloud. It was so brilliant this reflection that you could have read a paper outside our house – and we must have been at least 15 miles away from it. It was frightening that was, really frightening. Then we knew the raids had really begun, and as we were going up to London, it was the time when the daylight raids had just started, but then we set off for the seavacuation.'

Kentish Town, where Bess and Louis Walder lived, was even closer to the danger than Derek Capel's little estate on the western outskirts of London. The Walder household always had a flair for the dramatic, and Bess remembers the first air-raid warning creating another typical Walder family moment: 'Well, no sooner had the words come from Mr Chamberlain's mouth than off went the air-raid sirens and of course everybody panicked. The school next door had a massive big boiler room in its basement, so we all shot off down there, down this vast spiral iron staircase. I was carrying the dog; my mother was carrying the cat; my brother was carrying the kittens and his favourite cage of birds – so we must have been quite a funny sight! It was quite comical really. We stayed down there for ages, waiting for something to happen and it never did, so there was a huge feeling of anti-climax. Because I must admit, when the announcement had come over the radio that we were at war, I felt a huge wave of excitement. I thought, "It's happening, and it's happening to me, and it's happening now."'

➤ Bess found that first year of the war in some ways fascinating, despite the stresses and dangers of her situation: 'I did quite a lot of interesting things. My father used to take me and show me the bombing damage that had been done in various places in London. We went into the Bank of England area one day, and the devastation there was really quite horrible to see. But oddly it never really frightened me – well, I was never actually involved in any air raids. I just couldn't imagine the house being hit, or me being killed or anything like that. Because the strange thing was that it was all quite thrilling in a way. It was so different from the life I'd had before. All sorts of things happened that wouldn't have happened in peacetime. For instance, I used to watch the girls who were running the barrage balloons on Hampstead Heath. And they were dressed in soldier's uniforms sending up these barrage balloons and I thought, what a wonderful job. But my heart was really set on being a Wren, because I liked the sea and I was fond of the sea and I was just hoping that one of these days I could be a Wren.'

Whether the war came right on to your doorstep or not was really a matter of chance. The children had to develop a fairly fatalistic attitude, otherwise the whole experience was just too terrifyingly random. Despite living so close to the centre of London, Bess was able to be an onlooker. Yet at the very same time, the girl who was to become her lifelong friend, Beth Cummings, was having a totally different experience up in Liverpool. Beth remembers: 'The first serious raids we had in Liverpool were towards the end of July 1940. They were very unnerving really when I think about them. The first thing you heard was the drone of the aeroplanes. It was this low drone – a terrible noise – a very low, thundering sort of noise. Then as they came the searchlights would be there and then the anti-aircraft guns would start. That was really very noisy. The mobile anti-aircraft guns would be going along the road and it was very, very noisy. Then you'd hear the bombs coming down and they'd be screeching and you just didn't know where they were going to land. You had no idea where they were going to land, but it was very, very bad.

'We were spending whole nights in the air-raid shelter, we had one air-raid shelter between two houses. We spent a lot of time there until my grandfather built a brick shelter for us. He was great. He would be wearing my father's tin helmet from the First World War and as soon as there was a lull in the bombing he'd pop out to see how his other daughters – my aunts – were doing. He was always doing that! When you went into the shelter you took warm clothes and something to eat and drink. Of course, you took your school books as well. All our neighbours would be there as well, and they and my mother were chatting all the time. My mother was very close to the neighbours next door.

'So to begin with in a way it wasn't too bad, at that time. But later, by August, it was very, very bad. It was very frightening. But the thing was we didn't sort of – people didn't show fright. That was the thing during the Second World War, people didn't show that they were frightened. It wasn't something you did. I don't know whether that's unusual or not, but it did happen that way. You more or less expected what was happening and you couldn't really worry too much about it. Obviously you worried whether a bomb was going to hit you, but I think the noise of the bombers was the worst of the lot really. You could hear the screech of a bomb coming down, and it was this awful noise, the terrible noise of these bombers coming over. There were two houses up the same road as us, and they were hit. Fortunately the people in them were in the air-raid shelter, so they were all right, but the two houses were completely demolished. The problem was that we were so close to the railway line and it was the main railway to the docks. All the trains came along that railway from the docks, from Bootle, and they were getting it worse than anybody. So we weren't all that far away from the real bad bombing of Bootle.

'And of course, in the beginning, everybody thought there might be a gas attack. You see most of us, my age group, their fathers went to France in the First World War and some were actually gassed. People of our age, our generation, expected it would happen to us as well. So we did carry our gas masks wherever we went. We did feel they were necessary. When we were issued our gas masks, we had to try them on to see they fitted all right. We had them in cardboard boxes, and with carrying them wherever we went, the boxes would get a bit tatty, so we used to have all sorts of ingenious ways of covering them.

'The thing is, it probably sounds rather strange today, but to our generation – well, we'd heard an awful lot about war. Not just the First World War. There was a lot of war at the time – the Spanish Civil War, all sorts of wars were still going on in the 1930s. So we actually knew about war, and in some respects we expected problems. But you took your chances and hoped you would get through – we might not be killed, we might be killed. This was the way we were, even at the time of the threatened invasion, after Dunkirk and the fall of France. The Germans were there and it wasn't a question of whether they would invade, but when they would invade. That was the way we all thought. I remember thinking, "I wonder which way they'll come." It was as simple as that. We weren't frantic or getting ourselves in a state over it all because there was no point. It was a question of having to accept what was happening. We all knew that we were on our own – as a country, I mean – there was nobody else left, no other country, to help us. Europe had been overthrown and that just left us.'

But even Beth's stoic courage and resourcefulness were tested to the limit on the night of Wednesday 11 September, the day before she was due to sail for Canada. She was spending the night with all the other seavacuee children in the children's home at Fazakerley, but as a Liverpool girl herself, Beth could hear the bombs falling very near her home. 'That air raid on the Wednesday night worried me an awful lot because we didn't live too far away from Fazakerley and I was hoping desperately that the bombs weren't falling anywhere near my mother. We Liverpool girls were sleeping in the cottage homes that were part of the orphanage, but a lot of the seavacuee children were in a nearby school.'

For all the seavacuee children, the experience of this air raid – in an unfamiliar place, separated from their families – was far more unnerving than what they had been through back in their homes. Derek Capel explains: 'Liverpool was a new world to us, a completely new world. We arrived at this school and we all went in. There were about 50 of us from London, maybe a few more. We were taken into this great big schoolroom there and the first thing we had to do was fill up palliasses with straw. That was our sleeping arrangements for the night. We all settled down nice and quiet and then Liverpool starts getting bombed and there was bombs everywhere there was. We were in a panic and everything like that, but we got through it, and then the next day they decided we could go on board the boat.'

Of course, as a Liverpudlian, Beth Cummings had a much better idea of exactly where she was and what was going on – but this wasn't entirely helpful. 'When we Liverpool girls got off the train at Fazakerley terminus, which wasn't that far from where I lived, it wasn't a good feeling because there were two places there that no one in Liverpool at the time liked to think about. One was an isolation hospital, which had a lot of TB cases in it. Then the other side from that was an orphanage, the Fazakerley Cottage Homes it was called, and that was nearly as bad. Obviously nobody wanted to be in either of those places. So I was a little bit apprehensive going through the great big gates into the cottage homes. Mind you, the cottage homes were actually rather special as orphanages go, because they actually were a collection of real little cottages. In the centre was this big assembly hall, which is where I was taken.

'As I entered I was amazed to see it full of children. I think I must have probably been the last one to be collected, because the place was already chock-full of children. The boys and girls were segregated and then we were split into groups of around 15. The girls had a lady escort and the boys had male escorts. The male escorts, two of them were actually priests, one Anglican and one Roman Catholic. My group was the only group with a boy in it. He was little Jimmy Spencer. He was a lovely boy, but he was only 5 and he didn't want to be split from his sister. So they put him and his sister Joan, who was 7, together in our group with me and the other Liverpool girls. We were all making friends, and I soon made friends with Joan Irving and Betty Unwin, also from Liverpool. There were a couple of London girls in our group, and Bess Walder was one of them. Mrs Hillman, Maud Hillman, was our escort. The senior escort was Miss Marjorie Day, and she had various assistants and a lady doctor, Dr Margaret Zeal, and a nursing sister, Sister Dorothy Smith, so we were obviously going to be well looked after. It was really fascinating.'

As soon as they met up, Beth and Bess were busy comparing notes with each other about what they thought of the whole adventure. Of course for Bess, coming up from London, it had all been a bit more mysterious than for local girl Beth. Bess remembers how when she had left Euston station that morning she didn't have the faintest idea where she was going: 'The "unknown port" they mentioned could have been miles away, for all we knew. We left London at about 11 o'clock in the morning, and we didn't arrive at the unknown port until sometime in the middle of the evening. It was a slow journey because the bombing raids had started, some of them in daylight, and we had to be very careful, so the train took a long, long time. It was just crawling along. Sometimes it stopped altogether and we all had to get out of the train and go into the station air-raid shelters. So by the time we got to the unknown port we were all very tired. The unknown port was of course Liverpool. But the length of time it took to get there, it could have been anywhere. I even thought it might have been Aberdeen. It does amuse me today, when people grumble about the time trains take, to think back to those terrible days when the train might never arrive at all. Anyway, it was getting dark by the time we arrived in Liverpool, and we were all whisked off in buses to a huge school. People said it was for orphans, an orphanage school.'

The overnight accommodation for Bess and the rest of the seavacuee children couldn't have been more different from the luxurious Adelphi Hotel where private passengers like the Bech children and Colin Ryder Richardson were staying. Bess describes what she found when she was taken into the Fazakerley Cottages children's home: 'In the assembly hall, which was enormous, there was a line of long white things on the floor. They were oblong things, about six feet long and three feet wide. I looked at these things on the floor and I said to my escort, "What are those white things?" and she said, "They're your beds, darling." Well, I'd never seen beds like that, but we were all so tired that we fell onto those palliasses – that's what they were – and we had a wonderful sleep. I sometimes wish I could sleep like that now.'

Would Bess Walder have slept so well knowing what was to come? The following day, Thursday 12 September, was the date set to board the SS *City of Benares* and sail to Canada. That morning all the children, whether seavacuee or private passengers, would find themselves in the same boat – and that boat was about to sail into the most terrible danger.

CHAPTER THREE

Luxuries *and* Lifeboat Drills

I n the Britain of early autumn 1940, childhood had been cancelled. The children who turned up at Liverpool docks that September, leaving their parents behind and setting off into the unknown, had been through the mill. Most of them had already endured the loneliness and misery of an abortive evacuation from their homes to supposedly safe retreats in the countryside. They had been uprooted from schools and school friends they loved. Their lives had been turned upside down as their parents and the authorities – desperate to protect them – rushed them from pillar to post. Rationing was hitting hard and favourite nursery suppers and treats had disappeared. Then at every turn, there was the bombing. Even once they had arrived in Liverpool for their voyage of escape, the children were bombed again, the very night before their intended departure.

Yet the children kept going. They were under incredible stress, but most of them managed to push it out of their minds and just concentrate on the present. Even so, it is very telling that the children found their first sight of the *Benares* completely breathtaking when they arrived at Liverpool docks for boarding on Thursday 12 September. Kenneth Sparks says: 'It was such a gorgeous day, it was just the ideal nice late summer day and then we saw the *Benares*, and it looked a picture 'cos it had come direct from India.'

Unlike Kenneth, Derek Bech was a private passenger aboard the *Benares*, travelling with his mother and two sisters rather than as part of the seavacuee scheme. But Derek was just as impressed as Kenneth by how different the *Benares* looked from the regular, sombre grey cargo and troop ships. He remembers how amazing the experience was: 'Well, that morning my family was told to go down to the docks and there we would find our ship and we'd be allocated a cabin. So we went to the docks, and I remember it was a lovely sunny day, and we saw this huge liner – a beautiful liner – and it was the *City of Benares*. She had only been launched just before the war, 1936 I think, and must have been the flagship of the Ellerman line. Ellerman ran regular sailings between England and the Far East, particularly to India, and hence the name *Benares*. She was very much on the Indian run. She was just this beautiful ship, gleaming in the sunshine, with her two funnels with white bands painted round them. And of course we went up there all excited, as if we were going on a cruise.'

For Bess Walder, a seavacuee, it was as though she had emerged from a grim, grey, bomb-torn landscape and was looking at another world: 'We arrived at the docks and there in front of us was the most wonderful sight in the world. A magnificent ship, beautifully made, lovely lines, looking absolutely splendid, although she wasn't in her proper colours of blue and gold – she was in camouflage colours. And it was the first time that she would ever travel the Atlantic, because she had been used to going on the India route. She had been built to travel the Indian Ocean. And her name was the *City of Benares*. We were looking at her and suddenly the gangplanks were put down.

'We walked up the gangplanks, and at the top stood the most magnificent Indian men, wearing huge turbans and beautiful clothes with shoes that turned up at the ends. They looked like something out of the *Arabian Nights*. And they bowed to us, called us little ladies, little gentlemen. They said "welcome to our ship". And we felt as if we were in heaven. We were taken to our cabins, which were beautifully furnished, comfortable bunks. We were treated to the most magnificent food, things we hadn't seen for ages, like bananas, oranges, grapefruit – my goodness, we'd almost forgotten what those were. So we really were in seventh heaven.'

Of course, the ship's mainly Asian 'lascar' crew only added to the sense of glamour for the children. Fred Steels was bowled over by the luxury of it all: 'Well, when we first got on board it was like walking into a palace, it really was. You know, a blasted great dining room with little tables with chairs round them, all laid out. It was everything really that you would expect in a top-class restaurant – I couldn't tell you exactly what – but I know it was magnificent at the time. The lascars, the Indian stewards that is, were very good to us. We could order anything we wanted, and I think most of us did! To be able to have what you wanted – and then as much of it as you wanted – well ... But the one thing I do remember, the first time I walked on board that ship, was the smell. Curry. But you know we couldn't have asked for anything better from those lascars, we really couldn't.'

All the survivors stress what a huge change it was to come aboard the *Benares*. It must have been the first moment of real relaxation and fun the children had had for many months. Certainly to Derek Capel, the whole experience was like a wonderful Christmas party: 'By the time we arrived the boat was moored out in the river, so we chugged out to this boat and you've never seen a thing like it. It was beautiful. A great big liner, it was wonderful, we'd never seen anything like it. We'd been on paddle steamers before, but this! We went up and everybody was greeted by these Indian stewards – they were the lascars – and they were lovely because they loved children, and they really looked after us. Then we went on board and into a big room that was gonna be our common room. We were all lined up and met Father Rory O'Sullivan who was in charge of the group of 12 boys I was in.

'Then we had lunch. Now, lunch on board was chicken and everything you wanted. Well, chicken was something you only had at Christmas. You know, if it's chicken, it must be Christmas? And there *was* chicken – there was anything you wanted! The lascars loved us boys, really spoilt us. If anybody didn't like anything, there was always something else appeared. If you wanted two sweets – they were lovely sweets, all sorts of lovely things – you could have two sweets. It was wonderful.

'Then after lunch we were allocated our cabin and we went down there. Now we were very lucky, my brother and meself, because Father O'Sullivan had one just opposite us in the little gangway. He was one side and we were the other side, but we had portholes because we were on the outside, which was marvellous. There was a two-tier bunk, a lovely big wardrobe down the end of the bed and washbasins, I remember. And what was extra, you had your water in a carafe, changed every day. It was things like that you remember being special. There was a chair, and a little desk. Of course my brother had the bottom bunk and then I could climb in the top bunk. So there we were, in our cabin, and we were in our glory – we sat in the cabin and we were having a wonderful time. I remember trying the water and it was so good, nice chilled water.'

Of all the luxuries aboard the *Benares* it was the food the children noticed most, even those travelling privately like the Bech children, who were from a much more privileged background than the seavacuees. Derek Bech explains: 'Well, it was non-rationed food you see, we'd never seen food like it before. We had a menu presented to us and we could choose what food we liked and we were served by Indian waiters all in turbans and white costumes. We thought we were living a life of old Riley! At every mealtime there was a choice of about 40 or 50 different ice creams and as a child in the wartime, ice creams were a real luxury and we indulged and indulged in all this lovely ice cream. We lived very well.'

Barbara Bech teases her brother: 'Derek always says that our first meal was a special banquet, but actually I don't think it was. It was just that all the meals were like that, because it was just the same at breakfast the next day and at every meal. It was the high life – and very, very nice too! The *Benares* was a boat that had been on the India run and so first class, where we ended up, was very first class indeed. The dining room hadn't at that stage been altered at all from when it was a cruise liner. All the waiters were Indians in blue uniforms with white turbans, white gloves, and napkins over their arms. There must have been about three to each table, because it was real service. And then of course they all liked children, so we were fussed over. Any little thing we wanted at any meal we only had to say "What I'd like is so and so" and they were "Oh right, we'll get it", and back would come the ice cream or whatever it was that we thought we'd like.

— 'It was the kind of life that I don't think we'd ever lived before in our lives. It was incredible really – I don't know how they stocked the boats up, but there was no suggestion of any rationing. My recollection is of a long menu. There was a great deal of choice. Not so different from nowadays – but very different indeed from the way life in England was already becoming.'

For 13-year-old Kenneth Sparks from Wembley, it was something he'd never even dreamt of: 'Yeah, they were nine-course meals. After the wartime food, it was, oh dear, there aren't words to describe it. Some of the food – well, we didn't even know what it was, because it came from India. Nine courses. It was gorgeous. We'd never eaten so much in our lives.'

John Baker, who was only 7 at the time, remembers how much he looked forward to mealtimes: 'Whenever we went to the restaurant it was something special. The food was something that we hadn't experienced for a very long time. At home we always ate properly – good food, but economy minded, obviously. But the food on the ship was something else again. Ice cream to me was a luxury that I never would have dreamt of and it was wonderful, and I wanted ice cream – I think I would have eaten ice cream as starter, main course and pudding, and a cup of ice cream to swill it down with if I had my way!'

Could it really have been ice cream, ice cream all the way? Survivors conjure up a picture of the *Benares* as a floating paradise from cartoon land, stocked with every flavour and colour of ice cream imaginable: pistachio green, apricot orange, pink strawberry, creamy vanilla, golden fudge ... Perhaps it is natural that the children wanted to savour their fabulous mealtimes rather than dwell on the other side of *Benares* life: the constantly repeated lifeboat drills. Beth Cummings explains: 'Even that very first day, we had hardly got into our cabin when there was an alarm bell and we had to go to our first lifeboat drill. It was the first of ... I reckon there were three in that day alone, though there might have been four.

'We had to attend our muster station, which was the children's room on the next deck above us. At that first muster we were handed our lifejackets. We were given a navy-blue waistcoat-style kapok one, which we had to wear all the time, even in bed, and we were also handed a canvas pillow-style lifejacket which we had to carry with us wherever we went, and put on the end of our bunks at night together with our coats. We had to sleep in our clothes with our lifejacket on, and the chief officer who was in charge of these lifeboat drills was very, very insistent that we knew exactly what we'd have to do. He and his officers were marvellous actually. They were very insistent that we knew everything, and even at one point I remember this tall chief officer kneeling down to little Jimmy Spencer, who was only 5, with bright blond hair, and he said, "Now Jimmy, what do you do when you hear that bell, what do you do?" It was all very personal – we were talked to individually, not just as a crowd.

'During one of lifeboat drills we had to get into our lifeboat. The lifeboat I was assigned was actually on the starboard side, the opposite side to where my group slept. But we were told exactly what it was about, you know, what would happen. So we got into our lifeboat and we were shown the Fleming gear. It was basically two sort of wooden struts going down the centre of the boat, and these pulled backwards and forwards – and everybody was supposed to help work them when they got into the lifeboat to paddle it forward. We were shown all the provisions. It's strange, but to this day corned beef and sardines always remind me of that. Of course there were the ship's biscuits too.

'Anyway, that first day we had hardly got back down to the cabin after one drill when we had another one. But they wanted to make sure we always knew the drill. We noticed of course that there were two Lewis guns on the stern of the ship. The river was full of ships. We didn't know then, but the problem was that we were supposed to sail on the Thursday evening, on the early-evening tide. But apparently there were mines dropped at the mouth of the Mersey. Shipping couldn't move and the river was actually chockablock by this time.'

So the *Benares* was forced to stay overnight on moorings in the Mersey estuary, where yet again, as almost every night, the children found themselves being bombed once more. Derek Bech took it almost for granted that there would be bombs: 'Of course that night was another air raid. All the bombs were falling all around the ship in the docks and on the water, but fortunately luck was with us and nothing hit the boat. Because we couldn't have sheltered, there's no shelter on a ship. You just had to take your luck in your cabin. So we went to bed normally with all this happening above us. We were too excited about sailing the following day to be afraid of the bombs.'

But Beth Cummings remembers: 'I think it did make us feel vulnerable, being stuck out in the middle of the river with the bombs, but the next day was the day we had been told we were sailing. Friday 13th. Then Friday was very nasty weather. It was dark, it was raining. It wasn't nice at all, but we still sailed. We set off out to sea at about six o'clock in the evening. We waved to everybody we passed. We were all excited, waving to every ship.'

For Sonia Bech there were still some misgivings about the whole adventure. She says: 'I think our family hadn't got onto the boat until the afternoon, and I remember I had a slight sinking feeling. I was leaving England. What was I doing? I was a bit, just a little bit nervous for a moment, and then of course everybody was rushing round so really there wasn't time to go on worrying.'

John Baker was another to be having second thoughts. He found the whole experience overwhelming as much as exciting. Only 7 years old at the time, as the ship sailed out of Liverpool Bay he was already rapidly earning himself the nickname of 'the lost boy'. He admits: 'The thing was, when we eventually got on board, I actually found the ship a very confusing place. It was huge as far as I was concerned. When we were first going round the ship, well, people expect you to be a bit confused, but it wasn't until we were out to sea that you could tell I was the one always getting lost. I just got lost easily, specially going to mealtimes and that sort of thing. I mean, I would be dinging my way about. Every corridor in a boat looks the same to a 7-year-old.

'It's one of my main memories about the ship, getting lost. Every time I moved out of the cabin, there I am lost again. And quite often I would end up by myself. I suppose I should have been waiting for my older brother Bobby, but I wanted to explore, as kids do, and the number of times I got lost was unbelievable. Usually it would be when I went to the restaurant, and eating in the restaurant was exciting, but there you go, leaving the restaurant I would be lost again.'

Luckily for John, his brother Bobby was making every effort to keep an eye on him – and this would be an important part of John's survival story. Robert 'Bobby' Baker was nearly 13 when he boarded the *Benares*, five years older than John. The two lads had a fairly typical brotherly relationship. John remembers: 'Bobby and I got on as well as any relationship between a 7-year-old and a 12-year-old. You know, Bobby obviously was becoming interested in girls and I certainly wasn't at that age. He and I, we rubbed along quite well. Mind you, I do remember the experience of going round to one of his prospective girlfriends and trying to suss out how she felt about Bobby and trying to arrange something – well, that was as far as I got, and I did get a bit of a thick ear from him for doing that! But anyway, he would look out for me. I know when we went to go on the *Benares* my parents would have said to my brother, "Now you look after him". Which he did. He did look after me.

'And the proof of the pudding of him looking after me was that when we were torpedoed and I'd left my lifejacket downstairs in those corridors where I'd got myself lost on so many occasions, there was no way he was going to allow me to go down there to get it. He restrained me very forcibly from going down there and getting lost again. Instead, he gave me another lifejacket. Now, whether he gave me his own lifejacket in replacement of the one that I left behind, I do not know and I shall never know. But he knew the drills, and it was drilled into us every time, to bring your lifejacket and to put a lifejacket on. And so he put a lifejacket on me.'

Derek Bech remembers mealtimes and lifeboat drills as being the two fixed points round which ship's life revolved: 'We used to have lifeboat drill at least twice a day. It was at the drills that we were told about the U-boats and the risk of being torpedoed. We were told what to do, exactly what the procedure would be. Even when we went to bed at night we were to have our outdoor clothes close at hand and in fact a lot of the children used to go to sleep with their main clothes still on. My mother always had a pile of clothes on the side, and a little grip, which was her emergency bag where she kept a sort of survival kit in case anything happened, including a small bottle of brandy.

'We took the drill deadly serious. We were told that in an emergency the alarm bells would ring and when they started to ring we had to assemble in a muster station. Our station was in the main private passenger lounge, which was this lovely big, open room on the main deck. We were told which number lifeboat we would go to and we went to see where it was. Then they explained how the lifeboats would be lowered over the side – we would get in them and then the lifeboat would be lowered into the water. All this was in theory, of course. But anyway, we children were well drilled.

'I think we were pretty confident that if anything happened we knew what to do. The lifejackets weren't like the ones we know today. They went round your neck only and in each corner of your neck there was a big cube of cork, two in the front, two at the back. You put this over your head. To hold it on round your neck you had a strap that went round your body. So they were very unwieldy things and you couldn't walk around deck with these corks because you would be crashing around. We had to carry them day and night. It was the big rule: you must always carry your life jacket.'

But of course, the one thing the drills couldn't achieve, no matter how often they were repeated, was to prepare the passengers for what a real sinking might be like. As Bess Walder points out: 'Yes, we had lots and lots of practice of lifeboat drill. We were told exactly what to do and how to do it, where our lifeboat stations were. How the best thing to do would be to walk not run; not to panic; to take the proper exits and entrances. We got into the lifeboats, sat in the lifeboats, and got out of the lifeboats. So we did our practices and all would be well. But never at night, and never when the ship was in a storm. Our drills were only in the utmost favourable conditions.'

Sonia Bech also remembers just how treacherously straightforward the lifeboat drill seemed during practices: 'We did them every day if not twice a day. We were told where our muster station was, it was the lounge of the first class – a rather nice room with sofas and bridge tables at one end. And we knew where our lifeboat was. I remember it being number three and my brother says it was number four. I think we'll have to go on fighting about that because we'll never really know. At any rate, we knew how to get into the boat and they showed us what to do. But I don't think they ever lowered the boats, and I don't remember that our group ever actually got into the boat. And it was in the daylight always. I don't think we ever did one at night – and then of course there was the storm, we had never done it in a storm.'

Looking back, her sister Barbara wonders if perhaps the repeated routine drills hadn't left the children with a false sense of security: 'For us it was just the boat drill and we did it on the same basis as putting on your gas masks or going down to the air-raid shelters at school. It was just something that you needed to know how to do, a bit routine, but it didn't mean that you'd ever actually have to do it. After all, in peacetime they do have emergency drills and I think we just regarded it in that light, as a sort of safety routine which you did when you were on board a ship. The thing is, it was never in any way suggested to us under what circumstances it might be needed. I mean, they didn't sort of say, "If we're dive bombed or they send six torpedoes in it from end to end". They didn't describe why the boat drill might be necessary, so it became just one of the things you did to amuse yourself while on board. That was the attitude, nobody would have dreamt of discussing not getting to Canada. We were on our way and that was it.'

And indeed, they were on their way at last, leaving Liverpool behind and heading out into the Irish Sea and then the Atlantic. Derek Bech remembers: 'The day we set sail was the 13th – Friday 13 September. We left our mooring buoy and sailed up the River Mersey out of the estuary and into the bay. As we went there were one or two other little boats which also cast away and they followed us. We knew then that we were forming a convoy. By the time we had got out into the Irish Sea and were south of the Isle of Man, we were all assembled into the full convoy. Ours was what they called the commodore ship, and also in our convoy we had the *Duchess of Athol*, which was the other big ship of the convoy. But the man in charge of the convoy, that was Admiral Mackinnon, he was on our ship. Mostly though the convoy was a motley selection of ships, old tramp steamers and coal cargoes with a few tankers thrown in.'

Watching as the convoy formed up round the *Benares* and they all set out to sea, Fred Steels felt a kind of pride: 'I'm not saying we were in the league of the *Queen Mary* or anything, but we were the lead ship and we had a commodore on board us, who actually ran the convoy. So yes, I did, I felt proud being on that ship – and thinking we're off on this new adventure, hoping all would be well. We'd heard a few reports about U-boats and the like, but we took them with a pinch of salt. We were keeping our fingers crossed that we were going to make it, but I'm afraid it wasn't to be.'

For Barbara Bech it wasn't until a little later that the full realisation of their adventure hit home: 'The funny thing is I don't remember finally leaving Liverpool. I sort of remember crossing the Irish Sea and I suppose we must have been going round Northern Ireland. But then, as we were leaving the coast of Ireland behind us, I remember sort of taking a last look and thinking, "Ah, that's the last time for the moment I shall see land." It wasn't a huge drama or anything, though. It just faded away down the horizon.'

The children's great adventure had begun, and the truth was they were far too busy enjoying the glamorous life on board to dwell on the idea that something might go seriously wrong. As Beth Cummings stresses: 'We were fascinated with the ship. There were 90 of us all running around, you know, enjoying the fun. We seavacuee children were told we had to stick to the promenade deck. I think it was something to do with the private passengers, so we had the promenade deck – but we could still see the other passengers, of course. We had the veranda café to ourselves and the children's room. We went to the dining room for our meals a little earlier than the private passengers, but the passengers were fascinating, you know. There was one, I was intrigued by him. He was a French naval officer in a leather coat with his cap on and he looked so serious, oh dear! Well, I was imagining all sorts of things about him. At 14 you do that sort of thing. I thought, "I wonder where he is going? I wonder who he is? He looks sort of mysterious!" You know, we had all sorts of making-up games.'

Beth's mystery man was probably Hervé de Kerillis. Had she known it, Beth was quite right to be spinning adventure yarns about him, because he was a lieutenant in the French air force – and he was indeed on a secret mission to Quebec, though he didn't survive to complete it. There were several VIPs among the adult private passengers aboard the *Benares*. Arthur Wimperis was a well-known playwright with a string of West End hits. He was on his way to the States to work in Hollywood with the famous film director Alexander Korda. Lt-Col James Baldwin-Webb, the MP for Wrekin, was on a mission to New York to raise money for Red Cross ambulances. The BBC's overseas correspondent Eric Davies, then aged 32, was on his way to Malaya via America.

Although travelling as a private passenger, Lt-Cdr Richard Deane, 56, was a reservist in the Royal Navy and was going to Canada to take up a naval appointment. Almost as soon as he had boarded the ship, Lt-Cdr Deane went to the bridge to offer any help he could during the voyage. The convoy's commodore, Admiral Mackinnon, turned him down out of hand – in a manner that seems to be typical of his character as it was to emerge during the voyage. If only the admiral had been more receptive, not just to Richard Deane but also to Captain Landles Nicoll, the captain of the *Benares*. Both men had so much to contribute to achieving the vital task of getting the children safely across the Atlantic. It is a bitter irony that in the end it would be Richard Deane who actually saved children's lives, not Admiral Mackinnon.

From the outset of the voyage Lt-Cdr Deane was concerned about the way the lifeboat drills were handled. He pointed out immediately what some of the children had noticed themselves: that the very basic routine drills, carried out in calm water, were in no way a preparation for what might go wrong if the ship really had to be abandoned. He was also highly critical of the method of launching the lifeboats, knowing from his long experience that in rough seas, particularly if the ship was 'listing' – leaning dramatically to one side – they would be almost impossible to get safely clear of the ship's hull. Lt-Cdr Deane had also inspected the Fleming gear that operated paddles in each lifeboat and he was very suspicious about its state of maintenance. But no one – certainly not Admiral Mackinnon – wanted to hear him, and as Richard Deane well knew, no ship wants a Jonah on board.

There were already enough highly stressed adults sailing on the *Benares*. As Sonia Bech points out: 'The grown-up passengers were all rather preoccupied. Some of them had been through lots of horrible things. You know, they had escaped from Germany and some of them were from Hungary and Czechoslovakia and places. They were in transit for America where they hoped they'd be safe – they didn't really want to stay in England.'

Among this group of passengers were some very influential refugees. Rudolf Olden, the Jewish owner of Berlin's *Tageblatt* newspaper, had fought the rise of Hitler through his newspaper's pages until forced out of his home in 1934. He had then been interned in Britain, and now at last he and his wife Ika were heading for a new life in Toronto. Another German refugee was the writer Baroness Emmely von Ingleseben, who had managed to escape from the concentration camps. Shipping manager Bohdan Nagorski had been driven out of Poland in the Nazi invasion; he at least was familiar with the routines of a large ship. There were also Hirsh and Emma Guggenheim, an elderly couple fleeing Holland, and Ernest Szekulesz, a Hungarian refugee. Ernest's compatriot, Laszlo Raskai, had been a journalist back home in Hungary. Colin Ryder Richardson remembers Laszlo: 'He had the cabin across from me. Later, when the sinking was happening and we were in the lifeboats, he was there, diving. He kept diving again and again and bringing back children. And then he dived and we didn't see him again.'

Laszlo did not survive the sinking. Nor did Alice Grierson, the sister of documentary filmmaker John Grierson. Alice, 36, had been commissioned by the Canadian Film Board to travel aboard the *Benares* and make a documentary about the seavacuee children and their journey. To the children she was perhaps the most glamorous of all the intriguing adults on the board. She certainly made a big impression on Bess Walder: 'She was such an interesting character to look at. She strode about the ship as if she owned the thing. She wore a beautiful beret and smoked cigarettes from the most magnificent long cigarette holder you'd ever seen. And she wore trousers. That was a daring thing, because in those days women didn't always wear trousers. Well, she looked every inch our concept of a transatlantic lady!

'And then she had this brilliant idea, she thought, of getting us all together, and teaching us a song so that we could sing it to everyone when we arrived in Canada. She chose 'In an English Country Garden'. Well of course, we were in no mood to sing 'In an English Country Garden'. I mean, we could sing other things –

the songs that were popular at the time, like 'Wish Me Luck as You Wave Me Goodbye', or we could sing 'We'll Meet Again, I Don't Know Where, Don't Know When' – but we just didn't seem to manage oh these lovely things that went on in an English country garden! And here she was trying make us sing 'In an English Country Garden' and it really wasn't going down terribly well. I think she was very disappointed!'

The Bech children, as private passengers rather than seavacuees, didn't get caught up in the compulsory choir practice inflicted on Bess and her friends. Barbara explains: 'In those days first-class accommodation was completely separate from third-class accommodation, and since most of the boat had been given over to the seavacuee children, we private passengers were put in first class. It was very comfortable, with quite modern furniture in fact. But what struck me was when you wanted a bath you just told your steward that you'd like a bath and he would go and run it for you and then come back and say "Bath ready, missy". And it was a salt-water bath with a rack across the bath with a bowl of fresh water to wash your face and hands. But actually you simply wallowed in glorious hot sea water, because of course you knew there was a limit to how much fresh water could be used. Then you rinsed off in your basin of fresh water and just left the bathroom to be tidied up for you. That was really very nice.

'Oddly enough, we weren't terribly aware of the seavacuee children. I suppose we were told that there were some child evacuees on board, but I don't think we knew how many or anything about them except that they were in the other half of the ship. Because you couldn't really see one outside deck from another, I don't think we realised that there were so many children on board – we didn't see them where we were.'

Her sister Sonia adds: 'Also, pretty soon we had got our own little party of friends including Colin Ryder Richardson. We had our mother with us, but Colin was lonely because he was on his own and he only had a guardian to look after him. So we made friends with him and I rather liked him. We talked and played – imaginary games, that sort of thing – rushing round the deck and probably being a pain in the neck to all the grown-up passengers. We had time to really enjoy the boat – especially being in first class because the tourist class was taken up by the seavacuee children. They were all put in dormitories at the stern and we were sort of in the middle of the boat. We had a very nice lounge and dining room, we didn't meet the children at all. It's strange to remember it now, but we didn't really think about those children. There were 90 or so of them I think, but we just never met them.'

Already separated off from private passengers like the Bechs and Colin Ryder Richardson, the seavacuee children down in the stern found themselves snared in another form of segregation – between boys and girls. The official attempts by their escorts to keep the boys and girls strictly apart amused Bess Walder even at the time: 'Oh yes, they tried it alright, oh dear! Obviously someone in authority had said that there's to be sex segregation on board the ship, so they tried to. The boys had one side of the ship, the girls had the other. What they thought would have gone on had we mixed together goodness only knows, but these were innocent days, they really were. I was relieved in some ways because my brother was out of sight – and so could be out of mind – particularly as he was quite a naughty boy, full of spirit. My father had said to me before going, "You look after that young man." But with him on the other side of the ship I couldn't. And I must admit, at the time I was quite pleased I couldn't because I had other plans of my own.

'I was very intrigued by the little children who were on board. Some of them were only 5, even some of them were just 4. They had their own little nursery school. We sort of had a school too, but nobody wanted to go to school. Who would want to go to school on board ship when all this wonderful excitement was going on all the time? So the school room ended up being empty most of the time. But the little ones' nursery room had the most magnificent rocking horse. It was the biggest rocking horse I'd ever seen. It was enormous, and it had two huge panniers either side of the horse, one for one child, one for another and one on the horse. Oh, it was my ambition to get into the nursery and ride it. But I was not allowed to because I was too old and the nursery was locked at night so that I couldn't pop out and try it myself.'

Derek Capel was on the other side of the ship from Bess: 'Of course the boys and girls were strictly separated. We never saw the girls at all except up in the common room. There were strict rules about that. Once we had got settled in they sorted us out into our little classes, which was if I remember right: 5 to 8s, 8 to 11s, and 11 to 14s – boys and girls still strictly segregated.

'As we set sail most of us didn't even really know where we were going, even when we were well out to sea. We were sailing on and we were going north up the coast of Ireland. We knew we were going north because you could tell from the bit of sun we had. When we went on deck the sea was ever so rough, ever so bumpy and lumpy. But we only found out we were going to Canada through Rory O'Sullivan. Father O'Sullivan came up to me and he said, "Where are you going, do you think?" Then he said, "We've been told not to tell anybody, but borrow this book," and I can remember the book to this day, it was called the *Wonder Book of Empire*, and Father O'Sullivan said, "Look under C, you might get an idea there." And there it was all about Canada, so I thought, well that's it then, now I know.'

Father Rory O'Sullivan was one of the volunteer escorts assigned by the Children's Overseas Reception Board (CORB) to look after the seavacuee children on their journey across the Atlantic. Aged 32, he had been teaching at a seminary in France when war broke out, but managed to escape back to the UK. Another escort was an Anglican vicar, the Reverend William King, 28, who was returning to his native Canada. They were helped by Michael Rennie, 23, a theology student at Oxford. Senior escort Marjorie Day, a schoolmistress, was assisted with the girls by Margaret Zeal, a doctor; Maud Hillman, 44, a teacher; and Mary Cornish, a music teacher.

Mary Cornish was very popular with the children, who all called her Auntie Mary. Gussie Grimmond, 13, wrote home to her parents: 'Please, Mum, do not worry as we have been fitted up with clothes. Our escort is a very nice lady, Miss Cornish, but we call her Auntie Mary.'

Gussie was from a family of ten children from Brixton, of whom five sailed on the *Benares*. They were Gussie, Violet, 10, Connie, 9, Eddie, 8 and Lenny, 5. As the oldest of the Grimmonds on board the *Benares*, Gussie had organised her siblings to write home as the ship left Liverpool. She began her own letter:

Dear Mum and Dad,

'It is very lovely here on the ship. I wish you were with us. We have men from Calcutta to wait on us, and we go into a big room for meals and we have silver knives and forks – table napkins and three different kinds of knives and forks. We have a menu card in which we can choose what we like off the card.'

Gussie's letter home closes: 'There are men to guard us at night in case our boat got sunk. Please do not answer this letter as I will be in mid-Atlantic. Excuse writing and spelling.'

In Gussie's words it sounds hardly threatening at all. The boat getting sunk, the men to guard them, the Atlantic ocean – they all seem to be just yet more excitements in the adventure that includes men in turbans and silver cutlery. But long before Gussie Grimmond's letter reached home, she and all the other children of the *Benares* really were in the mid-ocean, and the worst storm the North Atlantic could throw at them was on its way.

CHAPTER FOUR

The Eye
of the Storm

What with the 40 or 50 different varieties of ice cream on offer – or at least that's how many Derek Bech remembers – life on board the *Benares* was beginning to feel more and more like a luxury cruise, even for the adults. But at night the reality of their situation couldn't be ignored. If they really had been cruising, instead of escaping war, the *Benares* would have spent its evenings sailing through the ocean decked out in fairy lights and with the accompanying sounds of a band playing in the dining room. But there was nothing like that for the ship of children. The *Benares* had to keep a strict blackout – and the children had it dinned into them every bit as thoroughly as their lifeboat drills.

Colin Ryder Richardson remembers: 'We were told about the blackout: that a cigarette could be seen for miles by the U-boats, not that I smoked, but you were told all these things, why the windows were blacked out, everything like that. All sorts of instructions were given to you: that we must be as secret and quiet as possible and that making a noise at night was not such a good idea, specially on a calm evening when the weather was quiet. Those, what I'd call elementary precautions, were really hammered into us and made quite certain by the crew too.'

Derek Bech agrees: 'We were warned that at nighttime we weren't allowed to walk round the deck because of the blackout.

All the ship was very much in blackout. You couldn't show a light and the adults couldn't even smoke a cigarette because some people were accused of being German spies by having a cigarette – smoking on deck, that is – and you wouldn't want that accusation!'

So in the very early hours of Tuesday morning, the *Benares* was a dark, silent ship as she ploughed her way with the rest of the convoy through the gathering storm. While the children slept, their ship reached a point of no return. It really was a point – the map reading 17 degrees west – at which it had secretly been decided that the Royal Navy escort of fighting ships would leave and turn back towards British waters, escorting some incoming ships, while the convoy itself, led by the children's ship, headed on towards Canada. The Navy destroyer and two other ships known as corvettes (but most of the children thought of them as just 'little destroyers') actually left the civilian ships at one o'clock in the morning of Tuesday, 17 September 1940. The convoy sailed on alone into the night: an odd little fleet, composed of a grand liner (the *Benares* itself), and a bunch of assorted cargo boats, including some that were hardly more than tramp steamers. The *Benares* was certainly the only ship important enough to have two funnels. From now on the ship of children and its companion vessels would have no protection from any German U-boats that might have made it this far out to sea.

The children awoke to a worsening storm. The north Atlantic is well known for its massive gales, and the *Benares* was sailing right into the teeth of a heavy Force 5 storm. Lashing squalls of sleet, hail and rain thundered onto the deck, while the bows forced their way through waves that broke 20 feet high. The ship was being thrown up and down in the howling gale. The slower a ship travels, the worse the Atlantic swell feels for its passengers. And the rollers were crashing against the *Benares*, sending the horizon skewing wildly up and down to the eyes of those inside the vessel. At one moment there was nothing but sky through the porthole, and the next it was all angry grey sea. As a top-class liner, the *Benares* could have gone faster to reduce the effects of the heavy seas, but if the convoy was to stick together she had to go much slower, so that even the old steamers could keep up.

Derek Bech had noticed this from the moment they sailed out of Liverpool Bay into the Irish Sea: 'A lot of the convoy was what you would call tramp steamers and they were very, very slow moving – only about three or four knots, that was the maximum speed, and of course the convoy had to go at the speed of the slow ship, so our *City of Benares*, even though it was easily capable of doing 18 knots or more actually, was reduced to this snail pace. But anyway, that morning – the Tuesday morning it was – I remember we had run into bad weather. There was quite a storm blowing and in fact I had my first bout of sea sickness. I was in bed most of the day. Then the cabin steward – he was a lascar – came in and asked, "Do you want any food, sahib?" and maybe I was feeling a bit better because I said, "Well, I might do a bit of ice cream" and up came the ice cream. The Indians, they love the children, so you know I was well looked after of course. Really, whatever you asked for, it was there instantly!'

Derek Capel also remembers being irritated by how the *Benares* had to stay at a slow speed despite the weather: 'It was rough and a lot of the children were sick, and the adults too were very sick. The thing is we were just going along – you know, in the convoy – and going ever so slow, about five knots, I don't know, about that, but with us being a ship that should cut through the water, we were just bouncing around on top of it with going so slow. But that was it, nothing to be done. So me and my friends went down to the common room as usual.

'But there were fewer people this time funnily enough, fewer adults and fewer children, but there we still were, and they were wondering what to do with us! The girls had been having school and the younger ones had their little lessons, but with us older boys, they didn't quite know what to do with us because we were a bit – I suppose we were a little bit radical, like all boys are! They decided to let us carry on with our hobbies, so we all had things to do. We could read or whatever, like I'd a stamp collection and things like that. But mainly we older boys liked to get to know the crew. Now we were lucky with that, because we got chatting to 'em and they used to take us out a couple at a time to look around the boat and see the convoy and everything like that and we really got to know some of them, you know, they were really good.

'They'd talk to us, tell us about the boat and who the captain was and everything like that. They thought the world of him, of Captain Nicoll. The crew told us about the seamen as well, because most of the seamen were lascars; that is, they were Indian seamen. The lascars were really feeling the cold. We felt ever so sorry for the lascars because they used to go on the route from Liverpool to Bombay, and here they were in the middle of the north Atlantic only in thin clothes and everything. The crew and us gave them all the blankets we could, so you had the Indian seamen always going round with a blanket wrapped round them! They were all lovely people, they all waved and laughed with you. But everyone on that ship was lovely – like the younger officers, they taught us a lot about the ship, about the convoy, and everything like that.

'By that Tuesday we were old hands. We knew about getting a lot of fresh air which stopped us getting sick. So even that morning we didn't stay stuck inside the common room, we went out there with the wind really blowing you. I remember we were joking: if you were gonna be sick it'd get blown back again with that gale because when the Atlantic is stormy it's really stormy! After we'd gone to the common room we went up on deck to wave to the other ships, we always waved to the other ships. In front of us there was a little ship called the *Marina*. She looked more like a coaster than anything, with more under water than over the water. But one of the crewmen said, he said: "Well, if anything happens to you, she'll pick you up. You know if it happens – if anything happens, she'll pick you up, you know." We thought that's lovely, but poor little ship – it felt as though we needed to pick her up, not the other way round!'

On that fierce Atlantic morning the children hadn't really even noticed that their escort had left them. For those who could handle the gale – as Derek Capel could – their wonderful life at sea went on as normal.

'It was after a couple of days of wonderful life and it was blooming lovely,' he remembers. 'The girls had been enjoying themselves, and I know they'd started their little choir, and they got them well trained for singing 'In an English Country Garden'. I can remember it all now. The girls got really quite good and they could sing it all the way through. I thought it was beautiful, and they said, "Oh, we're gonna sing that when the ship goes into harbour," so I said, "That was wonderful," they said, "Phew." Then they wanted – they decided they wanted the boys to do the same, but well, you know, the grown-ups weren't proper schoolteachers, so they weren't that strong – firm, I mean – and have you ever tried to teach a crowd of rebellious 12- to 14-year-old boys how to sing, when half of them have got voices breaking and everything like that? So that were soon scrubbed round; that was soon finished that was! And so we went on. It was a wonderful trip, lovely food, lovely comfort, and we were having a lovely time, we were.

'We were proper little, you know, wanderers on the boat, 'cos as long as the crew was with us, they'd take us just two at a time, one of the crew would take two and two, you know, they wanted to take us all around, show us all the different bits of the boat. But we could never go near the girls' side. That was strictly forbidden that was. They had some stewardesses on and they certainly made sure, because they were looking after the girls. Yeah, not that we wanted to, mind, but you know, strict rules it was.

'And so we went on, through the storm, watching the boats, watching the sea, having the time of our lives and eating all we wanted to, because we had got over the sea sickness. It seemed to hit the adults far worse than us. I know poor Father Rory O'Sullivan, who was our escort looking after us, he was really badly hit and by that Tuesday he'd finished up in bed with his sea sickness.'

Fred Steels was one of the first of the boys to notice that the escort had left their convoy. Coming from a family of seamen and naval officers, he always felt 'the sea was in my blood' and he was enjoying getting to know every aspect of the voyage – especially the more technical seamanship aspects: 'We had the run of the ship virtually. They took us all over the ship – if I remember rightly Captain Nicoll even took us up onto the bridge to see how it works, sort of thing. I think the only place we never went was the engine room, but the rest of the ship was ours virtually. It was a damned fascinating experience, you know, on board that ship. And of course, for us kids from London in the middle of the war with the rationing and the bombing it was like the lap of luxury, we thought it was just a great holiday we were going on.

'And as I say, it was just fascinating to stand on the deck and watch all the ships, because there was 19 ships in that convoy, and it's surprising the lot of space that 19 ships will take up, even though it was a small convoy. We used to watch them and I was thinking at the time that our top speed on the *Benares* was about 19, 20 knots, and I think the slowest ship in the convoy was somewhere about 8 or 10, which restricted us very greatly because we had to keep down to her speed. We were the commodore of the convoy, which put us right in the van of it, so we had to chug along at that speed so the ones behind could keep up with us. I spent a lot of time up on deck watching the other ships. If the weather was really bad we would be down below, you know, playing in the ballrooms and state rooms, but I liked to be on deck most of the time, in fact I think I got told off once because I wanted to stay up there and they wanted me out of it!

'The thing is, I've always liked the sea breeze and being up there watching the convoy just really fascinated me. I think it was the fact that to us it was like a vast armada – a vast, exciting experience, wondering where all those other ships with us were all going in the end, who was on them, how long it was gonna take us to get there, if anything would happen. To begin with we had a seaplane in the early stages as well as the destroyer escort. But then, on the Tuesday, we had reached the 600-mile limit I think it was, and we realised the escort had gone. We were told then that it was because we were out of the danger zone, because they didn't believe in those days that the U-boats could get out that far, and so they left us and about quarter past ten that night the U-boats proved 'em wrong!'

But the crisis on the *Benares* had already started that very morning, even as the boys were standing on the spray-washed deck watching their escort disappearing across the stormy horizon. Back in England, the instructions for the convoy had been that once the escort had left, the fleet of ships would split up. As a group, bunched together, with no protecting destroyers and going only as fast as its slowest member, the convoy would obviously make a very soft target if a U-boat had managed to get this far out to sea — not that anyone expected such a thing to happen. By far the best plan was for the convoy to fragment. The *Benares*, with its vital and fragile cargo of children, could then treble its speed and get to the safety of the St Lawrence seaway and the shores of northern America as quickly as possible.

Captain Nicoll had actually argued for this right from the beginning. Even before the *Benares* had left Liverpool, he told his daughter: 'If only we could get away by ourselves at sea — just the *Benares* on her own. I could employ a zigzag course at high speed and we would have a better chance.'

Now Captain Nicoll found himself in head-on conflict with Admiral Mackinnon, the commodore of the convoy as a whole. Since the *Benares* was the lead or commodore ship of the convoy, the two men were in the tricky position of sharing a bridge. While the children played or watched the seas and the adults nursed their sea sickness, a flaming row was taking place on the bridge of the *Benares*. Captain Nicoll pushed for the convoy to break up now, as soon as possible, by midday at the very latest. He couldn't see any reason for delay. But Admiral Mackinnon dithered. The more forcibly Captain Nicoll argued, the more Admiral Mackinnon seemed to stick to the idea of the group staying together, even though they no longer had any protection — and Admiral Mackinnon was the senior officer. Yet he seemed unable to make the crucial decision, leaving Captain Nicoll fuming.

Through his friendship with the crew, Derek Capel got a unique insight into the bitter quarrel — which was later to be hushed up. He remembers: 'The announcement came out that the escort had left us and we were talking to the crew at the time. One of them said to me, "Oh, that's OK, we're breaking off at midday and everybody's going for themselves, so we can make our speed then, you know, so it'll be a much smoother ride and get there much quicker." Well, that was lovely, but then midday came along and nothing happened. And we were out with the crew in the afternoon and they turned round and said, "Don't know what's happened, we've got to stay in convoy for another 24 hours." One of the crew turned round to me and said, "The old man's not pleased." He meant the captain, and he said, "He's flaming mad about it." And the crew were too – they were feeling quite mutinous. They were saying things like they were "nearly flaming ready to mutiny" – you definitely got the impression feelings were running high. They wanted to get out of the convoy, you know, and get where they could work up their speed.

'One of the things for the Indian seamen – the lascars – was they were getting colder and colder. They thought the quicker they got there the quicker they could go below and stay below and get warmed up and then go back on their Liverpool-to-Bombay run. And so it went on. There was this almighty row.'

A young member of Admiral Mackinnon's personal staff, Signalman Johnny Mayhew, was present at the furious scene. He later gave an eye-witness account of how he had told his senior, Chief Signalman Bartlett: 'The admiral and the skipper's been having a few words down there. The skipper wants to get cracking, off on our own, but the admiral says, no, we'll have a better chance in the dark.' Johnny Mayhew was told to keep what he had heard to himself, but the rest of the senior crew members were already beginning to second-guess what was happening. The ship's two senior engineers, Chief Engineer Alex Macauley and Second Engineer John McGlashan, both of whom knew better than anyone what the *Benares* was capable of, simply couldn't understand why the ship was still chugging along at around 5 or 6 knots when it could be speeding away from danger at 18 to 20 knots.

Was it the storm that influenced Admiral Mackinnon to hang on? Or was it, on a very human level, the clash of personalities between him and Captain Nicoll that caused him to want to win a battle of wills? He may genuinely have thought that the *Benares* was out of danger. But this seems unlikely, because only hours before, when it was leaving the convoy, the escorting destroyer HMS *Winchelsea* had radioed Admiral Mackinnon to warn him of a U-boat thought to be operating at 20 degrees west, hardly any distance at all from the *Benares*. But Captain Nicoll couldn't override Admiral Mackinnon, and so the convoy sailed slowly on through the storm.

Only one or two of the passengers – inquisitive, get-everywhere boys like Derek Capel and Fred Steels – had any idea of what was going on. For most, the big event of the day was the news coming through about the Battle of Britain. Derek Bech explains: 'We were four days out by then: four days of the good food and the good life on the ship. We had been having regular radio messages coming from home – from England – and I remember we had a posting of a notice on our noticeboard to say that the Battle of Britain, well, we had shot down I think it was 185 planes in one day, and of course with that news there was great jubilation and people were cheering and we thought maybe the Battle of Britain was being won. And of course being four days out at the same time as that announcement we were told by the captain that hopefully we were out of range now of the U-boats. They didn't think they could operate more than 600 miles from base, and we were now outside that area, and we could relax our care. We didn't have to carry our lifejackets and that, but still be vigilant.'

His sister Sonia remembers that in any case the children were enjoying life on board too much to have any great sense of danger: 'Well of course, at first you would look on the horizon and there were the three other destroyers running round us and we were in convoy, so obviously there was a danger, because you wouldn't have had three chaps running around otherwise. But we were in a convoy with mostly cargo ships, smaller than us, and even though we weren't all that big, we were still bigger than them which made you feel good, and really somehow we just didn't worry. Then when the destroyers left, the captain came on and said, "You can leave your lifejackets today, we are in American waters. We are going to be all right now, so please leave your lifejackets in your cabins." So then we felt much better. We felt well, we're not gonna be torpedoed now or dive-bombed or anything. We know we're in American waters. America wasn't in the war then, but they were doing all sorts of things to help us and one of the things was getting ships into their waters, up the St Lawrence. We definitely relaxed – but of course you have to remember that a lot of us, particularly the grown-ups, were too busy being sea sick to think about anything. People were really feeling so, so ill.'

Barbara Bech also remembers the sense of release that came over the ship during that day. For her, it was round about six o'clock in the evening that marked the feeling of being out of danger. She explains: 'Well, I think what really happened was that we'd seen these three destroyers every day up till then buzzing around and flashing lights at each other and all the rest of it, and what had really happened was that that evening – I suppose at about six o'clock – by then they had actually left. And we were told over dinner that we were now considered to be safely out of the range of U-boats. I think it was suggested that we needn't keep our lifejackets on – because we'd got these awful cork life blocks, you could hardly call them lifejackets. They were sort of blocks of cork in canvas things which you slipped over your head and tied round you which we were always supposed to have near us. That evening was when they said well now, hopefully you don't have to carry them round everywhere with you, though you must know where they are. I don't know how much we were aware that the destroyers had gone, or whether it was them saying about the lifejackets and so on, but that's the time that I remember us having the idea that we were now supposed to be safe.

'Of course in some ways, I don't think I'd ever been that tense. It was just that it now felt as if we seemed to be getting nearer, you know. But the awful thing with the seavacuees – the children in the Government evacuation programme – I believe that was the first night they were allowed to sleep in pyjamas. Which was a tragedy, because if they had still had their outer clothes on they mightn't have all got so cold and wet. As it was I think, or from what I gathered afterwards, that was the first evening they had undressed and gone to bed properly.'

So by the early evening of Tuesday, the general mood among the passengers at least was almost a party atmosphere. Apart from the good news about the Battle of Britain, there was another reason to be cheerful: the storm had finally dropped a little. It really must have felt for everyone as though the worst was over. Perhaps Admiral Mackinnon subconsciously caught some of this optimistic atmosphere. Could that have been what influenced him to linger so long in the slow-moving convoy – a sitting target when all protection had disappeared? After all, it did seem as if the children had been got clear from the terrible bombing that had threatened their lives every night back home in England. The ship itself now appeared to have outrun the invisible dangers of the submarine U-boats. The storm was beginning to quieten. America and Canada were getting nearer all the time. It even sounded as if the war was finally beginning to go England's way after the desperate dark times of Dunkirk and the Blitz.

Most passengers, whether children or adult, would have agreed that evening of Tuesday 17th, as the setting sun broke through briefly to coat the decks in rainbow colours, that yes, the voyage to safety had reached a turning point. But while the darkness gathered and night set in, things were about to change, though just how terribly was imaginable only in the fears of Captain Landles Nicoll – and in the mind of one other man.

Kapitanleutnant Heinrich Bleichrodt, 30, was the commander of the German U-boat that the destroyer *Winchelsea* had reported operating a little way off earlier in the day. Heinrich Bleichrodt was already having a very successful tour with his U-boat, U48, and was on the verge of being decorated by Hitler. The men in the U-boats were Hitler's personal favourites – depicted in the German media as glamorous aces who would win the war for Germany, the submarine brothers of the fighter pilots. Bleichrodt's radio operator was Rolf Hilse. Rolf was only 17, but he had already been thoroughly caught up in the German propaganda machine. He explains: 'I had been selected to serve on the U-boats because of my height – under 5′ 8″. They said, "Anybody under 5′ 8″ who wants to go in a submarine step forward." Nobody did, but we were volunteered anyway. I spoke English, so I became a radio operator.'

Rolf's first tour aboard U-boat U47 saw him making history, helping to sink *The Royal Oak* at Scapa Flow: 'Then I was flown to Berlin, direct to the Chancellery. Hitler congratulated me personally and I was awarded the Iron Cross. It was 1939. I was 17.'

So by that night of Tuesday 17th the following year, Rolf was already a German war hero, and his commander Heinrich Bleichrodt was well on his way to becoming one: 'During the day on Tuesday we had already had a very good day. We had intercepted a convoy that was coming in towards Britain from America and we sunk either three ships or it may even have been four – but anyway, it was a good score. Heini, Kapitanleutnant Bleichrodt that is, was a good commander, very good. But then a British plane came over and we had to dive. We stayed at depth for the rest of the day. The weather had turned bad, you know, it was very rough, much better for our boat – a submarine is called a boat – to stay deep below the waves. We were just staying in position at about 20 degrees west, waiting for the opportunity to surface and move on.'

Meanwhile, on the other side of the *Benares* from where U-boat U48 was planning to surface, a young cadet, Edward Smith, was on lookout aboard the *Clan MacNeil*, one of the other ships in the convoy. Edward was just 19 years old, only a few years older than boys like Fred and Derek on board the *Benares*. He was serving in the Merchant Navy as a cadet aboard the steamer *Clan MacNeil*. That night Edward was on watch on the bridge.

He remembers: 'I was a young, innocent cadet at that time serving a four-year apprenticeship with the Clan Line, and that particular night of Tuesday, 17 September 1940, I was on the port wing of the bridge keeping lookout. We were part of the convoy – it was about 20 ships, I think – and we were leading the column next to the *Benares*. We were on the starboard side of the convoy, so that means we were on the right-hand side of the *Benares*. With my watch being on the port I could look across at the *Benares*. I remember during the day I often used to see all the children running about and the boys up on the deck looking out and waving at us and the other ships.

'Anyway, that night, it was a wild night. There was a moon out and the clouds were moving across the moon, scudding across as the gale blew them, so the moon appeared and disappeared. Of course, all the ships were all in darkness. Everything was black. All you saw around you was shapes of other ships and then just glimpses as the moon suddenly shone and then went again. But you had to try to keep station with the other ships – that is, stay in the same position in the convoy. You had to try and guess their distance, but with the sea throwing you about and the waves and the blackness it wasn't easy. The *Benares*, of course, was a big ship, it was the biggest ship in the convoy. It had two funnels, you see, and thinking back, probably that was one of the reasons why it was the target of the submarine. He'd be looking through his periscope I imagine and he – well, what he'd have seen here, he just saw a big ship, didn't he?'

Across the rough seas from Edward's lookout position on the *Clan MacNeil*, the children of the *Benares* were settling down for the night. Bess Walder was one of those children: 'The storm was really brewing up again and people – including the grown-ups – who were up on deck were advised to come down quickly and get down below and if possible go into the cabins and get in bed. The younger children were already down for the night anyway. That night, of course, of the 17th, the sea was at its worst. It was heaving. The boat was slashing and bashing and the noise of the waves against the hull was absolutely tremendous.'

Sonia Bech also remembers the way the storm whipped itself up again during the early evening: 'We'd just been rip-roaring around as usual. I used to play with Colin, Colin Ryder Richardson that is, a lot. I thought he was nice. Anyway, that night the weather really did turn nasty, it got very rough and stormy. We were told to keep off the deck because it had got so wet and rather dangerous.'

Sonia's friend, Colin, had his own special way of measuring the gathering storm: 'Well, it sounds a bit strange when you describe it now, but I had this ball bearing which I put in the drawer of my bedside cabinet, and when the ball bearing didn't move, well, that meant we were in calm water. But when the ball bearing started to go – you know, hitting the side of the drawer from one side to the other in time with the ship rolling – well, then you knew you were in a storm, and the more violent the storm the more the ball bearing would be knocking from side to side. So you knew the ship was entering a bigger and bigger storm. It was quite a simple way of knowing that we were in for a really rough time.'

The weather was putting a damper on the normal antics of Derek Capel and his mates up on the decks, so it was decided to call it a night and everyone went below decks for a bath and an early bed. 'That evening everybody said we were safe at last and we could go to bed wearing pyjamas for a change. We'd been sleeping fully clothed with two lifejackets on all the time before. And they said we could all have a bath, our first bath that was for a few days, you know, so in we all trooped. We all had baths and nice clean pyjamas on. That's what happened, groups went in, had a nice bath, clean pyjamas, lifejackets down beside you out the way, all lovely and comfortable. We sat around for a little while, then we all went to bed. About quarter past nine, Father Rory O'Sullivan came round to make sure everybody was nice and comfortable. He looked really rough though he did, poor fellow.'

Up on the bridge, this was the time when Admiral Mackinnon took the step of changing the orders of the convoy. Instead of breaking the convoy up by midday, as Captain Nicoll had wanted, Admiral Mackinnon had insisted they stay together, but he had at least agreed to Captain Nicoll's original plan of following a zigzag course to make them all a more difficult target. Now he countermanded that order. With the storm increasing to Force 6 it was just too dangerous to have 20 ships criss-crossing the rough seas in the pitch black with every chance of running straight into each other. So by ten o'clock that night the *Benares* ended up in a situation that, as far as Captain Nicoll was concerned, was the worst of all worlds: it was plodding along slowly, in a straight line, an obvious target surrounded by a fleet of smaller ships.

This was the exact moment at which Kapitanleutnant Bleichrodt on U-boat U48 was planning to surface. His radio operator Rolf Hilse remembers: 'It wasn't until very late that night that the captain thought it would be peaceful enough for us to surface and move on. So, it was just before midnight, our time that is, which was 10 p.m. British time, and I was looking at my scanner and I spotted another convoy of ships. Heini – Kapitanleutnant Bleichrodt – said, "We'll have a look." So we went up and we had a look, and it was a convoy. I don't know how many ships were in it, about 18, 19, something like this, I don't know for sure. Anyway, we had a good look round and we said, "There's nothing there – there's no escort, where's the escort?" Heini said, "It's odd. There's nothing there, there's no escort." The lull in the storm was ending and the weather was getting worse again. The sea was very rough, and the storm clouds were low over the water, but you could see the convoy when the moon came out.

'Naturally, we targeted the biggest ship first. That was obvious, the big two-funnel ship – we later learnt it was the *Benares*. To us it just looked like the most important ship, the best target, an Allied ship. There was nothing painted on it to indicate it was anything other than an ordinary ship. It might have been a troop ship, a cargo ship, or anything, but nothing to show. I mean, it should have been painted with a Red Cross and had all lights blazing. Then we would have known. But it was just part of an Allied convoy. So we fired. And we missed. We fired again and the second torpedo missed also. The master sight officer was useless at operating, and he made a mistake. He miscalculated, so two torpedoes missed. But nobody had seen us or the torpedo trails so we still had time. We only had four or five torpedoes left, but we said, "Hell, we risk another one. No more."

'The first officer shouted, "Rolf, watch out, 110 to 120 seconds." That was the warning I had to take my earphones off – the sound under water travels a lot further than above and the bang of a torpedo is tremendous under water, it's far stronger than above. It took 119 seconds for the torpedo to reach the stern of the *Benares*, then there was a huge bang and when we looked again the *Benares* was already gone well down in the sea. We got her right on the back in the engines and she went down very quick.'

If only Admiral Mackinnon had taken the obvious step of dispersing the convoy — but this he wasn't planning to do for another two hours. If only Edward Smith, on lookout aboard the *Clan MacNeil*, had seen something — but when U-boat U48 surfaced, it rose on the opposite side of the *Benares* from Edward's post on the *Clan MacNeil*, so he was in no position to see either the U-boat or the torpedo trails.

As the children went through their evening routine, there was nothing much for them to worry about apart from the storm. Down in the boys' dormitories at the rear of the ship, Derek Capel and his mates had finally settled in bed: 'By tenish it must have been, we were all nice and quiet in bed and just nodding off and there was an almighty whoomph and everything started falling. The wardrobe at the end of the beds suddenly was on my bed, stuck across the bed at an angle. It was terrible. I grabbed my brother and myself, we didn't know what had happened, there was rubbish everywhere, everything was thrown everywhere, there was dust, dirt and everything.

'Me and my brother grabbed a lifejacket each. We could just make out this faint blue light, the place was in turmoil. Where our wardrobe had ripped away from the wall was a hole. Billy Short came through from next door and we put our lifejackets on and went out through the gap where the wardrobe had been to try to get to Rory O'Sullivan's. His wall was still standing. We could see a little bit because the blue emergency lights were on in the passageway, but all the cabins were all still in darkness. So we went over and we thumped on his door and we heard him shout "Push it, push it," and we were trying to push it and the door was jammed solid, it was, and we were pushing like mad. Even with the three of us we just couldn't get it open.'

Fred Steels had also been enjoying the rare pleasure of sleeping in pyjamas at ten o'clock that night: 'All I had on was my pyjamas, cruising along quite comfortably, thinking oh good, it's gonna be glorious now. There was a bit of a gale going and next thing I know there was this one hell of a crash and the top bunk fell on top of me and I was soaking wet through.

'You couldn't make out what the devil it was, but what had happened when the torpedo hit us was, it came right in underneath us and exploded, blew a dirty great hole in her, you could look down the hole right down to the keel. Yeah, it's a thing you never forget. All we lads were in bed – it was about quarter past ten at night – and there was this dirty great thump and the alarm bells went off, and I woke up with the top bunk lying on top of me, luckily it was empty, and there was water everywhere. I didn't have a clue what had happened, but I managed to struggle out from underneath the bunk and I found that the explosion had ruptured all the water pipes, and the whole lot was streaming onto my side of the cabin.'

In their first-class cabins up at the front of the ship, the Bech family were some way from the torpedo strike. They weren't even sure whether or not they had actually been hit. Barbara and Sonia had settled down for the night a little later than the seavacuee children at the other end of the ship. Barbara Bech was just thinking of going to sleep: 'It had turned stormy and we had gone to bed as usual and I was reading. Sonia had already gone to sleep and I was just thinking, gosh, ten o'clock, maybe it's time to put the light out. I was just reaching for the switch when I suddenly heard this boom-oom, and I thought, oh, what's that? And then the alarm bells began to ring, so I shot out of bed and shook Sonia and said, "Sonia, wake up, I think something's happened, the bells are ringing, we'd better get as many clothes on as we can."

'So we started getting dressed and then I opened the door almost simultaneously with my mother opposite and she said, "Oh, you're up and getting dressed, right, carry on getting dressed." So we all got ourselves dressed and then headed off down the corridor and up the stairs to the lounge and everybody else was there. But strangely, I think the only noticeable thing was that there was a faint, well you might call it a sort of haze in the air, and a smell of – what? I suppose it was explosives? There was a curious kind of smell and a kind of haziness, but otherwise everything looked just the same as usual. All the lights were on and well, we just all went up to the lounge and started saying, "Well, what is it? What's happened?" Everybody was saying, "We don't know. Have we run into somebody else in the convoy?" '

Barbara and Sonia's brother Derek Bech was already sleeping when the strike happened. He says: 'We were all asleep. I'd been asleep and my mother was asleep. It was ten o'clock at night and suddenly we had this – this shudder and a thud. It wasn't an explosion, it was more of a boom and a sort of resounding noise, as though you were being put inside a steel drum and somebody had banged it with a stick or something. It was a sort of bummm and it echoed. You didn't have the impression of an explosion but my mother, who was always vigilant, she thought there might be something sinister about this. So she threw me out of bed and said, "Get dressed." And I had my school uniform alongside me, which I put on over my pyjamas. I put on my school gym shoes. I put on my school raincoat and I think I even put my school cap on – that was how you got ready back then.

'My mother went through to Barbara and Sonia. They'd heard the explosion – Barbara had been reading, she was always a bookworm – they were getting dressed as well. My mother collected Barbara's holdall and we all walked up to the muster station. By this time there were bells were ringing. As we went into the corridor we could smell this smell. I've always been told it was cordite, a sort of acidy, acrid kind of smell. If I ever smell it, even now, whenever I smell that pungent sort of smell, it always brings back memories. Anyway, we went up to the muster station and just ended up sitting down on the sofas. Some of the adult passengers who hadn't gone to bed were still there. They were sitting at the bar, you know, drinking and smoking, chatting. Some of them were even playing bridge I think, playing cards or reading books. I mean, it was an odd thing, a kind of a social event going on up there. So we just sat down. But then when my mother wanted to go back down to the cabin for something she'd forgotten, they said, "No, you mustn't go down, you can't go back".'

Sonia Bech had been fast asleep when the *Benares* was struck, so her first awareness that something was wrong was the alarm bells ringing. On waking it was the acrid smell that hit her more than anything: 'There was a funny smell in the cabin immediately – not a nice smell at all, strange, and everything was still. I think the engines had stopped straight away, so there was an eerie feeling with no dub dub dub – the noise the engine makes, duka, duka, duka – that had gone dead quiet and there was a sort of murky smell and I just had this instinctive horrid feeling.

'Then Barbara said, "Come on, Sonia, don't dither around, get into your clothes as much as you can find, we've got to get on deck." So I put on my knickers and jumper and kept my pyjamas on. Then I put on my duffle coat – it was my favourite, a really nice coat, which came down quite a long way down my legs. It was brand new, really smart. Barbara had pretty much the same on. We got outside and Mummy was there pulling Derek out into the corridor and we went straight to our muster stations. But then we were waiting in our muster stations and that's when it hit me that things had really happened, not nice things. It was something bad, and I remember I started saying my prayers.'

With an awareness and instinct beyond his years, Colin Ryder Richardson realised almost immediately just how serious a situation the *Benares* was in: 'I was in bed reading my comics when there was an enormous bang and almost immediately a smell of explosives. I knew at once what had happened, you see it was such a familiar smell, because I'd smelt it in the air raids – the smell of explosives. We had had the drill to go up to our muster stations, as they were called, so I knew that was what I had to do straight away. Luckily my cabin was at the front of the ship, so I wasn't near where the torpedo had hit. But there were clouds of smoke rolling down the passageways and it was pretty obvious what had happened. I quickly got out of bed and put my personal lifejacket on and of course I had my cork lifejacket that the ship provided. I put my dressing gown and slippers on and also my string gloves and my balaclava helmet – of course I was still in my pyjamas, but I felt that was the proper thing to wear at the time!

'Then I went up to my lifeboat muster station where everybody else was gathering and saying this and that. Some people said, "Oh, we've just been hit by another ship in the convoy or something." I said, "Well, I don't think so," but you keep yourself fairly quiet when you're with adults – they're voicing all sorts of opinions, so you are not going to be listened to. People were saying was it worth going out on to the boat deck to see what was happening or perhaps it was a bit too stormy? But to me that was a big worry, because it was really windy and stormy and high seas running. We'd never had a lifeboat drill in weather anything like that.'

From his lookout station on board the *Clan MacNeil*, Edward Smith was able to see clearly what those in the *Benares* could only guess at – that a torpedo had struck the ship well back towards the stern and exploded. The huge gash in the hull was just below the dormitories of the seavacuee children. 'It was about ten past ten,' remembers Edward, 'and I was standing on the side of my ship looking at the *Benares*. Then there was this big bang and I looked, and to my horror the ship, the *Benares*, shuddered and suddenly all their lights came on. She had been hit. But the thing was, our orders were to scatter. The convoy had to break up and run immediately if there was an attack. I'd never seen anything like this, never seen a ship hit or anything. So I just had this, this confused feeling. And we went on. And gradually as we went on the *Benares* dropped back and disappeared in the distance behind us and there was nothing more we could do.'

Meanwhile, the crew of U-boat U48 were congratulating themselves, as Rolf explains: 'As we hit the *Benares*, of course it was an excitement. It was a big ship and these U-boat captains, they tried to beat the other ones in the tonnes sunk, and this was big. We saw the lifeboats going down straight away, but to us it was just an ordinary ship so we didn't take any notice. We went onto the next one, which was the *Marina*, 5,000 tonnes, and within two minutes we had this one, we knocked this one down. Then there was a tanker and he was empty, so he could get a fair speed on. We tried to catch up with him but it was no chance. So we weren't taking any notice of what was going on with the first ship, we just carried on. We did not know that there were children there, nothing at all, no, and after we got the second one, we're already starting to look for the third one, so we didn't know anything was wrong. We found out later on. If we had known we would have left it, we would have left the ship. Well, you don't kill children, do you, so that's why we would have left it.'

But for the victims of U48 the long, desperate fight to survive had only just begun. In the bowels of the ship Derek Capel, his 5-year-old brother Alan and their friend Billy Short were struggling to get the jammed cabin door open to rescue their escort, Father Rory O'Sullivan. They were only a few feet above where the *Benares* had been holed, and water, steam and smoke were rapidly engulfing them. Torn cables dangled from the bulkheads, sending electricity flashes arcing across the passageway. And still Derek pushed on the door: 'Then suddenly it gave just a little bit and Father Rory got the door dragged open. What had happened was in the darkness, he'd got hold of the wardrobe handle, which had fallen at an angle and he was trying to pull the wardrobe door handle. So he was on the wrong door and these three little boys were still trying to push his cabin door open, which had got wedged. But in the end we pulled him out and we were out – me brother, meself and Billy.

'So we went along with Father Rory and we picked up other boys until there were the seven of us. Everything was falling, stuff falling everywhere, we had to climb over, under stuff, everything like. It was such a mess. There was water pouring, there was cables flashing. There was dust, dirt, everywhere there was – and you had to be careful where you walked because there was bits and pieces on the floor all over the place. And gradually we got up the stairs onto the deck and we walked up there and then we went into our common room, which was where we all had to meet if there was any problem. We got in there and it was empty except for us boys, I think, and then – suddenly I looked around and my brother had disappeared and – I didn't know what had happened to him, but he'd disappeared.'

CHAPTER FIVE

The Sinking of the Benares

At first the routine for abandoning ship seemed to be going calmly on board the *Benares*. Kenneth Sparks was one of many who didn't immediately assume that the ship had been hit. He says: 'I remember the bang, but you didn't know right off that it was a torpedo. There was just this bang. Then the lights went out in all the cabins and there was a lot of steam and noise, and screams because people had got hurt. Once the emergency lights came on, we could see at least. I was the oldest in my cabin, so first of all I was getting the children organised. There were four younger children and I got them pushed out into the gangway. There was a bit of panic among the children because they didn't know what was happening. But the crew were very good. They organised everything. It was put through the tannoy that you should get into the gangways and then work your way up to the upper deck. Well, I had all my lot out of my cabin, so we started to move up to the upper deck and I was walking with them to the muster station.

'Then I thought, oh dear, I haven't got my overcoat, mother'll kill me when I get home – I mean, not thinking that we might never get home. It was just "My mum'll kill me if I don't take my overcoat back home", so I decided to nip back down to the cabin to get it. I began working my way back along to the cabin. There was still a lot of noise and the rushing of water and steam escaping, but you could see what you were doing. I managed to get the coat alright and then got back into the gangway and in this big queue to work me way out back to the dining room where our muster station was. We were all shuffling along. Nobody was running, there was no real panic. But there was a lot of noise of the escaping steam and shouting from different people. You could hear a bit of screaming too, I think it was people trapped in their cabins. Once you got in this queue in the gangway you couldn't get out again, you had to keep going.

'We eventually got through into the dining room where you had to go up this big staircase to get to the upper deck to get to your lifeboat. But while we were going through the dining room you could see at the far end of the room – which was the stern end of the boat – there was a massive big hole where the hatch had been blown off. There was electricity flashing all along the metalwork on the edges of it. Well, then of course we realised we must have been hit by a torpedo.'

Up at the front of the ship, away from the actual impact of the torpedo, the private passengers had even less idea what was happening, so they stuck calmly to their routine drill. Derek Bech remembers: 'We were just sitting at the muster station, which was in the lounge. Of course, rumours were getting around. Most people thought that due to the very rough sea something might have been dislodged and banged into the ship. Or some people reckoned one of the other ships in the convoy had rammed us in the dark as we were all in blackout. Nobody had any fear, because nobody had even thought of a torpedo at that stage. We had been sitting there for about five or ten minutes when the door from the deck suddenly burst open with the gale roaring in and one of the young English officers came in. He shouted, "God, what are you all doing here? The ship is sinking. Go quickly to your lifeboats".'

The passengers had calmly followed their drill to the letter. But what they had never practised for was reality. And the reality was that things had already begun to go very wrong with the process of abandoning the *Benares*. The passengers had very little idea of what to do when lifeboats were actually being launched in earnest. Far worse than this, the launching of the lifeboats was fast becoming a disaster. By now the north Atlantic had whipped itself into full-scale Force 6 storm and 30-foot waves were crashing against the hull of the *Benares*. Worse still, the ship had already begun to list over badly to one side as the sea flooded into its stern where the torpedo had struck.

Barbara Bech remembers how the initial false calm turned to instant chaos: 'The doors out to the deck suddenly flew open and it was one of the officers and he said, "Oh my God, you're all still here! Get to your boats because the ship's going down." In the boat drills we'd all been allocated a particular number lifeboat – there were about six down each side – and we each had a numbered boat that we should go for. Anyhow, we all clambered up on onto the lifeboat deck, but there were no boats there.

'So we sort of peered over the edge and way down below the station for our boat, which was number 4, we could see there was a boat already down in the water, still sort of holding into the side of the ship. I don't know what had happened with the other lifeboats – whether some hadn't been lowered or whether they had all already gone. But there was number 4 down there, tossing up and down in the massive waves.

'There were rope ladders with wooden slats, two of them, hanging over the side of the boat, going down to where the lifeboat was. The people for our lifeboat were slowly clambering down, and we were all just standing there and waiting our turn. There was a chap directing operations and I heard him say, "We'll never get them all off, I wonder if any of them can climb ropes?" I had always fancied myself as a gymnast, so I said, "I can climb ropes." He said, "Well, that would help." So I turned to Mummy and said, "Shall I go down on the rope?" She said, "Do you think you can?" and I said, "Oh yes." So the next thing, the sailor said, "Right, over you go" and there I was hanging on to the rope for dear life. But I wasn't wearing gym shoes and I realised that with my stiff lace-up shoes I couldn't grip the rope at the bottom with my feet. So I had to come down hand over hand. I kept telling myself, Now, don't let go, don't let go because … But then as I got down near the boat I had to let go and I landed on top of a couple of people! I apologised and picked myself up to see what was happening next.

'By then I could see my brother Derek was coming. He'd just been heaved over the side into the arms of a sailor, and the sailor was holding him into the ladder inside his arms. They were just beginning to come down very slowly and carefully when I suddenly realised that our boat was drifting away. I don't know what had been holding us in the first place, but whatever it was had been let go or something. And it hit me. He's not gonna get in, is he? The sailor that was with him looked down and I think he must have decided to take them back up again because the last I saw was them was climbing back on board. Then my lifeboat got too far away to see. So the rest of my family disappeared from my sight.'

Still on board the sinking *Benares*, the Bechs could only watch helplessly as Barbara drifted away from them. Derek will never forget the moment his older sister disappeared over the side down the rope: 'What had happened was that by the time we got to our boat – lifeboat number 4 – it had already been launched by the Indian lascars who had got there first. I think they must have thought there were no passengers coming, so they had better get in and launch it themselves. So that meant boat number 4 was already in the sea, crashing up and down in the waves, with no way for us to get in. That was when somebody said can anybody here climb a rope? And of course, Barbara had been to St Paul's Girls' School and learnt to climb a rope in the school gymnasium, so she said, "Oh yes, I can climb a rope." The davits – big steel arms – they use for launching the lifeboats still had the ropes hanging. So they put her onto one of these ropes dangling into nowhere. Here was Barbara, my sister, a 14-year-old girl, in the middle of this storm in the Atlantic, going down a rope into a lifeboat that was flinging up and down on the waves. But she made it.'

Barbara, as the oldest of the three Bech children, was always the calm one in a crisis. She had the ability simply to concentrate on the task at hand rather than worrying about the future. For her little sister Sonia, only 11 at the time, the whole experience was frightening, from arriving at the muster station to the moment she watched her sister disappear over the side: 'When I got into the muster station, I did become very scared and Mummy and Derek were sitting there, you know, looking a bit scared too, and I remember thinking I must say my prayers at once because I knew by then that something awful was going to happen. There was no panic whatsoever, but everybody was very still and I felt something really dreadful was happening. I thought, this is bad. This is going to be very bad, so I was saying the Lord's Prayer. Then this officer came in and said, "What are you doing here? You should be up on the deck." But no one had told us to go on the deck. In our lifeboat drills all we had ever been told was to wait in the muster station and so that was just what we did. But as soon as we'd been told, we immediately got up to our lifeboat – and it wasn't there. It was gone.

'There were people standing around, but the lifeboat had gone. Then one of the sailors stood up and said, "Can anybody climb a rope? The ladders are full, can anybody climb a rope?" I'd never climbed a rope, but Barbara was very good at gym at school. She said, "Oh, I'll do it," so she began climbing down this rope and we saw her go. I think I must have looked over and seen her into the lifeboat because I can remember thinking well, she's going to be all right. They took Derek next and they had an old sailor who took him in his arms and lowered him on a ladder. But then they said no, the ship has pushed off, there's no way can you get on it, and they had to get my brother back up. So there we were, on this boat which was by this time beginning to list and we were going – the stern was going down and the bows were going up.'

Derek had to climb not just down towards the lifeboat, but also back up against the outward-sloping hull of the ship to try to get back on board again. 'It was pretty much everybody for themselves by then. They put me onto a rope ladder down the side of the ship. Luckily there was a lascar crewman just below me on the ladder. He stood me between his arms and we walked step by step down the side of the ship, looking down to see where the lifeboat was.

But the lifeboat was crashing up and down. The waves were huge, really high. It was obviously suicidal to bring the lifeboat alongside a rope ladder. It was crashing into us and we'd have all been crushed. So the lifeboat pulled away and I then had to climb back up – up the ship's hull, with the lascar behind me helping. One of the big waves just crashed right over us, but we got up and were hauled back onto the deck. It was pretty shaking. I was quite frightened by then. It was hard having to go back on the sinking ship. But my mother was there and I got pulled over the ship's rail and reunited.

'We were still on the upper deck level, which was pointless with no lifeboats. So we went back down onto the main deck. But we didn't know what to do. All the lifeboats had gone. There were children screaming and a lot of noise and commotion of people trying to leave the ship and obviously in difficulty. Then one of the passengers saw my mother and us two children, my sister and myself, and he said, "Follow me, I know where there's some rafts."

Sonia picks up the story: 'My mother said, "Right, we must go." She couldn't take her bag so she told me, "Sonia, you must have my little box of jewellery in your dufflecoat pocket." So I put that in my dufflecoat and mummy threw away her bag and kept our identity cards and passports and some money and a little bottle of brandy which she put in her own pockets. Then the man started taking us to the raft. We'd never heard about rafts because they were for the crew as a last resort. The rafts were just fairly basic, made of wood, and with metal buoyancy cylinders like petrol cans tied on. The man threw down the raft. By now the ship was really sinking and where we were was rearing up. We began climbing down the ladder. My brother went first, but the ladder ended, it didn't reach as far as the water because the ship had gone up higher. So Derek was at the bottom and it was my turn to go and I was a bit frightened – especially when the ladder stopped short and I just literally had to let go and let myself fall into the water.

'But the raft was nearby. There was a young man – he was the seventh engineer, Tommy Milligan – already in the water and I think he must have helped me onto the raft. I got on somehow, and Mummy was behind me and she said, "Don't worry, I'm coming, I'm right behind you." There was another lady in the water as well and we all just clung on to the raft. Then the man who had found the raft for us swam up alongside. We found out later he was Mr Davies, Eric Davies. Mr Davies told us, "I'm going to have to swim you out because if you stay here you're going to be sucked under." That was frightening, because I couldn't imagine he could do it. But he did, he was strong and he pulled the raft out away from the suction. Up until now when you looked up you could see the boat with all its lights on. It was massive. You couldn't see all of it from down there at the bottom, but we could see the lights at the top. Then the lights just all went out and the next minute she was in the water, sunk, and there was this incredible silence and – blackness. I'll never forget it as long as I live. I was so frightened. Here we were hanging on this little raft. There were five of us on this raft, all hanging on. The seas were so rough. We were being knocked against wreckage. We could hear the people crying out sometimes, but not very much, and soon it was absolutely still, a horrid stillness. There was nothing, nothing, and there we were, and – well, during the course of that night while it was still black, I lost consciousness.'

But at least the Bechs were alive, and on a raft. Derek Bech remembers vividly how they very nearly didn't make it off the ship at all: 'We were hurrying after this man to try to get to where the rafts were supposed to be. As we were running along there were these explosions – which were obviously the boilers exploding. Then a great cloud of smoke came out and we had to turn round and go back up to the bows. We found the rafts and they were quite big rafts, enough for four to six people. Eric Davies launched two of those rafts single-handed. By this time the ship was very much going down at the stern and when we walked up to the bows we were going up a fairly steep gradient. We heard over the side this man calling. He said, "I've got the rafts, jump." And so we saw where he was and we just let go of the ladder and jumped.

'My mother and Sonia and me managed to get on the raft. Then there was a splash in the water as another lady jumped in. Then Eric

Davies swam up and he was holding onto the raft with one arm and with the other arm he did a crawl stroke and pulled us away from the side of the ship so that we wouldn't be sucked down, and he then left us to go and see to the other raft. I found out later he was just a passenger like us. He worked for the BBC and was going out as a war reporter. He was a very brave man. Eventually we were joined by another person swimming in the water who happened to be an engineer from the ship. So in total we were five people on that raft. There was myself, my mother, Sonia, the engineer and Doris Walker, an Australian lady, who was the woman who had jumped from the ship.

'We were sitting on the raft, and then the ship slid down into the sea and that was the end of it. We were left in darkness and in the darkness you could hear people calling out for help. And we kept having to push away all the junk and debris that was bumping into us, because it was very, very rough still. And that was the beginning of our night.'

Barbara Bech, drifting helplessly in lifeboat number 4, had no idea whether the rest of her family had even made it off the ship. Among the seavacuee children too, brothers and sisters were losing each other as the chaos mounted. Derek Capel was desperately trying to find his 5-year-old brother, Alan. 'He suddenly disappeared. He was holding my hand and then he was gone. It was half dark, or very nearly dark, with just these blue lights. I couldn't work out what had happened and I was thinking how I had promised to look after him, and I really had been looking after him every minute of the time. I was absolutely gutted. I didn't know what had happened. It was so confusing – he was gone, and then immediately I was grabbed hold of by seamen and they said right, this is the last boat, and I was literally thrown into the boat. And I do mean thrown, because the boat was hanging halfway down the hull and we were literally chucked down into it. There was one woman already in it, Mary Cornish, plus a lot of lascar seamen. There was a Polish shipping man and a few white officers, us boys and our escort, Father Rory O'Sullivan. We boys were just shoved down the bottom, sitting there in our pyjamas in the half-waterlogged boat.

'The sea was terrible. One minute the waves were as high as a church steeple and you were looking down from the top. Then the next minute you were at the bottom looking up at this wave towering above you. That was the way the sea was. There were people in the water, there was shouting, there was screaming, there were boats that were turned over. All this was going on around us in the water. It was frightening, really terrifying. I think we picked up a couple of people, but that was all we could do because we couldn't manoeuvre the boat. Our boat only had two proper oars. You were meant to use this machine, like winding gear with handles that you turned to propel the boat, but we couldn't get the handles to work so we were just drifting. We could only drift, which meant we could only pick up people who could get to us. The screams and yells were awful.

'Then we looked out and there was the ship, about 150 yards away, slowly going down. And gradually she slipped away, and eventually disappeared. There was this terrific wind, a big squall, still blowing, and the lifeboat was pitching and tossing. It was pitch dark now and we could feel the boat going up and down. There were bits of wreckage all around us in the water that kept crashing against us. Everybody was just sitting there – terrified, I think. In the end we boys clustered together down in the bottom of the boat, we didn't know what to do. We were the last boat to be launched. I think a lot of the other boats got into terrible trouble because the ship itself was still moving when they went in the water, so they were dragged almost under the water. As I say, we were the last one and we just about got away with it.'

Derek Capel's lifeboat was number 12, the last to be launched from the *Benares*. Kenneth Sparks also ended up in this lifeboat, but it was by a sheer fluke that it happened: 'It was my coat, you see. If I hadn't have obeyed my stepmother's instructions to get me coat, I wouldn't be here today, because that's what saved my life – going back for me overcoat. It saved my life for the simple reason that I went back to get it. If I hadn't done that I would have been on the upper deck that much earlier and I would have walked across to my own allocated lifeboat. I wouldn't have been picked up and put in the wrong boat because it was the last boat.

'The boat I should have been in was lifeboat number 8, but when I started to walk towards it, an officer shouted that it was full and said, "You can get in this one." He just picked me up and put me in what I found out afterwards was number 12 boat. Which in fact was very lucky, because number 12 was the only lifeboat out of all of them that landed the right way up. So we were able to pull away. Although we were the last boat to be loaded and lowered, we could see the others all at different angles, all still trying to be lowered because the falls had jammed. Whether they had been lowered too fast or the rough sea or the angle of the ship I don't know, but the lifeboats were tipping people out and they were screaming and falling into the sea. While the *Benares* was still there and still lit, you could see what was happening. The sea was very, very rough and it was falling with rain. The *Benares* wasn't the only ship that had been torpedoed and everything was very noisy because of all the steam venting from both boats. So there was a lot of mess and confusion.

'The Indian lascars — poor devils — were all just in their cotton things. I think they had been below us in the crew quarters even nearer the explosion. There were people being tipped out of boats. The sea was shipping into our lifeboat at the front, carried in by the gale. But the people who'd been tipped out were struggling in the sea, having to hang on to the bottom end of the boat. We were wet through as well — but from the rain, not the seawater. In a way we were very, very lucky. If I had been in the boat I was meant to be — which was four more along on the starboard side — I wouldn't be here now, because that boat never made it. I don't know if they ever found any individual survivors from it, but as far as I know number 8 boat itself never made it at all.'

Fred Steels was another of the seavacuee children who had been delayed in getting to his muster station and ended up being late arriving at the lifeboats, which meant that he, like Kenneth, was put on the lucky last boat — lifeboat number 12. In Fred's case it wasn't the pressing need to rescue an overcoat that held him up, but his efforts to get some of the younger children out of the cabin.

'The first thing I did was get Paul Shearing out of his bunk, because for some strange reason he was still asleep, I don't know how he managed that. And we had another lad in there. Neither of us knew him because he wasn't attached to our group, but this kid was sat up in bed crying about he couldn't find his glasses. We managed to get the door open, which had been jammed with the force of the explosion. Once we'd got out we were trying to coax this nipper out, but he kept saying, "No, I've got to find me spectacles." We really tried for quite a while to get him out, but he wouldn't leave without his glasses and in the end we just had to set off and trust he'd follow us, but I'm not sure he did. We were hoping that he would get out, but I don't think he did, quite honestly. Paul and I managed to get out into the gangway, and we were heading for the upper deck when we came across this damn great hole. It was massive, you could have put a couple of buses in it.

'The torpedo had come in right underneath where our cabins were and exploded. You could look right down this hole down to the keel itself, and the water was just pouring in. That certainly wasn't a pleasant sight, we were really worried. But we managed to get up on deck and the first thing that happened was some dirty great seaman – don't know who he was – picked me up and threw me in this lifeboat along with Paul. He grabbed hold of us and he didn't put us in the lifeboat, he threw us. Then everything went on from there, people started piling in after us. The lascars were the first ones in there – they were in the centre of the boat and they had started lowering the lifeboat. We got it down so far and one of the pulleys jammed a bit, and the lifeboat tilted right up at one end. We had visions of all going for a swim, but they managed to straighten her out and they got her down. And then we had a couple of blokes, I think one of them was the gunner actually, came down the lifelines into the boat. One came down and landed on top of Billy Short – well, he always said he'd been crushed!

'We got everybody on board we could and then we managed to pull away from the ship a bit. We could hear kiddies and passengers in the water shouting for help, and that's when we picked up Purvis. He was one of the crew and he'd been diving in the water over and over again trying to save as many as he could until he was completely exhausted. We managed to pull him on board. We were being thrown all over the place and we didn't have proper oars on those lifeboats. They had like pump handles. They had a row of eight handles down the centre of the lifeboat and you used to pump them up and down, which turned a shaft, which turned a propeller. There was half a gale going at the time we got hit, so we were getting quite high waves. One minute we were down in a trough and waves were up 20 feet above us, the next minute we were on top of the wave looking down into a canyon. So we were trying to fight the waves. All we could do was use the handles to get us away from the sinking ship and we were just tossing up and down there, watching the rest of the lifeboats trying to get away.

'And the other lifeboats, some of them, the falls jammed or slipped and the boats just nose-dived into the water, virtually. Others were coming down and just fell into the water. Some boats were tilted same as we had been, but they couldn't right them. Others hit the water too steep and went right under, and when they came up again they were full of water right up to the gunnels. And all we could do was just lay off there and watch it because we couldn't do anything. It wasn't just the sight, but the sounds as well, I think they were the worst. All you heard was the screams and – it was pretty dark – we saw a lifeboat just disappear and the kids were screaming. There was one lifeboat, and as it was coming down the side it slipped right out of its falls and hit the water fast. It was too near the torpedo hole. The lifeboat was just sucked straight in. The boat was being dragged into the hole in the side of the ship and they didn't have enough power to pull it away, the suction from the ship took it straight in. You could hear the screams from the kiddies and everybody else on board the lifeboat, but there wasn't anything anybody could do about it –

and that was the worst part of it, was listening to the kids screaming, and you knew you couldn't do a damn thing about it.'

The seavacuee boys, Fred, Derek and Kenneth, all ended up together in lifeboat number 12 by sheer chance. For one reason or another they had been delayed in getting to the muster station and had literally 'missed the boat' when it came to the lifeboat they had been officially assigned. It's natural to assume that being among the very last to leave the rapidly sinking ship would have put the boys in much worse danger than those, like the private passengers, who were away from the torpedo impact and could make their way to a lifeboat relatively easily. But surprisingly, the boys, last off the ship, were among the first to be safely clear of it. By the time lifeboat number 12 was launched, the *Benares* had slowed to a dead halt, and in fact its stern was already sliding down into the sea. This meant that boat 12 was actually easier to launch than most of the other lifeboats – it wasn't dragged and buffeted by the ship's motion, and it didn't have so far to drop. So when it landed in the sea it was by far the least waterlogged of any of the lifeboats. Again, this was doubly good luck because it meant that not only was the boat more buoyant and able to ride the waves, it also drifted more easily, helping it to get away from the powerful suction forces caused by the sinking *Benares*.

By a tragic twist, it was the initial lifeboat launches that met with disaster. Lifeboats number 1 and number 2 – both up at the bows of the ship – were among the first to be launched. The pulleys, known as davits, for lowering the boats worked okay with these launches, but both boats hit rough seas while the *Benares* was still moving forward comparatively fast. The combination of wave and suction dragged them both down until they were waterlogged. Both these boats capsized completely, leaving their occupants trying desperately to cling onto the hull or simply swimming for it. The third lifeboat also had to be abandoned. This one was sucked right under the bows of the *Benares*, standing it on end and flipping its passengers into the sea. Lifeboat number 4 – the one the Bech family should have been in – was the only other boat to do as well as number 12. It had been launched early for some reason – possibly by lascars – but the launch had been successful at least, and it was soon drifting with 33 people in it, including Barbara Bech who was watching the rest of her family still struggling to get off the *Benares*.

The launching of lifeboat number 5 was among the most disastrous of all. The pulleys failed completely, leaving the boat dangling, and catapulting its occupants into the water. This was the boat that held Beth Cummings from Liverpool, and her new friend, Bess Walder from London. Lifeboat number 6 was another where the pulleys failed to work properly in launching. This meant that it hit the water at a bad angle and submerged completely; this was the boat that Fred remembers suddenly popping up to the surface again. It had mainly contained private passengers. Admiral Mackinnon had also seen fit to board this boat, departing from the naval tradition for commanders to go down with their ships. But ironically, he went down with the lifeboat, because he was never seen again from the time it resurfaced. Though it was badly water-logged, a few survivors managed to stay afloat in it, including Anthony Quinton.

The reserve naval officer Lt-Cdr Richard Deane was in lifeboat number 7 with his wife and, as with so many of the boats, the pulleys once again failed. The boat was sent crashing into the water and Mrs Deane drowned, but Lt-Cdr Deane managed to keep it afloat, though like nearly every boat it was almost completely waterlogged. What made it worse for Richard Deane was his belief that the launching of the lifeboats need not have been such a tragic disaster. He felt that mismanagement, poor machinery maintenance and inadequate drill were more to blame than the rough seas. After all, the other ship in the convoy to be torpedoed, the *Marina*, managed to launch its lifeboats without difficulty.

There is no record of what happened to lifeboat number 8, the boat that Kenneth Sparks should have been on – it may have been the one that Fred Steels saw sucked into the torpedo hole. Though Derek Capel didn't know it at the time, lifeboat number 9 was the one that his little brother Alan ended up in. Like so many of the others, its launch was botched, and it was yet another boat to be dangling by a single rope before plunging into the sea. Most people fell out, and those very few who did manage to cling on found themselves sitting in a boat so totally waterlogged that it was barely more than driftwood.

The seavacuee children had mainly ended up allocated to the boats numbered from 8 upwards; these were launched from nearer the stern. But even lifeboat number 10 suffered the same problems as all the rest – a faulty launch, near capsizing and resulting waterlogging. Young children in this boat, basically floating in the sea, yet within the surrounding gunwales of the lifeboat, mainly died from exposure. Yet again, lifeboat number 11 ended up full of water, but it managed to stay afloat and even picked up an extra child – Bess Walder's young brother Louis, minus his Hornby train set.

Was Lt-Cdr Richard Deane right to criticise the process so bitterly? Could the launching of the lifeboats have been handled better? And why did Admiral Mackinnon board a boat so early on in the abandonment process? Colin Ryder Richardson's lifeboat was one of those that got into terrible difficulties, and he has his own theories about what might have gone wrong. He explains: 'We were led out when our boat number came up, I think it was lifeboat number 6. By this time the whole ship was lit with the emergency lighting, so we could see quite clearly that the lifeboats had been lowered. It was obvious even then that it was going rather erratically. The ship was really rolling. The person looking after me was a Hungarian journalist, Laszlo Raskai, and he came and saw me safely on board. He wasn't allowed on because it was women and children only, and then almost immediately the lifeboat was lowered.

'As soon as it struck the water, the sea came straight into the lifeboat and it disappeared almost completely under water except for the stern and the bows. The boat was only being supported by the air tanks that were under the seats. My view was that the boats were not watertight. It was an Indian ship and I think the boats were letting the water in because they were wooden lifeboats and they had probably just dried out – shrunk where they had been in a hot climate. I think maybe they had not been tested to see that they were watertight, that they would float. So we're all sitting there in the water and looking for buckets to bail out with and things like that, but you could see it was totally hopeless because the sea was running through the boat from one side to the other. There was no way we were going to get the water out and keep the boat dry. It was impossible.

'Our next big problem was to get the lifeboat away from the side of the ship. The ship was still moving forward and we couldn't manage to undo the falls, that's what they call the ropes that lowered us. So the boat was being pulled along with the ship, which was still travelling even though it had been torpedoed. There were oars and a mast lying on the seats of the lifeboat, but they hadn't been tied down and they had floated away when we went under. So that meant we had no means of getting away from the *Benares*. We knew if the ship sank it would drag us down with it by suction, so we were desperately trying to push the boat away. And at the same time other people were trying to pick up those who had gone in the water. There must have been about 40 or so people in the lifeboat by then, so we were already overloaded and we had to tell people that we couldn't take them. There was just no room. We tried to get them to hold on to the sides – but those were underwater – and the waves were so big. It was all so difficult, you couldn't even open your mouth without getting a lungful of water.

'I was sitting next to an elderly lady who I think was a ship's nurse. She kept asking me, were there other boats around to pick us up out of the water? I was trying to reassure her. Another ship had been torpedoed at the same time and they had lifeboats that were properly crewed and were riding properly in the water, and I could see the lights in these lifeboats, so I said, well there's boats over there, they're bound to come and help us. We just have to wait. But she was getting a bit hysterical, and she was an elderly lady. I sort of had her in my arms and she was slowly slipping down into the boat itself, and she was very big and I was only 11, so I was having problems trying to keep her head above water. I just kept reassuring her that we would be picked up and that we would be saved in some shape, way or form, whether by other lifeboats that hadn't sunk like ours or by destroyers. But of course, I knew that the destroyers were already long gone.'

John Baker and his older brother Bobby were also caught up in the worst possible phase of the lifeboat launching. By this stage nobody could claim there wasn't chaos. Though people were trying not to panic, the fresh disasters that came with each lifeboat launch were obvious to everyone. There were children tossing in the waves, screaming and shouting, unable to get near a lifeboat. Those lucky enough to be in boats were desperately trying to keep afloat. Meanwhile, other lifeboats dangled over the edge of the sinking ship, spilling yet more children into the sea. It was during this lethal confusion that John, who was only 7 at the time, lost contact with 12-year-old Bobby. Even now he finds it hard to make sense of what happened that night in the Atlantic storm.

'It all started with the alarm bells going and we were all in bed, fast asleep. The alarm bell woke me up and so I knew we had a drill or whatever, drills can happen at any time. I had my blankets wrapped round me Navy-style in a sort of cocoon, so I was trying to kick my bedding clear. I fought my way out of bed and then ran around everybody waking them up. I must have been the first one to be awake. There were four of us in the cabin and I woke my brother up and the boys in the other bunks. The alarm bells were still going, and we all mustered out in the passageway and proceeded on deck as we'd been taught in the lifeboat drills. We knew the procedure, but the first thing that occurred to me when I got on deck – and it was the first rule we had been taught, but unfortunately I'd forgotten – that is, I'd forgotten my lifejacket. So I said to Bobby, "I must go and get my lifejacket," and off I went like a rocket.

'Fortunately Bobby very sensibly grabbed hold of me and kept me close, even though I think I probably struggled a bit, because I was that determined to go down to get my lifejacket. He stopped me going because he knew I'd get lost, which I wasn't thinking of at the time, but I was bound to have got lost. There's no doubt about that whatsoever – because every time I was by myself in the bowels of that ship I got lost, so why would this be any different from all the other occasions that I'd got lost? And I was trying to wriggle free to go and get the lifejacket, because I knew how important it was, from all the drills. So Bobby really had to hang onto me and make me stay on deck.

'Then we had to go and get onto the lifeboat, and that's when it all went wrong. Things were happening really fast and it's hard to work out exactly in what order it all was. Because I can remember by the time I was climbing back up the hull of the ship to get back on board again after the lifeboat fell, I have a vague feeling that I'd got a lifejacket on. I was climbing up these sort of stairs – slats on a rope ladder – up the side of the ship, and that memory is vaguely connected to the fact that I probably had a lifejacket on as I was climbing. But that must have been later, because what had happened first is that when we were all in the lifeboat and they began lowering it down the side of the ship, one of the pulleys jammed, tipped the boat up at an angle and shot a lot of people out into the water. I clung on to the bow and stopped myself slipping into the water, but the boat was being dragged along with the stern in the water. I was just hanging on for dear life and I don't know whether Bobby was at the bow or the stern, because we were all clambering like mad trying not to fall out. So I was in the part of the boat that was uppermost out of the water, clinging on like a limpet, but I think Bobby must have been in the stern, because I can't remember him being with me. So I think that must have been when Bobby was either bounced out of the lifeboat, or missed his grip, or didn't have a lifejacket.

'Because the thing is, if I had a lifejacket on, where did I get it? And I did have a lifejacket on by then. I don't know whether this lifejacket came from somebody else or whether it was Bobby's. But I would imagine it was Bobby's lifejacket, because he obviously wanted to calm me down when I was struggling to get back to the cabin for mine. I don't know – well, I think he had given me his lifejacket to keep me quiet. Looking back I can see how it must have happened, that when Bobby restrained me from going back down into the bowels of the ship to fetch my lifejacket and probably to pacify me he, well, he gave me his own lifejacket. I have this feeling that he gave up his own lifejacket ... for me.

'But where Bobby was I don't know. If he was at the stern of the lifeboat when it went into the sea, well, the stern was certainly awash with water. But your survival instinct takes over and I was just hanging on, concentrating on nothing but clinging on like grim death. Then the next thing, there was a rope ladder that was thrown down from the top deck and I was then on my own and I was told in no uncertain terms to climb that rope ladder. This sailor said to me, "Now, you look at the top of that ladder and you climb that ladder, and you don't look down. You climb and you don't stop until you're at the top." Which I did. I remember that vividly. I clambered up and it was a long way and I was on my own. There was nobody with me, just one rope ladder and me climbing it and I got up on top again.

'Back up on top of the deck, we all gathered again and by then they had managed to get the boat back out of the water and haul it up again. So they reloaded it and we were lowered back down into the water again and cast off. I don't remember actually being unhooked or anything like that, but I just remember being in the boat away from the ship. I can remember being wrapped up in sacking and pushed down into the middle of the boat. But then I must have lost consciousness. We were in that boat a long time, but it's almost as though I'd been given an injection or something, because I must have passed out and I don't really have any memory of it. That whole time is just a blank.

'The launching of our lifeboat had gone wrong, I think, because the ship was actually still moving forward quite fast. Even when a ship has been torpedoed, it doesn't just stop dead. So the ship was moving when the boats were lowered, and some of the lifeboats would have hit the water with a heavy way on — that is, going forward themselves — so if you were unfortunate enough to be bounced out of the lifeboat you'd be left behind quickly. I can only think that's what happened to Bobby, but it was pandemonium at the time. I suppose when the lifeboat hit the water, if Bobby was at the bottom of the boat – that is, at the end which hit the water first – then he would have been bounced out of the boat with the impact. And he would have been left behind probably as the boat moved forward. And if he'd had no lifejacket – he'd given it to me – he wouldn't stand much of a chance, would he? No ... he wouldn't have stood much of a chance.

'There was such a lot of chaos. It was pandemonium. We'd clambered back on to the ship and they were trying to get us off again, and everything was going on, and I can't remember seeing Bobby then. Because the lifeboat had been hauled up again and we were all gathered together and put onto the boat, lowered and cast off from the *Benares*. But it was from the time of being on the deck before the first lowering of the boat, when he gave me his lifejacket, that I cannot remember seeing Bobby ever again.'

There were no more chances left now. The *Benares* was sinking fast. Every available boat and raft had been launched, though most were either waterlogged or had capsized completely. The abandon-ship procedure, supposedly so well drilled, had been a disaster, wrecked not just by the horrific Atlantic storm but also by the faulty functioning of the lifeboat gear. To this day no one knows quite how many lives had been lost at this point, but it was probably at least half of the final death toll. For those surviving by a thread, clinging on to half-sunk lifeboats or bits of plank, there was nothing to do but watch as their ship went down.

Barbara Bech, in lifeboat number 4, separated from the rest of her family, paints the scene: 'I was wedged in with a lot of other people all round me, and thinking, oh dear, I wonder what's going to happen next? There was a bit of murmuring and talking, though not much, nobody did anything very much. The lascars were crouched down in the middle of the boat and they were crying out to Allah all the time and muttering in Hindustani, praying.

'But the worst thing was that it was the first time that I saw all the children, how many seavacuee children there were. Because all the ship's outside lights were on by this point and you could see them in the sea. Some of the children were in lifeboats going up and down, up and down, with the children wailing. And I thought, "Oh, there were a lot of children." I think that was the first time I'd realised how many very young children had been on the ship, even though I was only seeing some of them. But it was pretty much a vision of horror. And you could hear the wails on the wind. They were a couple of hundred yards away, but just caught by the lights of the boat, and you could see them tossed up and down in the waves.

'It's always surprised me how quickly everybody got separated. The lifeboats all drifted away from each other very quickly, despite the fact that we'd all started from the same place. Very soon there didn't seem to be anybody else around, and so we sat there and got wet from time to time because the waves were pretty large. If you happen to be where a wave breaks, it all goes straight into the boat and you get soaked. Our feet were wet all the time because there was water in the bottom of the boat. It was for about 15 minutes, which seemed like a long time, that nothing at all happened to us except our lifeboat was drifting. Then I heard somebody say, "Ah, she's going." The *Benares* had all her lights on by then, and you suddenly saw her tip down towards the stern and the bows go up in the air, and she slid away down to the bottom of the sea. And then suddenly it was completely dark. You could see the odd little light here and there and still some shouts on the wind. But it went quiet so quickly.

'Oddly, even though it was all so alarming, I can't remember being really frightened. You see, I think you are only truly frightened when you're afraid something *may* happen, but once it is actually happening, you're much too busy to be frightened. It is when your imagination has time to work that you notice the fear, but if you have to do practical things, I don't think fright really comes into it. I mean, terror does. It's what galvanises you to do extreme physical things like leaping across gaps and cliffs and climbing trees and all the rest of it. I think sheer fright drives you to do things which you wouldn't have the strength to do normally – perhaps that was what got me down the rope. And once I'd come down the rope and landed in a boat which seemed to be floating, it was very much a question of "What happens next?" rather than being frightened. And there were a lot of other people there. I wasn't all alone in the water – I think I would have been frightened if I'd been alone floating on my cork lifejacket.

'I was thinking, what's happened to the others? I had this feeling that somehow they must be all right, because they couldn't have drowned in front of me and me not know it. I just clung to that feeling that you couldn't lose your entire family in front of your eyes without a quiver. I mean, we were quite a close family and I couldn't believe it could happen. I know, sadly, it probably could have happened, but at that time of my life I was sure that if you had that bond between you it couldn't suddenly be severed without some kind of sensation. So I didn't know how they would have got away, but I was so sure they would have done.'

In fact Barbara was right, the rest of her family were still alive, just. Derek, Sonia and their mother Marguerite were managing to cling to the little raft – barely more than a few planks of wood – that Eric Davies had found for them. Like Barbara drifting in her lifeboat, Derek and Sonia too were watching the last seconds of the *Benares*. Derek remembers: 'We felt very much on our own as we saw the ship go down. And Sonia just said to me, "Well, what a waste of ice cream." I know it sounds silly, but that was our childhood reaction to seeing this beautiful ship sink. And I don't think we had any inclination of what was ahead of us. My mother afterwards said she would never, ever have attempted to go on a raft if she had realised that other ships wouldn't be stopping to pick us up. She thought it was just a question of going in the sea, and going across to another ship. But of course, the command to a convoy is that if anybody is sunk or torpedoed, then you must immediately break the convoy and go at your best speed independently. So nobody stopped or waited for us.

'We were very close to the ship when it went down. I can remember looking up at it and it did a sort of a corkscrew. One of the masts – one of the forward masts – was coming right at us, but then it slid back again. As the ship sank it went down by its stern.

All the deck lights were on, and what had been a blaze of lights just suddenly went completely dark. And there was silence. That silence for the first time was eerie, because up to then things had been going on and we'd been watching. But now that everything had gone quiet you could just hear the cries all around us in the darkness, of people calling out help, help. You could see the silhouettes of some of the lifeboats. They each had a little lantern on their bows and you could see them, but then they all dispersed very soon – it happened very quickly. And within five minutes we had nobody in earshot, they'd all drifted away.

'We were confronted with all this flotsam. We had deckchairs and all sorts of furniture which was bumping into us, which we had to push away. We realised we were all alone in this terrible sea hundreds of miles from land, just the five of us being tossed about on this little raft. It was a stormy night. We were going up and down these huge waves, 20- or 30-foot waves, like a helter-skelter. We would go up the side of them and then down into the troughs, and as we went into the troughs the buoyancy drums of the raft would rise for the next wave and pinch our fingers in the wooden slats which we were hanging onto. But it wasn't just banging our nails, it was knocking the wood out from the raft – unknown to us there were just too many people and the raft was breaking up.'

The boys who had managed to catch the twelfth and last boat were much luckier. While Derek Bech was watching a mast toppling dangerously near his raft, Kenneth, Fred and Derek Capel had already drifted quite far from the *Benares* when it sank. Derek Capel remembers: 'The seas were carrying us away, so we just drifted off and the noises got fainter. But as we gradually drew further away we could still see this beautiful ship, the *Benares*. And suddenly, I don't know why, every single light on the ship came on. Maybe it was a short circuit when the water got into them or something, but anyway, the lights came on, dazzling, shining out over the water, while the ship slowly began to go down. It just sank down into the sea until only the stern was showing, then it was gone. They say it took about 20 minutes, I don't know, but we just kept being carried along by the waves.

'We were wet through. The storms that night were terrible. You were looking at waves. One minute you would be looking up, up to where the waves were breaking high above you – then you'd be up there looking down as if you were at the top of a cliff and it was a sheer drop down the side. And we had no control of the boat at all, we had to go where the sea took us.'

Fred Steels also found the sense of helplessness upsetting: 'You could still hear these cries from the kids that were still being tossed around in the water, but we couldn't do a thing about it though, I'm afraid. As we got our boat away from the sinking ship we were looking for survivors, but there were none around where we were. We must have been lying off about 20 or 30 yards from the ship and we were watching her all the time. We saw her going down by the stern. Then suddenly all the lights were on. The *Benares* looked like a Christmas tree, everything lit brilliant. She began to slide under as we were watching, and one of the things I do remember was that we saw this torch going round the bridge area and the top decks. I am pretty sure it was the captain, Captain Nicoll, looking to see if there was anybody still there. The seamen had already been searching down on the lower decks when we were leaving, trying to find as many children as they could, but they reckoned it was pretty clear. Then all at once the ship was really slipping under, and we saw her bows come up in the air and she just disappeared.

'You could still see all those lights shining under the water for a while. Then that was it, everything went black. We just sat there and watched her go; probably within 40 minutes from the time we got in the lifeboat, the *Benares* had disappeared and that was that. There was lots of rubbish around from where the torpedo had struck. Then we did see another lifeboat with people in it, but it wasn't from our ship. Harry Peard, the gunner, shouted to them and found out the lifeboat wasn't one of ours. It was from another ship that had also been torpedoed. We had had two ships that were flankers one either side of us, port and starboard, and it was from one of them that this lifeboat had come. Then we had an empty lifeboat pass us, plus loads of timber, bits of furniture and all that sort of thing, but we just gradually drifted away from it all. It was the gale was blowing us, one hell of a gale, but we just had to make the best of it that night until the morning, when maybe we would have a chance to try and sort ourselves out.'

Kenneth Sparks had not been watching the *Benares* very closely as it went down, he was too busy trying to help the men keep the lifeboat away from the vortex caused by the sinking ship. He explains: 'Well, I wasn't exactly the oldest or the strongest on the boat and when the ship went down I was pushing on this kind of pole to move the boat away from the suction. To me the *Benares* seemed to go down quite suddenly – one minute the ship was there and the next it was gone. And then of course, without the ship's lights, it was pitch dark because it was the middle of the night – it must have been round about eleven o'clock at night by then. We were soaking wet and cold, being thrown about by the waves. So that first night all we could do was try and make ourselves as comfortable as we could. And we began to pull away, setting a course, well, towards Ireland basically.'

CHAPTER SIX

Beth *and* Bess *and the* Lifeboats

Beth Cummings from Liverpool and Bess Walder from London had quickly become firm friends on board the *Benares*, and now the new best friends ended up in the same lifeboat – lifeboat number 5. It was about the worst possible place they could have found themselves. Oddly enough, Beth has always had a sneaking feeling that number 5 wasn't in fact the boat they had been allocated in drills. Certainly it couldn't have been an unluckier destination. Beth says: 'I have always thought – well, I'm pretty sure – that we got into the lifeboat next to the one that was our own lifeboat. But that was the way it was, there was an awful lot going on, a terrible lot going on. There were people yelling and men shouting orders. We got into the lifeboat and the rest of our little group were there. There was Joan Irving. She was sitting in between Betty Unwin and me. And behind the three of us, Bess had a little girl she was keeping an eye on. Then it was a question of lowering the lifeboat – and that turned out to be the big problem.'

As they reached the lifeboats though, the girls were just relieved to have got as far as the upper deck – they had almost been trapped in their cabins. Bess describes what happened: 'There wasn't much I could do after the explosion because suddenly there was furniture all falling about inside the cabin. I got a lifejacket on and that old green dressing gown to keep me warm. One of the other girls in my cabin had been injured badly by the falling furniture, and there was no way could she get through the small space of the door, because the wardrobe had stuck across the door. I hammered on the door and someone started making a big hole for us to get through. Who it was that did that, I don't know. I managed to get through and shouted, "There's another girl in there," but the girl that had been injured couldn't move. I'm afraid I think she died in the cabin. But the thing was, there just wasn't the time to start thinking about the awfulness of that. I had to get upstairs into the area of the muster station and find my lifeboat. I rushed up towards the deck and I looked for the row of steps that went up to it, and as I looked at them, they started to collapse inwards. Where there had been a staircase there was now a huge gaping hole. I didn't know what to do.

'I turned to try and go another way and then I was grabbed by a man who said, "Come with me." And he got hold of my hand and he took me round side turnings, side walks, down steps, up steps that I'd never seen before – I think he was a member of the crew – until we got up to the top deck where the lifeboats were. That is when I saw the full horror of what was happening. There were people everywhere, people queuing and waiting, trying to get into lifeboats.'

Beth Cummings' cabin was opposite Bess Walder's, and while Bess was trying to rescue her cabin mates, Beth was doing the same. Whenever Beth thinks about those terrible moments trying to escape from the lower decks of the ship, the first thing that comes to her is a memory of the horrible, frightening smell: 'The thing that really upset us was this awful smell of sulphur, it was a terrible smell. It was really frightening. To this day I've always remembered it – a really nasty smell, sulphur, obviously from the explosion. You could hardly see anything in the emergency lighting. Betty Unwin was in the next cabin, and she and I had managed to get Joan Irving out and got a blanket wrapped round her and got hold of her coat. Then as we were getting Joan out, we met up with Bess from the opposite side and she had another little girl with her. But then we could see there was just no way you could get down any of the gangways. They were completely blocked, and there was nobody around. It was a dreadful situation. You couldn't see anything, and there was nobody there – we couldn't even hear anybody, just the alarm bell was going like mad. But we managed to get up the staircase to the next deck, which was the deck where the children's room was. By now I was a bit bothered, there was nobody about there either. I said, "We have to go to the children's room," because that's what we had been drilled to do, we were supposed to muster there. So I said, "I'll go and have a look" – but there was nothing there. I mean, nothing there at all – the deck had gone, everything had gone. It was all black, it was awful, and it really worried me. But there was no way back, so I said, "I think we'd better get out, let's go up."

'The trouble was that the staircase up to the next deck, the promenade deck, didn't look very happy either. But there was this little side entrance that Bess and I knew, because we used to go and sit there when we wanted to get away from everybody and go and have a little chat. It was a little iron door onto the side of the ship. So we headed for there and that's when an officer found us. He lifted Joan and carried her. He was wonderful. I wish I could remember who it was, but he was carrying Joan and he took us up past the Lewis guns, right round the stern of the ship. And all the time the ship was moving. You could feel it going. Anyway, we got up and outside onto the promenade deck and we joined our group. Most of them were already there by the time we got there. I always remember Patricia Allen. She was another Liverpool girl like myself, and she'd already been torpedoed on the *Volendam* and nothing really had gone wrong – nobody had been injured or drowned – and she said, "Oh, don't worry, it's all right, the Royal Navy will pick us up. They'll rescue us like they did the last time."

'But I couldn't understand that. It didn't feel to me as if that was going to happen. I was thinking, I don't know whether this *is* like the last time. It was so stormy, it was pitch dark, the waves were terrible and the ship was moving in this odd way. It was the only time in my life that I have really felt it in my stomach, you know, when your tummy turns over – that horrible, draining, sinking feeling. But I thought, well, it's no good being like that. For one thing the young children were being absolutely marvellous. They really were super. Even the very young ones – an awful lot of them were much younger than Bess and Joan and Betty and me. But they were so brave. They didn't cry, just a little whimper now and again, but they were doing everything they were supposed to do, and they weren't screaming. The children were very good and very, very well disciplined. They didn't move, they did exactly as they were told, while we were waiting to be organised into our lifeboats. I remember the moon spilling in and out of the clouds, suddenly you could see it all and then you couldn't. Then finally it was our turn for a lifeboat.'

When that moment came there was no time for second thoughts. After the brief pause waiting for a boat up on the deck, events suddenly began to move very fast, as Bess explains: 'The officer who had found us and brought us up – and I still don't know who he was – lifted me up and literally threw me into a lifeboat. I had no time to think about what was happening to my brother, Louis. All I knew was I was in a lifeboat. And so were other people, and then more and more people getting in. And as the ship was beginning to sink, it was sinking at a steep angle. What happened was that the davits that should let down the lifeboat steadily were also at the same angle as the ship. That meant that as the lifeboats were launched into the ocean they met it at this same steep angle, so the ocean came right inside and filled up the lifeboat. It was because of the angle that the ship was sinking in, and it was sinking very fast.

'Then when the lifeboat filled with water it fell off the davits and plunged right into the sea. Many people lost their lives at that point. I was lucky because I was at the end of the lifeboat that hit the sea last. Eventually it sort of righted itself, but with great difficulty, in a very, very difficult position. There were people sitting in the lifeboat – as I was – and we were up to our necks in water. The little children had no chance. The adults were up to their chests, and with the huge waves and the gale, and these lifeboats that were absolutely full of water – well, there were only a very fortunate few could be thinking about saving themselves. I was one of them. And that was when the lifeboat collapsed and I was thrown into the sea.

'The lifeboat capsized and turned turtle. It ended upside down with its hull in the air and I was in the water, going down under the waves. But my father had taught me to swim. I was a good swimmer. When my father taught me how to sea-swim he told me that if I should ever find myself in danger of going down, I shouldn't panic. He told me not to worry, I should allow myself to relax and I would come up. He said the human body is like a cork. "Just let yourself go," he said, "and you'll come up." And I did it, I could hear my father saying it to me. I can't believe it now. And I did. I came up and what's more, as I came up, I realised that my hands were touching something solid and what it was, was the side of the lifeboat. And I managed to carefully inch my way up to the top of the curve of the hull and hang onto the keel. With just my bare hands – child's hands, not big, strong hands at all, not really, but that's all I had. I had nothing else and I had to hang onto the keel. And other people had done the same. Not many, but some. I think perhaps of all the people who came out of that lifeboat alive, at that stage, there were about 12. The number of people sitting in the lifeboat originally must have been something like 90 to 100.

'So having got to the stage of hanging on to that upside-down lifeboat, there was nothing else to do but cling on. The people who had been thrown out of the lifeboat and who had managed to swim back to it, as I had, and had managed to grasp the keel, were ranged each side of the hull. The keel was on the top, and we got our bodies across the hull lying down on the keel, with our heads just above the water. There I was – and my worry now was what should I say to my parents about my brother. Because I'd seen so many children drown that I was worried he had too. But I really didn't have much time to brood about this, because it was urgent that I should keep myself alive. And fortunately, this wreck of what was left of the lifeboat was moving away from the sinking ship, which was lucky because if it had stayed close we would have inevitably been drawn under. The ship was sinking fast, and the rush of waves underneath the ship would certainly have overturned us back into the sea, and we would have died.'

As the lifeboat was being jerkily lowered down towards the waves, Beth was being thrown around inside it, banging her head against part of the launch gear: 'To begin with one of the problems was that we were on the windward side of the ship — that is, we were exposed to the wind, and it was a terrible gale. And the ship was going down by the stern on the other side, so she was moving away from us and we were against the sloping side of the ship. That meant getting the lifeboat down was almost impossible. There was stuff crashing around, and I got a bang on the head. But the lifeboat was sort of jerking down, teetering from end to end. And we ended up hanging, more or less dangling for what seemed like an awful long time before we were going down to the water. That was when I thought it would be all right, things would be all right — but it wasn't, of course.

'Things were happening so quickly, things that we couldn't do anything about. We couldn't control anything, we were being controlled by the storm and the sinking ship. We were trying to pull these mechanical oars — Fleming gear, it's called — and they wouldn't work and we couldn't get away from the side of the ship. And there was an officer in the boat, and he was shouting, "We must get away from the ship." That's all I seemed to hear, but we just couldn't get the Fleming gear to work. I thought, what's going to happen if we don't get away, will we go down with her? We'll go down with the ship, I thought. But we did manage to get away. I don't know whether in fact it was partly due to the ship moving away from us. Our boat was at the stern of the ship, so that may have been a factor perhaps in our getting away — but only just.

'We'd only just got away when she went down. I thought she was on fire. She had this terrible glow, completely red and a horrible orange colour all over as she went down. It was the most awful feeling as she went down. We were dumbfounded, sitting there looking at it. But then almost instantaneously there were these awful waves caused by the ship going down and they overwhelmed our boat, and all I knew then was I was flung out, um – and I was going down and down, a most odd feeling.'

For Beth what followed was a desperate struggle for survival. Her friend Bess, clinging to the front end of the lifeboat, remembers everybody being thrown out of the stern into the sea. And this must have been what happened to Beth, because her next impression is of fighting not to drown: 'It was my most frightening time – being thrown in the sea with this awful wave, it just threw you, you had no control at all. I was thrown into it, inside the wave, and I was going down and down and down. It was awful and it was all strange – everything was light. It was almost as if you were in a lift out of control, you were going down so fast and things were going down with you. What was alarming was you could see things, you could see people, sinking down with you. And you could see chairs from the veranda café, all going down with you. It seemed as if you never ever, ever going to stop; but it was happening so quickly. It was as if you hadn't time to be frightened, you hadn't time to understand what was going on. But looking back I know underneath I was frightened. I really thought I was drowning.

'Then all at once I just sort of popped up to the surface, virtually bobbed up right onto the surface. Of course, it was the lifejacket which brought me up. I suddenly realised then that I was actually on the surface among all these people, all these boats, people shouting, flares, all sorts of things going on. And it was an odd sort of feeling – well, you felt a bit better. That sounds rather ridiculous really, but everybody was in the same boat – well, of course not literally, literally that's exactly the opposite of where we were! But we were all in the same situation, all trying to cope with our problems. Everybody at that point was having their own individual difficulties. It was a question of doing whatever you could to get to your lifeboat again or to get on a raft or get somewhere.

'I managed to see our lifeboat, which was in fact still sort of floating – this was before it finally capsized. It was so peculiar, there were all these people either up to their necks in water, or sitting on the side with one leg in and one leg out. It was weird, they looked as if they were sitting on the water. You could see it because the moon kept coming out, just flitting in and out of the storm clouds. Then you could hear all these people shouting and there were voices – people giving orders, presumably the ship's crew. Then other people shouting. It was all disturbing really, because they were all in their own dramas – they were all having problems. Every single person at that point was having their own individual crisis. Even if they were in a lifeboat, most of the lifeboats were being overtaken by the sea, just like ours. So they were all either in waterlogged lifeboats, or people on rafts, or in the waves. They were all trying to save themselves.

'The lifeboat was looking an awfully long way away, but I took a big breath and I virtually floundered – that was the only way you can put it – across towards the lifeboat. I wasn't a swimmer and to be perfectly honest, I'm not sure about whether swimming would be any good. I think the lifejacket was really the main thing, but one way or another I got to the lifeboat and she was buoyant, very odd really, and all these people were sitting round one leg in and one over the side. And I saw Bess and I got up beside her. From that point we never saw any of the other children who had been in the lifeboat with us. They must have all drowned, there is nothing else you can think, they must have drowned. But there were a lot of people still perching on the lifeboat. We sat opposite each other on the side, the lifeboat itself was pretty much underwater. We sat facing each other, one leg in and one leg out, for what seemed quite a long time. Another strange thing happened: all of a sudden I saw all these glittery things on Bess's lifejacket and they were plankton. They were bright, bright little things all over her. It looked like sequins, but they must have been from the sea, plankton.

'Of course, all the time there were people trying to get onto the lifeboat and it was getting more and more uneven. And eventually it capsized, and exactly the same thing happened all over again. I went under, down into the sea again. I really felt I would drown this time, but strangely it didn't seem as queer as the first time. The only thing was when I came to the surface I seemed to be a little bit further away, and it was getting a bit darker. But I did it again. I managed to flounder back to the capsized lifeboat just as Bess got there. It was uncanny that we seemed to meet all the time. Every time, it was the two of us back together again, it was most peculiar. Anyway, we reached the lifeboat – it was upside down – and Bess got there at the same time and she was climbing up and I climbed up beside her. It was then that we sort of started hanging on to the keel, and this seemed to be what everyone was doing. It was going on right along the lifeboat.'

Bess also remembers vividly how she and Beth seemed fated to go through their ordeal together: 'When I'd got up on that keel of the upturned lifeboat you couldn't see much, but what I did see, on the other side of the keel, opposite to me, was another girl about my age, 14 – and it was Beth. She was doing the same as me. And we looked at one another and we nodded.

'There were some Indian seamen who were at the end of the upturned boat who had got rope there and they had tied themselves onto the gear, which one would have thought might have been a very good idea. But in practice it turned out to be not good, because the waves came over and crashed against them and they couldn't lift their heads out of the way, and they literally drowned with their bodies tied up to the boat, whereas we could lift our heads above the water. But of course, our plan only worked as long as you were strong enough to hold on, and gradually the number of hands that were in a row on that keel became – quite few. Beth and I said nothing, but bit by bit as other people let themselves go, we realised that we were the only children left holding on. In a way, when you think about it, these other people were doing the obvious thing, because those people thought there's no hope for us, we are heading for death, and we will not be able to keep on this lifeboat, so we will let ourselves go. And they did. Beth and I were young, strong – daft if you like –

and thinking that we could possibly save ourselves, and we did. Otherwise we wouldn't be here to tell the tale.'

Beth was having problems trying to keep a grip on the upturned lifeboat. She remembers: 'The keel was very slippery. We knew there were other people there but we couldn't see them, except I could see hands on the other side where we were. And there were people talking and shouting – people all over the place still shouting – and then the weather was getting worse. The flares had disappeared and by then it was too dark actually to see anybody, but we could hear them climbing on to the lifeboat, hanging on to the keel. I think there must have been quite a lot of people hanging on to begin with, but we were down at the end of the lifeboat and you couldn't see much. I could just make out that Bess was by me and there were these two people opposite me. They were the only people I could see, and actually I could only see their hands. It was a man and a woman and they were sort of intertwined with our hands, and this hand with a ring there, glistening. One minute it was there and the next minute it had gone, and that meant they'd gone. It was as simple as that. It was just after that that I sort of slid off – that's the only way I can put it – I slithered down the side of the lifeboat and I felt my nothing under my feet, nothing at all.

'And then, what I have always thought of as a minor miracle happened. I couldn't see anything, it was black, I couldn't see a thing, but I just grabbed into the nothingness – and I grabbed a rope. I don't know what that rope was meant to be for. I didn't know where it belonged, I just climbed it – followed the rope up. It turned out to be a rope that must have gone through the keel onto the other side, and that rope really in my opinion saved our lives. If we'd been hanging on to the keel all night with just our bare hands there's no way we'd be here now. I can remember sliding, that keel was so very, very slippy, and I went and there was nothing and some instinct just made me grab blindly. I always look upon it as one of those sort of things that happen during times like that, and I'm a great believer in them. I think this particular minor miracle was that I grabbed – and I didn't know what I was grabbing because I couldn't see anything – yet I still reached out, and I grabbed a rope. It was almost as if it had been put there. I couldn't believe it. I was still way back down in the water below the capsized boat, and I grabbed this rope and I started to crawl up the side of the lifeboat to be with Bess again. Then I shouted to her, "Hang onto the rope, it'll be much better, much, much better than the keel, it's too slippy." Definitely that rope did save our lives. We had to hang onto it for dear life, and we had to keep hanging on to it, which we did.'

So the two girls found themselves in the middle of a north Atlantic storm with nothing but a rope and the upturned hull of a capsized boat between them and drowning. They could no longer see any other survivors, and even the shouting had stopped. Everybody else seemed to have disappeared, either drowned or drifting helplessly. It seemed that things couldn't get any worse – and oddly enough, for a while at least, things didn't get any worse. But they didn't get any better either. Bess explains: 'The thing is you expect something to happen next, but actually not much happened really for the next seven hours. The upturned lifeboat gradually moved away. Behind us was this dreadful scene, that of wrecked lifeboats and wrecked rafts with nobody on them because the people who'd tried to get on them had jumped from the deck down into the water and missed, because the waves had moved the raft away from where they were jumping.'

And so began the marathon ordeal for the two schoolgirls, Beth, nearly 14, and Bess, 15, as they continued to drift, clinging to the rope. Beth describes how they felt as the night drew on: 'There was nothing for us to do except hang on to this rope. So we were facing each other on the side of the lifeboat with this rope between us and we hung onto the rope. And we never let go of that rope in all the time that followed – which turned out to be 19 hours in all – we never moved our hands off it. Of course, we knew if we did let go, that would be the end of us. But the weather was getting atrocious. The wind was terrible and the rain and hail lashing on your face. The boat hull was moving backwards and forwards, up and down, so we were being thrown away and bumped back all the time. All we could do was to shout to each other, "Are you all right, Beth? You all right, Bess?" That was all we did most of the night. We couldn't say much because it was impossible to talk properly, if you opened your mouth it got full of seawater.

'I think what we were both really bargaining on, well, we both thought that there would be ships around and if we could stay like that and hang on all night, there would be a ship there waiting to rescue us in the morning. But it was a long night, a very long, dark night. I kept thinking I could hear this voice calling to Allah. It was weird at first, but then I realised that there must be a lascar on the hull somewhere who had survived and was still there. But anyway, I was doing my own praying. I must have sort of said the Lord's Prayer in my mind I don't know how many times throughout the night. I think this is something people don't always admit, but you do pray at times like this, you have to. You have to do something, you have to pray to somebody when you're in that sort of situation. It's like when people ask if I was frightened. Of course you are at some level, and you are praying. But what Bess and I both say is that we were too busy to be frightened, certainly we had too much else to concentrate on to be aware of fear. And you know, we were fighting a battle. Not the Germans now, a different enemy, we were fighting a hostile north Atlantic. That was really what we were doing, and it was a question of whether we would succeed or not.

'It was hard not being able to speak to each other properly, but we would try and shout during that night. So Bess would shout to me, "Are you all right, Beth? You all right, Beth?" and I would shout back, "Yes I'm all right, are you all right?" and then occasionally we'd say, "Oh there's a wave coming," but you couldn't see it, you felt it was coming. You could sense it in the way the hull would move and then you would be bracing yourself to try and ride out another wave. And this went on all through the night. We couldn't say any more to each other, but we kept on at it, shouting to each other, "Are you still all right, Bess?" and she would shout, "Yes, all right. Are you still there, Beth?" It was the only way we kept ourselves going, because to be perfectly honest we couldn't even make each other out very clearly, we couldn't really see each other. We knew we were there because of our hands on the rope and that was all. But as long as we could still shout, we knew we were both still there – me on one side of the rope, Bess on the other. And that's how we kept going, that was the way it was all through the night.'

Clinging there as the night wore on and the storm continued to batter them, it was thoughts of home and family that naturally came into the girls' minds. Bess was thinking of her younger brother, Louis. 'My one thought was I've got to get home, because I've got to go back and tell my mother and father what has happened. Particularly because of my brother. I knew I had to get home to tell my parents about why Louis had not come back, and how I'd tried, but found it impossible to look after him. That was what was motivating me throughout the whole of those terrible times. It was such a strong driving force, thinking that I must get back in one piece so I could be the one to break it to them. Beth told me afterwards she had the same thoughts. Of her brothers one was in Iraq in the army, and the other one was in Canada training to be a pilot, so she was the only child left for her mother, and her mother was a widow. So if she didn't get back her mother would have been on her own possibly for the rest of the war.

'So we weren't going to give up. But the waves just never stopped these huge crashing movements up and down, because the storm was still at its height throughout all this. It was as if the elements and the rain all combined together to make rescue impossible. It just wasn't a possibility. And yet, against all the odds, there were some people who made it – nothing short of miracles, absolute miracles. Some of the lascars were still alive where they had tied themselves to the boat, but one of them had become very disturbed mentally. He was crying aloud to his gods in his own language, which Beth and I couldn't understand. He was making most terribly pitiful noises, and finally I think he just gave in and opened his mouth and allowed the elements to come in and then he was gone. But there were two others who were still hanging on.

'During that night Beth and I were trying to communicate, but it wasn't easy. We were facing one another, but we had to be careful because if we opened our mouths too wide, water would come in and go in our lungs. So we had to be very careful how we communicated with one another. I would look at Beth and nod, as much as to say I want to talk to you, and through almost half-closed lips I would say to her, "We'll hang on," and through her half-closed lips she would say, "Yes, yes, yes." She was as determined as I was. We were indivisible. Totally. Without her I could do nothing. Without me she could do nothing. So it was wonderful in that sense that we were so closely linked.'

Then something finally did happen – the thing the two girls had been hanging on for, holding out until it came. Their aim had been to survive the night and make it through to daybreak. And they did. Eventually the dawn came. Neither Bess nor Beth will ever forget the bitter disappointment of that longed-for dawn. Bess remembers: 'By dawn, when the sky became lighter, I mouthed over to Beth, "Better now." She mouthed back at me, "Yes, good. We'll stay here." You know you say funny things in a crisis. Well, they do say 'come the dawn', don't they? And that's a phrase that I shall always remember. We were so disappointed, because both Beth and I had envisioned the dawn breaking and us being able to see other people on boats or rafts that were near us or were within sight. That would have been a tremendous boost to our morale. But as that dawn broke, and the light came into the sky, there was just nothing. Nothing.

'There is nothing more lonely than being in mid-Atlantic on a boat upside down, with nothing in view but the sun, the sea and the waves. Not a bird, nothing moving. Nothing alive except us three. Beth, myself and the lascar seaman at the rear of the boat. The sky itself I shall never forget, because it came out in huge streaks with the most brilliant colours. Peacock blue, yellow, orange, red. It was something out of a nightmarish artist's dream, and it's something I would find it hard to reproduce, but it was a murderous sky. Partly because it shone on nothing but ourselves.'

It was the same for Beth: 'Eventually when the dawn came we were hoping that was going to be the big breakthrough, but of course it wasn't, was it? There was nobody there. There was not a ship in sight, there was nothing. Not a ship. Not a piece of driftwood. There was just nothing, just the sea. And there wasn't any hope, because you couldn't think, well, perhaps there's something just round the corner, perhaps there's going to be a ship any minute, because you could see for miles, and there was nothing to see.'

So the girls had achieved their objective of surviving the night. But their only reward was the realisation that they would now have to survive the day as well. And as the hours passed, this was getting harder to do. Both girls were starting to go into their inner worlds. Beth admits that she was beginning to have strange, eerily beautiful hallucinations: 'You see things, really clearly, but you are only thinking you see them. I saw an iceberg, blue and icy, drifting by. And I thought I saw a big fish jumping, and little floats of ice. But they were probably hallucinations. I was numb by then. I don't think we were conscious of feeling cold. That sounds rather strange actually, but I think we must have shut it out. During the night we'd felt all these hailstones and rain on our faces, but in an odd sort of way we didn't feel bitterly cold, and eventually we just didn't feel anything except we have to hang on to this rope.

'It was the way we were. That was the way we went on all day then. But after a while we were getting more worried. There was a sort of watery sun came out and it looked as if it was the middle of the day and the day was wearing on, and we knew we wouldn't be able to hang on, not for another night. We knew exactly what the situation was – I knew and obviously Bess knew too. But we didn't say anything about it. We couldn't speak to each other much anyway. And there were these two lascars. I could see them over Bess's shoulder. One was obviously dead, his head was lolling in the water, and the other looked a bit dazed. They had tied themselves on to the rudder end of the lifeboat, and that was the only reason they were still there, they had something holding them. Certainly the keel had turned out to be impossible – if we'd stayed gripping the keel, we wouldn't be here now, we would never have lasted the night.

'It was the thought of my mother that kept me going more than anything. I owed it to her to keep going. I think this is what it was, this feeling, I have to keep going for as long as ever I can for her sake. I loved my mother, and she'd made the decision that it was a good thing to send me to Canada and so I felt I had to make it be the right decision. I had to find a reason to agree with that, and so I had to hang on as long as ever I could. I had to live for her benefit. I had to, and that was really what it was. It was as simple as that.

'At least as the day went on, the storm seemed to be going down. The swell was still bad, but it wasn't quite as wild as it had been during the night. We were wet through obviously and there was nothing to put your feet on at all, just the sort of rim of the planking. We were pretty much half in the water all the time. And the day went on, and nobody came, and you were thinking, if it's going to be another night, we'll never, ever hang on all night, but we must try, we must try. I think of the whole thing, the whole disaster, the sad thing really was the little children, the small children. They hadn't got a chance, not one chance. There was no way they would survive that weather, just no way, and certainly they sort of slept away, they actually slept away. They must have done, there couldn't have been any other way. Some drowned apparently, but I think mainly they would have slept away of exposure. It's a terrible thing.

'At one point during the day we saw a raft with one of the escorts, Mrs Hillman, Maud Hillman, on it. She had two children with her. She drifted by in the distance and she was shouting about the Germans to be honest, but she was hanging on to these two children. Well, eventually they died, and of course she did too. She died of exposure, I think. You see, it wasn't just a question of children either. When you think of it, it was the grown-ups too. There were men dying of exposure, women dying of exposure. It wasn't drowning always, some obviously drowned, but it was exposure that killed a lot. Yet Bess and I survived that. I think possibly it was because Bess and I were what you might call well built. I often think about that. We weren't exactly skinny wee lasses, either of us, we were quite well made. I think maybe that was one of the things that probably had an influence on it. When you haven't got much flesh on you, the cold is hard, so I do think it makes a difference if you're well padded. Certainly I think as far as the little children were concerned, that was a big factor. But then on the other hand some of the men who died of exposure, they weren't exactly thin either, so I don't quite know really the reason for all this.

'One other thing Bess and I had which was in our favour had nothing to do with your build or anything. I think it was to do with the fact that there were two of us and we relied on each other to survive. I think that's another thing. I think if one of us had gone, the other one wouldn't have lasted, I'm quite sure about that. And we had that rope, we were hanging on to that rope like it was glue, absolutely glued to that rope. I remember running through my mind was what Patricia Allen had said as we were waiting to get into the lifeboats about us being rescued, and I was thinking, well, I knew that we couldn't be – we were miles and miles and miles out into the north Atlantic. And I had the feeling I knew what the north Atlantic was like. Even though I'd never been across the north Atlantic, I pretty well had a good guess at it, and I was right. It was a very hostile ocean, the north Atlantic, a very hostile place.

'The waves were terrible. We were being thrown one way and then dragged back again. Then there would be a huge wave coming right over us. You couldn't see and you would be coughing and spluttering. Then you were out of the wave and next thing you were up in the air and back again. When I think of it, we were just two schoolgirls fighting the north Atlantic, which is something that many, many men must have done during the Second World War. It was strange that we didn't really feel the cold or the pain much, even though we were being bashed backwards and forwards all the time. Eventually I suppose we were numb. Our legs were numb, they were in the water most of the time. We had both injured our ankles badly, but we couldn't really feel it. But none of these things sapped our willpower at all, it didn't seem to work that way. Our brains were active, they hadn't gone numb, our brains were still very much alive and so we didn't mind. It didn't matter what was happening to our bodies or anything else, we had to survive, our brains told us that. We weren't going bananas or anything like that, we were very much alert. But we were so alone. There were particular moments when you felt it – when the ship went down, when the dawn came up – and that was I think possibly the worst feeling, being on your own. The fact that Bess and I joined up with each other and managed to survive with each other, I think that was the great thing that kept us going, and we did rely on each other so much for it, we did, we had to.'

Bess agrees that it was their mutual support that kept them going and made survival a joint effort: 'What I think helped me and Beth to survive as we did was that we were doing it together. Especially the fact that we had achieved so much already, in the face of great danger, meant that we were now prepared to sacrifice almost anything to stay alive. Having come so far, we were not in the business of letting ourselves go. So it was mind over matter. If we felt cold, we told ourselves we weren't cold. I have a theory about survival, because I think it's a matter of conserving your energy for the most important things, and not getting too wound up about minor things. So when I started to feel cold, I just shook the idea off, and told myself I'm not, so I didn't feel it. I think it's mind over matter. In order to survive after having been through all those things that had happened to me so far, I made up my mind that there was one thing I'd got to do, and that was to concentrate on staying alive at all costs.

'To do that I knew I'd have to concentrate hard on shooing away things that were not important and make myself believe that I was going to be saved. Even though these huge, cold waves were breaking over me constantly and battering my body, and I'd been lifted up and down on the sides of that hull by the force of the waves and the wind, I knew by now if I was going to die it would be my own fault. One of the reasons why I think I survived in those appalling conditions – where I had nothing but huge waves breaking over me all night long, in the cold wastes of the Atlantic, and really and truly I should have been drowned – was that I concentrated my mind entirely on staying alive. And to do that I think I needed to be totally convinced that I was going to win, that the sea was not going to get me. It was a matter of sheer determination. Not bravery, determination.'

And it worked, somehow. Somehow, through sheer willpower, the girls continued to cling to the rope that was their lifeline. They continued to keep their heads above water as the day wore on. The morning came and went, and the afternoon began to draw to a close, and still the girls were in exactly the same situation as they had been when dawn broke, drifting in the empty Atlantic.

In fact, one attempt to rescue the girls had already been made, although they weren't really aware of it at the time. After her extraordinary rope climb down the hull of the sinking ship, Barbara Bech had ended up in probably the luckiest of all the lifeboats, number 4. It and lifeboat number 12 were the only boats to be launched successfully, without taking on water or losing occupants. So Barbara's situation was nothing like as desperate as what Beth and Bess were enduring. This made it particularly frustrating for Barbara when she actually caught sight of the two girls clinging to the hull of their lifeboat: 'It was first thing in the morning that I saw them, not long after daylight. My lifeboat drifted quite close to the upturned boat where Bess and Beth were trying to stay on. It was awful, because we did get quite close to them and I could see the two girls holding on to the upturned boat. And there was what looked like a body flung across the hull on the other side. It did seem to me we were really quite close and I kept thinking can't somebody swim across with a rope and pull them in, because they really needed rescuing. But there was one of the sailors, I think he was, with us who knew about it and he said, "No, we'd better not try and get any closer, because I think it'll tip us up rather than rescue them." So we left them, but it always seemed to me rather awful that two small girls couldn't be saved by a whole boatful of other people. But then we drifted away again, and they were the only people we ever saw.

'We were very lucky in our lifeboat because we had got onto the water in good shape, whereas in the other boats where so many died, I think a lot of them had been launched badly. Because a lifeboat has flotation chambers, and so it can be virtually full of water and not sink, yet these boats were capsizing. Even those still the right way up were nearly completely full of water. People were sitting in water up to their waists, which isn't good for you. When you're soaking wet and the wind blows you get very cold indeed, and I think that was where the people suffered terribly because they couldn't get clear of the water. They were safer in the boat than out in the sea, but they were as wet as if they were in the sea. But in our boat we were lucky and I was never really wet above the knees, not seriously wet. The waves would break over you and you would get wet on your clothes, but I was never soaked to the skin. That probably made it a bit easier to be fairly positive, which we all were. A couple of people in the boat said an SOS had been sent out and had been picked up at Land's End. They were pretty sure that our position was known and that somebody would be sent out to look for us. So on that basis they seemed to be fairly certain that we would be saved and we took their word for it. All the same, we knew that if they had to come from Land's End it certainly wasn't going to be five minutes, so it was a question of sitting and waiting and hoping.'

Sitting and waiting wasn't an option for the rest of Barbara's family, who were in the midst of a full-scale battle just to stay above water. Their life raft was little more than a pallet made of wooden planks and a couple of empty oil drums for flotation. Now it was gradually being torn to pieces by the constant battering of the waves, leaving Derek, Sonia and their mother Marguerite Bech hanging on by their fingernails. Derek describes their situation: 'The raft wasn't a complicated construction. It had these two big buoyancy drums, and it was then ordinary wooden duckboarding all the way round. The only way you could stay on was by hanging on to the duckboard with your fingers underneath. But the buoyancy drums were loose, and they used to roll and pinch your fingers. My mother looked down at her fingers and they were full of blood – her fingers were completely raw.

'I was lying almost flat on the raft with my mother hanging onto me. Every time a wave came down – which was all the time – we were completely immersed in the water. We were told later on that probably saved our lives, because the water actually kept us warmer than if we had been sitting up in the wind. We were quite far north and the wind was very cold, and blowing a gale. What happened was that the people in lifeboats who were sitting upright had the full blast of that icy wind, and they died of exposure. On the raft, we were fairly low down and because of the troughs and peaks of the waves, about 50 percent of the time we were shielded from the force of the wind. We only got the full blast at the top of the waves, and even then we were lying flat. They said the reason we didn't suffer from exposure even though we were cold and soaking wet was because we didn't have the wind chill – that's what is so dangerous. But we were completely numbed. We couldn't move, all our limbs were stiff with cold.

'I still had my school uniform on. I had my raincoat, a gabardine raincoat. I have been told I was even wearing my school cap at one stage, but I think that must have fallen off well before I got on the raft. And I had my gym shoes on. I actually still wore all these clothes afterwards – and I still had them for years. It's strange, but it wasn't for a long time that the raincoat got passed on, and the person who got it actually remembered, and valued that it was Derek's raincoat. My mother had made sure we had all the warmest clothing we could – maybe two or three layers. I remember having my pyjamas on underneath my school uniform. And Sonia and Barbara had brand new camel-hair coats which they had put on over their pyjamas. But even with all that we were constantly being drenched by waves and we were soaked through the whole time.

'My mother just kept holding on to me because I kept on drifting in and out of a sort of sleep, I kept dozing off. So she hung onto me with one arm and also had to cling on to the raft, so she had the constant strain of looking after me and staying on

Part of the Ellerman Line's brochure promoting the Liverpool to Bombay route of the SS *City of Benares*.

Beth Cummings

Below: Louis and Bess Walder with their father. Bess and Beth spent 14 hours clinging to an upturned lifeboat together; they've remained great friends and are now related as Bess married Beth's older brother.

Barbara, Sonia and Derek Bech were travelling first class with their mother.

Below: Colin Ryder Richardson became a good friend during the voyage.

Fred Steels

John and Bobby Baker.
Bobby gave his lifejacket to his
younger brother John. He did
not survive the tragedy.

The crew of U-48 with Rolf Hilse centre.
(Reproduced with permission from The Imperial War Museum)

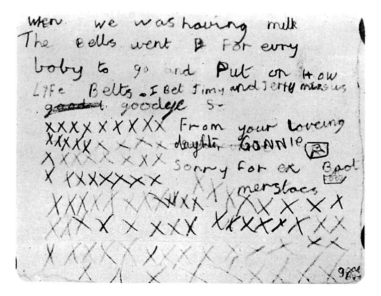

when we was having milk
The Bells went for evry
boby to go and Put on How
Life Belts. I Bet Jimy and Jetty misus
goodey goodeye S-
xxxx xxxxx From your Loveing
xxxxx xxxx dayter GONNIe
x xxxx xxxx Sorry for er Bad
x xxxxxxx merslacs
xxxxxx xxxx xx x x x
xx x xxx xxxxxx xx
xx xx
x x x

The last letter of one of the majority of seavacuees who died in the tragedy.

Illustration showing Eric Davies pulling the raft away from the sinking ship. Taken from the cover of *The War Weekly – including War Pictorial* dated 4th October 1940 and priced at 3d.

The moment of rescue – survivors clamber aboard *HMS Hurricane*. (Reproduced with permission from *The Liverpool Echo*)

Tommy Milligan pulled
Sonia Bech out of the water
on to a raft.

Survivors on a raft drawing
close to the *Hurricane*.

Above: *HMS Hurricane*.

Left: Dr Peter Collison.

Below: *HMS Anthony*.

Survivors on board the Hurricane — Louis Walder centre.

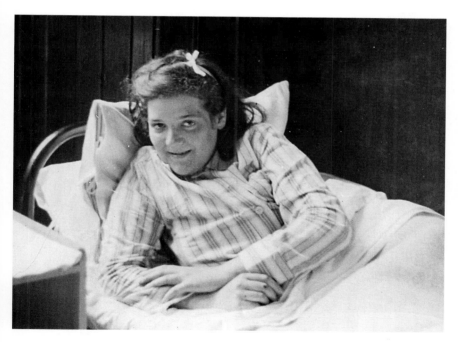

Beth Cummings in hospital recovering.

Ken Sparks' homecoming celebrations.

Colin Ryder Richardson looking at the press cuttings after the event — he was awarded the King's Award for Bravery.

Derek Capel and his younger brother Alan became separated and ended up on different lifeboats, Derek survived, Alan did not.

Bobby Baker who gave his lifejacket to save his brother.

Bess & Louis Walder and Beth Cummings – taken in 1941.

herself. And we were constantly being sprayed not just by the waves but also by hailstones and squalls all night long. We didn't talk very much, just a bit of chat, mainly warning each other if there was an impending wave coming along. The raft would be rocking up and down and every time we went up a wave everybody called out, "Hold on, here we go again." I remember at one stage my mother did bring out this famous bottle of medicinal brandy which she had. It was a little flask and we all had a swig of this, and as a child who had never had brandy or anything like that before it was quite different from what I expected. But during the course of the night it just slipped out of her pocket and she lost it.

'I suppose it warmed us all up and made us feel a bit better, but the only thing that really did warm you was when you let go and passed water! It was such a lovely relief to have a bit of warmth coming down you. That really was the only bit of warmth you felt the whole night – and what a sense of pleasure it was to have that warm liquid down inside your trousers. Just for a fleeting minute it was a real luxury. We revelled in it while we could, and then it would be washed away by the next freezing wave. The waves were terrible, you could hear the crest of the wave break with a great, tearing crash and then we would be going up through this torrent of water, like going up through Niagara Falls. And it happened again and again, it was a scary night. Twice Sonia actually got washed off, but my mother was trying to keep hold of both of us and she had her arm round me. Really, I think I owe my life to my mother looking after us. She kept with us all the night, she told us what to do and she protected us. As a young child you just do what your mother says and you don't have to think about it, so she protected us from having to make our own decisions. I think it was because she was a strong person in herself that we all survived, give her full credit for that.

'But I think my mother certainly thought we were going to die. There was a stage when she thought she might as well give up rather than prolong the deaths. She had this thought that we should just take off our lifebelts and let ourselves go into the sea and, I suppose, well, die in the sea. Because we had visions of people just dying on the raft and floating around for hours. But when she said it to Sonia, then Sonia piped up, "Oh, no Mummy, we'll wait a bit longer." Even then Sonia kept getting washed off and my mother was shouting to her, "Sonia, swim, swim like you've never swum before," and somehow – to this day Sonia doesn't know how – but she managed to get near enough to the raft for the engineer to reach out and haul her back on.'

The engineer who saved Sonia's life was Tommy Milligan, the seventh engineer on the *Benares*, and at the time he was only 19 years old, but of course Sonia remembers him as a big grown-up hero – the man who reached down into the sea as the waves closed above her and pulled her out. She remembers: 'I had lost consciousness and, even though I was hanging on for all I was worth, I went – I dropped off. The next minute I found myself in the sea, and this is another time when I remember praying. It's funny really, but the sea was all in monochrome. It was all white. I have seen programmes about people that have drowned or nearly drowned and they show them seeing the rushing water – and it's true, that's what you do see. I saw this water, rushing up past me, and I remember getting quite calm. I wasn't in a panic. I thought, "Oh, I'm going to die now, I wonder what God is like." And I remember distinctly that one moment I was thinking that, and then the next moment the seventh engineer pulled me out and put me on my back and was pumping the water out of my mouth. He propped me up and said, "Now hang on and don't do that again." But he was charming, very nice, and of course I thought he was a grown-up man.

'So anyway, he held me up and said, "Now you be careful and cling on, don't fall out again, it's not nice, next time I might not be able to find you." But it did happen again. I was getting so tired. It was probably about three in the morning, it was still dark and I was so tired, I just dropped off. I couldn't stop myself falling asleep. But that time I didn't go too far. I think he'd probably been looking out for me to lose consciousness again, so he had kept himself very near me. He was waiting for it to happen again. So he pulled me out of the water and I felt his strong arms round me, and he hauled me out and put me onto my tummy and made me spit out the salt water. Then he said, "Now come on, you've got to hold on, you mustn't do that again." Of course, I was in too much of a state to say thank-you. I don't think I said thank-you, but I knew that he'd saved me from drowning. I just knew it. I was so amazed, and he seemed to be so nice. I thought he was the most wonderful man, but I thought he was a big man, about 30 or something! Then when I heard years later that he was only 19 I couldn't believe it, but of course a boy of 19 can be very grown up – sometimes they have to be.

'With having fallen off twice I knew what would happen if I let go, but it was terrible, you had to fight every minute. My hands were being cut in shreds with these horrible rusty tin canisters. But I was holding on, even though I was only 11 and quite slight, I kept fighting, every minute of 15 hours in that awful sea – and I know that's why I'm alive today. During the night the weather changed a bit, and by dawn it was calmer. We could look around us, but we saw nothing, absolutely nothing. And then the waves started coming again, and I think this was when my mother had had enough. She was lying on top of Derek to stop him from falling in and her cork lifejacket was cutting into her breast. And she said, "Sonia, let's take our lifejackets off and go to sleep in the sea. It's no good staying up here any longer, it's too much of a fight, let's go to sleep in the sea." And I said, "No, on no account. We're not going to give up, I'm sure somebody's coming to save us, please don't let's do such a silly thing."

'You see, I was absolutely sure that we would survive and I would come back and get home. So when Mummy said let's go to sleep in the water, I was just furious. No, that was not going to happen to us. I definitely did not want to die and I'm sure that's why I am alive today – as well as being helped by my lovely engineer, and of course Mr Davies who found the raft for us. I believed in all of them and somehow I didn't think it would all be wasted. I didn't know what would end up happening, but I think, underneath, I knew we were going to go home. I don't know why, because we hadn't seen any sign of rescue. But we had been told that Land's End had been informed, so perhaps that's what I held onto. Well, whatever it was I hung onto it. I just thought we were going home and I was so looking forward to it. And I was not going to die.'

Sonia's friend Colin Ryder Richardson was in one of the waterlogged lifeboats, struggling to keep not only himself above water, but also a large lady passenger: 'I never knew her name, but I was trying to prop her up out of the water. But she became less and less conscious and I found it more and more difficult to hold her head up. Then somebody just said, "That lady's dead, let her go." But I couldn't. By that time I was so stiff with cold and my hands were grasping her body. When they said, "You must let her go," I said, "I can't," but eventually somebody helped me to get my arms from around her and to release her into the sea. Then she just floated out along with the other people that were dying all around me.

'The lascar crew had very little in the way of clothing on and I'm afraid they were among the ones who started to die first, because they really didn't have enough clothing on to protect them from the elements. At one time I found I was helping people push the bodies out of the lifeboat, but then they would float back in again. The boat was pretty much completely under water and the bodies were just floating in their lifejackets. It was awful, because I'm afraid our job was to try to get them out of the lifeboat so that we weren't ourselves knocked over by these floating bodies, so it was a gruesome task. And at the same time you were trying to hold on – I was sitting on the seats with my hands under the water trying to grip on under the seat. When the waves came over the water was up to my chest and it was just a question of hanging on for grim death. Luckily I had my string gloves on, and they gave me the grip to hold on and I tucked my legs under the seat as well to try and get an extra bit of security. Then every time there was a bit of a lull we would be trying to clear the boat of the dead bodies which kept getting washed in, knocking up against you.

'My mother had given me this modern red lifejacket which was filled with kapok – probably one of the first of its kind – and that kept me relatively warm. My balaclava had slipped off my head round my neck, so it was acting as a scarf. But I was aware all the time that I really had to keep awake, because it's very easy to sort of fall into a kind of sleep. You get into the kind of situation where you are drowsy, you're cold, and your fingers are numb, your feet are cold. I had slippers on but they went, the dressing gown went too. And you really are desperate for warmth. I was being immersed in the sea for one minute and then out of the sea and then back into the waves again. It is a terrifying experience, and there is this kind of feeling of losing consciousness from time to time. You would shut your eyes because of the salt water, and it seemed to induce a form of drowsiness – in spite of the storm. Very many people were letting go. They were falling asleep or wanting to drink water or do other things that were totally wrong. Then, because there was nobody really able to support them, they would fall forward into the middle of the boat and become another casualty.

'But I just kept telling myself that if I kept alert, kept myself going and awake, that there would be a rescue. In the past I had always been interested in stories of the Navy and survival at sea, and I tried to conjure up the story for myself – that any minute now, if I didn't drop off, if I just kept alert, that rescue was just around the corner. You had to go on believing that and saying that to yourself, because there wasn't really anybody else who would do it for you. You couldn't really talk to anybody else, there was no possibility, with the water around – we couldn't sing or anything like that. You just had to keep numb about the whole thing. My mother had said don't forget if there is any trouble the Royal Navy will pick you up, they will rescue you. So that was very firmly in my mind. All I kept thinking was, as long as I keep my head above water and my grip on the lifeboat, something good will happen.'

The commander of the German U-boat that had torpedoed the *Benares*, Heinrich Bleichrodt, noted the exact time of its sinking in his log. It sank at 10.31 p.m. on the night of Tuesday, 17 September 1940. The torpedo had actually struck at ten o'clock, so the *Benares* had taken just half an hour to sink. Twelve hours after that, in the middle of the following morning, the few survivors were still drifting alone in the Atlantic. By mid-afternoon, a full 17 hours after the sinking, the picture was exactly the same. Little clusters of survivors were clinging to rafts or sinking lifeboats, tossed on towering waves, unable to see either each other or any prospect of rescue. The situation seemed hopeless.

CHAPTER SEVEN

Rescue

S till the survivors held fast to the belief that they were going to be saved – they couldn't afford to think any other way. And amazingly, they were right: rescuers were coming. Lyness radio station in Scotland had received a distress signal from the *Benares* at 10.06 p.m. on the Tuesday night, shortly after it had been torpedoed, and had immediately taken steps to organise a rescue. So all through that horrendous night's storm, while Beth and Bess, and the Bechs, and all the other survivors were hanging on desperately, help was in fact getting closer. But the nearest Royal Navy ship, HMS *Hurricane*, was more than 400 miles away, and it too had to fight into the face of the north Atlantic force sixer.

Albert Gorman was a leading seaman aboard HMS *Hurricane*. He remembers: 'The first watch had taken over at eight o'clock that evening, on the Tuesday evening, and by ten o'clock most people were looking for a bit of rest, so we were all getting in our hammocks. Then the signalman came down and told us about the signal – this is what you do in the Navy, when you get a signal they always come down and tell the sailors first, then take the signal to the captain.

'Well, the signalman came and said, "We've just had a call. The *City of Benares*, a liner taking children to Canada, has been torpedoed and we're about to make our way towards her and see what we can do." She was sinking, and we were to go to code red: drop what you're doing and proceed at once and render what assistance you can. The next minute we felt the ship increase speed to, I suppose, 25, 28 knots and it was getting rough and the ship was being thrown all over the place. She started to go over, under and above the sea, and it was splashing all over the place and we thought, "Ullo, he's gonna smash the ship up." The skipper must also have thought this, because he reduced speed to probably 15, 18 knots, it's difficult to tell. At any rate, the *City of Benares* was 400 miles away and we had got the call at ten o'clock at night. Some of the youngsters were very worried about the speed we were doing in the rough sea, but I'd been at sea for a long while and it didn't worry me very much. Destroyers are good sea boats. They jump over mountainous waves, through them, underneath them, but they still manage to keep going. As we increased speed we knew that there was a danger of somebody getting washed over the side, or of damaging the ship, but we put that aside because all those kids were a priority. We wanted to save the children. I just kept thinking, let's get there before the kids drown. To be honest, I never thought that they'd even get into the lifeboats, because getting into a lifeboat with a load of children is no easy task.'

Albert's fellow seaman, Reg Charlton, also aboard HMS *Hurricane*, didn't immediately find out why the *Hurricane* had suddenly picked up speed: 'Well, I wasn't down below, I was at my action station, which was on the bridge. I heard the captain talking to the chief engineer and then the officer engineer, and I knew there was something afoot because very quickly the revs went up and you could feel the new vibration, because the seas were very choppy – the north Atlantic was cold and choppy – and we knew then something was afoot. But my duties took me down to the gun deck and it was a while before I got back up to the bridge and I read the signal. By this time the ship was racing into head-on seas, really pounding her way through, and Captain Simms was testing the endurance of the ship and his engines to the limit. We didn't know why for a while, but when we realised that an evacuee ship with mainly women and children aboard had been torpedoed, it was a terrible shock. Then we had all the emotions that you could imagine. Rage, anger and hate for the Germans, and the captain himself expressed it very clearly. He was saying he would kill them if he met any now. That's how it was, as our ship pounded into the waves. And the seas were coming in over the bows and onto the bridge, which reminded us what a cruel death it was – that bitter cold weather, the bitter cold seas. So we pounded away there and before we knew it we had covered 300 miles. We were up with the binoculars looking around for survivors, even though we must still have been 100 miles away from them at that stage.'

So, as that devastating dawn was breaking on the morning of Wednesday, 18 September, revealing to the survivors the bitter disappointment of an empty horizon, in fact HMS *Hurricane* was racing towards them at full speed. Even so, for the Bech family, clinging by their fingernails to their few planks of wood, the *Hurricane* would not have arrived in time. But fortunately, something else did. Derek Bech explains: 'It was just as dawn was breaking that we were conscious of the fact that there was another lifeboat or some sort of boat fairly close to us, because when we were on the crest of a wave we could see this mast. Then it got closer and closer to us. And slowly but surely it manoeuvred itself so it could pick us up. They had to carry us off bodily because we couldn't move, so they lifted us off. It was a boat from another ship that had been sunk that night, the SS *Marina*, a merchantman. The chief officer was a Mr Lewis, who we later found out was a ladies' hairdresser from Chippenham. He was in the boat and he picked us up. He saved our lives. When he saw the state of the raft he said it wouldn't have lasted another half an hour. So he took us on his lifeboat and told us that an SOS had been picked up and that a rescue ship would be on its way to pick us up.'

Having slipped off into the sea twice during the night, Sonia Bech was in as bad a state as the life raft. When she first saw Chief Officer Lewis's boat she had little energy left to believe in the prospect of rescue. 'We saw a sail, but then the next moment we were at the bottom of a wave and you couldn't see anything except the wave round you, so it wasn't promising. But when we came up on the top again we saw the boat again, a sailing boat it looked like. So we screamed and shouted, but we knew that the wind wouldn't let us make them hear. Still, we just hoped that this little boat had seen us, and we realised that he had, because in some incredible way with his navigation he was able to reach us. It was the most amazing feat of sailing, because in that small boat, with a sail up, he managed to manoeuvre in those seas. We didn't know to begin with what the boat was or where it had come from because lifeboats don't have sails usually, so we didn't know quite what it was.

'It turned out that sinking alongside us had been one of the cargo boats called SS *Marina*, and she had seen our plight and had wanted to help the children. Then she was torpedoed as well, but Mr Lewis, he realised that he could get out without any loss of life, because it was a small ship and he knew how to get everyone into the lifeboat. And it was his lifeboat with its sail that we saw. So he got us into the boat, and he'd also rescued some of the lascar crew. I don't quite know who else he rescued, because it was all a bit hazy for me, but he might have rescued a few other people too. And he talked to us and said, "Don't worry, if we don't get picked up out here, we will sail to Land's End." He said, "It's all right, they have picked up our message, they know we're here." So that gave us a little bit of hope too.

'But we were still on the little boat for another five hours. In fact, it wasn't until I got into that boat that I did start feeling the cold. On the raft you're wet all the time and moving around hanging on and your hand is hurting, so you are too busy concentrating on all that. But on the lifeboat the wind was catching you and you were dry one minute, then wet the other. We were getting wet because the big waves still came over us, and then we got dry again. Then just as soon as you think oh, bit dryer at last, then another wave would come, so it wasn't very pleasant. But we huddled together in the boat, and we sang, and we were given brandy, which I thought was absolutely disgusting. How anybody could want brandy I don't know, and we were given Nestlé's milk in a tin. They made a hole in one corner and we all had to lick this sweet stuff. But I was very fastidious – I did not like the idea of licking after all these other people! Mummy said, "Don't be so stupid, of course you've got to drink it." And so we drank the Nestlé's milk and ship's biscuits which were all salty and disgusting, but never mind that. That was the best part of it because I didn't like the brandy and I certainly didn't like the milk, but the biscuits, even though they were a bit salty, were all right.

'I think a child can be very resilient. People say children are very weak, don't they, but I don't think I was. I think I was tough. I don't remember feeling very bad, or anything really horrible happening. What I do remember is my hair! Oh dear, my hair was in two pigtails with elastic bands on the end, and I was dreading that the elastic bands would come out and that my hair would go flowing! Well, all the girls nowadays want their hair flowing around, but that was my idea of absolute hell. I wanted to have it firmly in plaits, but my mother wasn't very good at plaiting my hair, so all that time I was worrying. And Mummy had had a perm. Now in those days, perms were really frizzy things, and you can imagine, Mummy on a raft for all those hours and then in that lifeboat with the wind and the rain and everything else – her hair was like a big halo right round her head. I've never seen anything quite so funny, but I don't think she noticed. So about five hours went by, and with it being September, it was getting towards the end of daylight. The sun was setting, and I always remember setting suns ever since. I rather like September skies. Because there on the horizon was HMS *Hurricane*. She was silver and she was shining and she was a bit pink too because of the sun, and she was really a most beautiful ship, I thought. And we began screaming and shouting to get her attention, but she didn't immediately come to us and we thought oh dear, she's going to go away.'

HMS *Hurricane* had got into the position indicated on the signal by the afternoon, but still it proved impossible to get the rescue under way. Albert Gorman remembers the frustration of that moment: 'That particular position had been given to us by the Admiralty. But when we got there – nothing. Not a piece of flotsam, or jetsam, or anything else. No bodies, no boats, no nothing. So the skipper turned round to the midshipman and he said, "We'll do a 20-mile search." And this young midshipman, he started a 20-mile search. A 20-mile search is, you go north 20 miles, you go west 20 miles, you go north twenty miles. And each time you go, you can see 20 miles that way, 20 miles the other way. Well, we went along and we never saw a thing for 19 miles.'

But finally, just as the afternoon was drawing in and it seemed they might run out of light to search in, the crew of the *Hurricane* began to spot survivors. Reg Charlton will never forget what he saw: 'I was on the bridge and the ship slowed down. As we approached we looked around, and it was the most grim and heartbreaking scene. There were boats half full of water. It was difficult to take it all in at once, but then in particular I saw lifeboats that had children – dead children. Then when the ship came closer, we saw the detail. There was a boat – three-quarters full of water – that had a man sitting in the bows and he was up to his chest in water, but on his chest he was holding up a boy and he had his hand under the boy's chin to keep it clear of the water. Whether he was alive or the boy was alive, I don't know. It was a cruel sight to see. The next little boat I looked at had a girl, a little girl, maybe 8 or 9, and she was face down with her hair floating out in the water and that was such a distressing thing. I was very, very touched to see that girl, with her beautiful hair all floating. That image was heartbreaking. That's what still lives with me to this day. The image of little ones and the why – imagining what had happened.

'Little children of 8, there were, and the impact, the sad, sad impact on me of that image of them lying face downwards, in a three-quarters-full-of-water boat, still upright, and they were dead. I think there were two lifeboats which had similar kinds of pictures. Then there was that lifeboat that had the man sitting holding the boy's chin up to his chest. I never found that out if either of them was alive. I don't know, but I know our worst fears of what had happened were realised. A cruel death by all means.

'Then I saw another lifeboat that seemed to have some more children in, but at that point I had to leave the bridge to go down to help with the nets. We were throwing scrambling nets over the side and then helping people come alongside and hold them. They got their little boats up to the side of the ship, and the captain manoeuvred the ship alongside. Then I went to the gangway which had been got down a few feet into the water and I had two or three other sailors with me to hand people up the steps. They were mainly the women first, I think there were about three or four women, and these ladies were working the oars when they came alongside the ship. In the bows were a few lascar seamen, who had also survived. But we were hearing horrific stories of the way the lifeboats had tipped out from the davits when they had tried to lower them into the sea. That's where many of the crew and passengers died – a cold death for those people who had gone into the sea when the lifeboat launch didn't work properly.

'It's hard to remember the children individually, but there was one blond little boy, he was on the tiller. And I was surprised to see that the ladies were sitting working the oars. But of all the images, the one that will never leave me was seeing the lifeboats with dead children in, at least two girls in different lifeboats and the man holding up a boy in the flooded lifeboat. I will always think of these water-filled boats and the little girls with their hair drifting, floating in a fan on the water. It doesn't matter how many years pass, it happened, and the effect stays just as real as if it happened yesterday. The impact on me, so sad, distressing it was. I felt heartbroken. Everybody felt the same, terribly emotional and distressed. We all felt awful. We all of us went through that whole range – that whole gamut of emotions of anger and rage and distress. Some of the crew definitely wept when they saw it all. I remember that we all felt tearful indeed. It was such a horrendous thought when we saw what was left of them, in the lifeboats, and what had obviously happened to them.

'It was knowing in your mind what they had gone through, the image of what was happening to them when we were steaming towards them. Well, our worst imaginings had been realised when we thought of this dastardly death the people had suffered. But it was helpful, in a way, to our spirits that we'd saved some, that we were there to rescue some people. It was a bit encouraging for us then, to see that we had done some good in our dash against the storm – that testing out the ship's endurance against those heavy north Atlantic seas had paid off.'

Albert Gorman had actually had to leave the first survivor he came across without getting a chance to rescue him: 'The first thing I saw was an upturned boat with someone on it. We went there and it turned out to be a sailor sitting on the keel of this capsized lifeboat. We went alongside and over the loudhailer asked him where the other boats were and he pointed and away we went and we left him – and the thing I noticed was the complete devastation on that lad's face when we left him. People might say well, why didn't we pick him up? But we weren't after one, we were after dozens more. And we were very quickly called away.'

Albert was needed for a more urgent task. Another upturned lifeboat had been spotted and someone thought they might possibly have seen two little girls on it. It was a job for the small, manoeuvrable 'whaler' rowing boat that Albert commanded: 'The captain had a job for the whaler, so my crew jumped into it, by going down the netting. We slipped the releasing gear and pulled away from the *Hurricane*. I was a coxswain on the whaler and I had five good oarsmen, I'd trained 'em meself, they were part of my gun crew. Anyway, away we went. As we pulled away from the ship I had a good look round. There were boats everywhere, but one boat in particular I noticed had one person sitting on the keel. The boat was turned upside down, and he was sitting on the keel and I said to myself, well, poor bloke, I'll go and get him first, and as we pulled – rowed – towards this boat I saw two black heads. I looked and I thought to myself, what the hell's that? But as we got nearer I could see they were two female heads. They were little girls hanging onto the handrail or something, it might have been the ropes that were encircling the boat. I don't know, I just saw they were hanging onto something.

'So I said, oh, I'll have those. We went alongside. I was very careful not to touch the upturned boat. When a boat's upturned it's usually full of water underneath and if you touch it, it'll capsize completely. Any rate, I got alongside, very, very close. I turned the tiller over to the number one oarsman and said, "Keep us close up to the upturned boat but don't touch it." Then I jumped out of the whaler, climbed up onto the upturned boat, got onto the keel and started running along the keel – though the keel, mind, is only about five inches wide and very slippery. I got to the first girl and got my feet down into the water to reach her. I discovered they were hanging onto the lifelines that go all the way round a lifeboat; they go round in loops. I went down, picked her up as though she was a feather, got up again using the hand grips on the hull and ran back along the keel. The little girl was in a terrific state. She was sobbing, she was soaking wet. She'd been in that water in the cold Atlantic for eight or nine hours at least, and how they survived I will never know, but she had her arm round my neck, was hanging onto me as though I was her saviour.

'I looked at her and she looked very, very rough, but I didn't speak to her. I got back to where the whaler was, and I was just about to put the little girl down into the whaler and right where I was going to put her was the man – he was a lascar – that had been sitting on the keel when I first saw the boat. I said to him, "Get for'ard," I said, "there's not room enough here," I said, "I've got another girl to pick up."

So now I could put the first girl down – I remember tapping her on the shoulder and saying, "Don't go away, I'll be back." And there was a little bit of a glint of a smile on her face. Then I got back on the upturned boat and ran down the keel again to the second girl. I looked down at her and the relief on that girl's face, it spoke miles for me. She seemed to me to look in a worse state than the first girl, but she put her arm round my neck and she seemed quite happy to stay there. So I picked her up, run back along the keel, and at the same time this upturned boat was wobbling more than I would have liked. At any rate, I got back to the whaler, sat her down alongside of the first girl, then ordered the oarsman to row. The girls were in such a bad state, I thought I'd better take 'em straight back to the ship. They'd been in the water for all that time and how they survived I do not know. I remember one of them must just have had some sort of frock or nightdress on, because I remember picking her up, I put an arm round her legs and an arm round her body and I held her close to me and I said to her, "Yeah, your worries are over, you're safe now, you're going aboard a warship." I hoped that by saying that she would think that a warship was impregnable. But in truth, we could get sunk like anybody else.

'I don't really know whether it was Beth or Bess I picked up first, but I think it was Bess because of the glasses. Well, she was the more talkative of the two, such talk as they did say – it wasn't much. We got them back to the ship and willing hands took 'em aboard and took 'em down below. They had baths and were given something dry to wear and put straight to bed. But the truth is, when I first saw them I thought – I honestly thought at that time, when I picked them up – that another hour and they would have let go and died. There were so many women gave up. But those two kids said no, they weren't gonna give up, and they didn't. And afterwards when I spoke to Bess, I said, "Did you ever hope that you'd be rescued?" and she said to me, "When Beth said there's a ship coming." It was the *Hurricane*, and Bess had said, "What nationality is it?" So Beth said, "I don't know." That's when Bess said, "Well, I don't care if it's a German, as long as they rescue us."'

Albert never mentioned to the girls his belief that he had only just arrived in time, but of course, they knew it anyway. Bess Walder admits: 'I think at that stage we were both so disappointed, so weary, so generally failing in health and in strength and in our mental capacities. But then, just as we were at the end of our tether, it was almost as if it was something magical, I began to notice that I could see something that looked like a black speck on the horizon. I was curious because nothing had moved. In all this time, nothing. Then this black speck became larger and larger. My eyes by this time were almost totally closed, and of course we had imagined things before, like mirages almost. But as that speck grew bigger, I could hear noises. I could hear sounds, and I said to Beth, through my lips which were now hugely swollen, "Beth, a ship." Beth, knowing what we'd seen before, shook her head. But I persisted and said, "A ship." Do you know what she said? "German?" I said, "Don't care."

'And as we watched, so this thing revealed itself indeed into the shape of a ship. Not just a ship, but a ship of the Royal Navy, a destroyer that had been battling through these huge seas, to get to us. And it was on its way back to turn round because it was almost at the end of its capacity of fuel. But the commander had been told that somewhere on the horizon there was something that looked like two people and perhaps three, on an upturned boat. So he gave the command that a whaler be launched and be rowed out so that they could find out what this was – even though he was running out of time, he was desperate to get his ship back to port. So this whaler set off, and the coxswain turned out to be a Mr Albert Gorman. As the whaler came closer and closer to us, we heard the men on board saying, "Hang on, hang on," which was rather peculiar because we'd been hanging on for so long that night! Then, as they came closer to us, Albert, who was the coxswain of the ship, arranged very cleverly for the whaler to come alongside us without rocking us over. Now, that was wonderful seamanship in that sea. He held out his arms to me and he said, "Come on darling, let go."

'But darling couldn't let go because darling's hands had been in that position for so long they refused to move. So very gently, kindly, he leaned over, pushed my hands back. I felt no pain because I'd gone beyond pain at that stage. He could have cut my fingers off and I probably wouldn't have noticed. He carried me back and lifted me into his boat, the whaler. Then he did the same for Beth, and they rowed with all speed back to that destroyer. As we got closer to the destroyer all the crew were out on deck, shouting, laughing, crying, swearing, because some of them were family men and they realised how lucky these two girls were to be going back to their families.'

Beth Cummings remembers her pessimistic response to Bess sighting the ship. 'She shouted to me – well, sort of croaked, actually – "A ship" and my first thought was it'll be a German. I don't know why. It just came straight into my head, oh, it must be a German ship, can't be anything else. And I thought, I'm not very bothered. I don't care what sort of a ship, if it's a ship, that's all we want, a ship. It was then that this ship came nearer and I could see it was grey and a destroyer. It was number 06, I even saw the number on it! We saw they were dropping stuff on the water, apparently it was oil to calm the swell, and then the boat came out. This boat came towards us, and they were shouting to us. The chap in charge, he was very good, and he was shouting to us. But he was also shouting at the lascar too, and I was really shocked because he was swearing! Anyway, I don't know how on earth he did it, but he got our hands off the rope. We virtually had to be dragged off, I think. I ended up in the boat between two sailors and they were rubbing my hands. They put a coat round me and they were saying, "You'll be all right, you'll be all right." But there was a strange thing: one was cutting the lifejacket off me, and I heard this voice shouting, "No, you mustn't do that," because we were sitting ducks, obviously. We still had quite a long way to row to get back to the destroyer.

'The next thing I remember was being over a sailor's shoulder, with rows and rows of sea boots – sea boots going along there. All I could see were these boots and these feet and then I was laying on a chair with two sailors supporting me and being forced to drink half a glass of rum. It was Albert Gorman's whaler that had rescued us and got us back to the *Hurricane*. Albert was the leading seaman in the boat and how he got us off I honestly don't know, but he was shouting, and I've always laughed at him since. I say to him, "Do you know you were swearing at us?" "Not *at* you," he always says. But of course they were, it was just that they were trying to get us off very quickly.

As soon as Albert had seen the two girls safely on board the *Hurricane*, he had to rush to the aid of other survivors. He remembers: "We went to one boat and there were about 20 people in it, men, women and kids. And as I jumped onto the stern sheets – the ropes at the back – there was a young woman of maybe 22, sitting there with her knees together, hands in her lap, in a little frock. When the boat rolled, her frock came up and she had two big holes in the knees of her stockings and I looked and I thought, oh, she won't like that. I was moving through the lifeboat trying to find pulses and open people's eyes and slap them to try and revive them. There was a young seaman in the boat with me, about 18, it was his first ship. He yelled out to me, "Ted, what do I do with this one?" I looked and he had a little baby, 18 months old. It was wearing a little siren suit. Churchill had introduced the siren suits, which we would call tracksuits or boiler suits now. So this little baby was in its miniature blue siren suit and I said, "Is it alive?" He said, "No, it's dead." I said, "Well, put it down, we're only looking for live ones." "You bastard," he said, and he dropped the baby in the water – all the boats were three-quarters full of water. I just said, "Yes, I know, you'll learn."

'So I went back to this young woman, still sitting there with the holes in her stockings. I was feeling for her pulse in her wrist, but I couldn't get anything. I tried listening for a heartbeat with my head on her chest, nothing. Her eyes were still open. I picked up her left hand and it had a magnificent diamond engagement ring and a brand new wedding ring. It couldn't have been out of its box very long. I looked at her, and I pushed her face a little bit, and her eyes went down and then went open again with the ship was rolling. I just couldn't accept the fact that she was dead. And I didn't want to leave her, but I couldn't do anything about it. Then we got the recall signal from the *Hurricane* and I had to leave her. As we pulled away from the lifeboat I kept looking back at her and it seemed as if she was looking at me, but I knew she wasn't. We got about 50 yards from the *Hurricane* and the skipper shouted, "Anyone alive?" I said, "No sir, they're all dead." "All right," he said, "return to the ship."

'We went to two more boats, but they were all dead in those as well. In the end we had to abandon the search and go back to pick up the first sailor we'd seen. I was asking him about what had happened. He said, "Well, it was pandemonium getting those women into the lifeboats. The *Benares* was sinking like all those merchant ships do – they sink one side. They go over one side and then the stern goes down and up comes the bows, and the lifeboats get swung against the hull. We had to slide down ropes. Women were sliding down ropes, all just in their nightclothes," he said. He told me he had about 20 women in his boat and he was trying to get the rowing gear working to get away from the ship before it dragged them down. "Then night came," he said, "and during the night you would hear a splash and that would be someone going over the side." When the morning came there were only two women left. Then the lifeboat capsized and he was the only survivor of a boat of more than 20 people.'

Reg Charlton had stayed on board the *Hurricane* to help the survivors as they arrived on the ship: 'Members of the crew and officers were giving up their cabins to the survivors. We were waiting to help the people onto the deck. All the crew members were sharing the same worries, and all anxious about it. We all had these terrible images in our minds of the little children in that cold, cruel sea. As the survivors came on board they were all very cold. Some were just in pullovers. I was busy with helping the ladies up the steps onto the deck. One of the lifeboats had managed to pull in directly alongside the ship and I think we had a man and two or three boys come up from that. It was such a sense of relief – or even, if I dare use the word, pleasure – that we'd saved them from this terrible ordeal. It was wonderful that we'd been able to bring some of them back home with us alive out of this horror. But I'm afraid most of them were gone – all those boys and girls who met a cruel death in that bitter north Atlantic.

'The ship's doctor, Dr Collinson, came on deck and he was seeing to someone. Then they rowed the whaler in and I started to help the sailors down on the whaler to bring these two little girls up – and they were Bess and Beth, of course. I didn't see very much of Bess and Beth after that because I had to go back onto my action station on the bridge. So there I was on my watch through the evening trying to sort out my feelings – very mixed feelings of sadness, yet a sort of satisfaction that we'd been able to rescue some of them. Sadly, I think three of the children we had brought on board died during the night. But at least we got Beth and Bess. It was a wonderful feeling when we got the girls back, adding to the ones we'd saved already and brought up the gangway, a wonderful feeling. Thank God we could save some of them anyway.'

Colin Ryder Richardson's lifeboat was one of those seaworthy enough to be brought directly alongside HMS *Hurricane*. At that stage Colin still couldn't quite comprehend the fact that they really were being rescued. He says: 'Well, we couldn't believe it for a moment or two – one minute you're praying for this to happen and when it does happen you are asking yourself if it is real or an illusion, just another mirage? But yes, it was a destroyer, and a British destroyer at that, because of course it could just as easily have been a German ship. But we saw the white ensign and then that they were stopping and picking people up. The few of us that were left were waving and shouting and yelling and eventually they came alongside us with scrambling nets over the side of the warship. They said, "Come on, Colin, up you go," but unfortunately there was no way I could possibly climb the nets because my skin was so softened and soaked by this time that it was really impossible for me to hold anything. So they had to put a rope round my arms and haul me up, and I really couldn't walk or do anything. They had to drag me into the boiler room so that I could take off my wet clothes and get dry stuff on and put a towel round me.'

Because her lifeboat was the least urgently in need of rescue, Barbara Bech had to go through the unsettling experience of watching the *Hurricane* apparently setting off without them, not just once but several times, as the ship went to pick up the more desperate cases first. She remembers: 'It was in the afternoon that we thought we saw something. It's hard, because the Atlantic waves are massive and you go up and down like a switchback. So it's only the split moment that you're on the top of the wave that you can actually see the horizon, because immediately you're sliding down the other side, which means usually you can't see very much more than the next wave and the one you've just slid over. That's your view, it's sort of a little valley between two rather large hillocks. But anyway, on one of our ups suddenly somebody said, "Ah, I can see a boat." Then of course, the next time we got on an up we all looked, and we all said, "Ah yes, there's a boat." A little bit nearer somebody said, "Oh yes, it – it is a warship, oh, they've found us."

'I think we let off a rocket which we had in our emergency kit. We'd also had a little bit of stale, brackish water to drink, and some utterly appalling ship's biscuits, which I don't think anybody with ten sets of teeth would have got through! Anyway, the ship got nearer and suddenly we could see it quite clearly, so we let off another rocket. But then we had a good two hours of being rather concerned because it kept coming quite near and then shooting off in another direction and then coming back and still not stopping. Of course, we heard afterwards that they had got lookouts watching to see the condition of the people and the lifeboats, and they could see that we'd last out for a good bit longer. So they were racing around picking up the people that looked in much more danger than us. That meant that we were one of the very last lifeboats to be picked up, but suddenly the ship loomed up near us. And this time it obviously was going to stop. They put a rope mesh down the side and told us to wait for them to come down and help us out. We were manhandled up fairly quickly. Once we got on board they took us to a little room by the main funnel, where people go to warm up because it is where all the heat is coming up through the funnel. They stuffed us in there and it was so lovely and warm.'

With Barbara and the rest of her lifeboat safely on board, the *Hurricane* had finally picked up all the survivors it was aware of. There was no sign of lifeboat number 12. Since none of the survivors had seen anything of it, the *Hurricane* had to presume that lifeboat 12 had also been completely sunk. HMS *Hurricane* was at the limit of its fuel. Now was the time to turn for home and begin the process of nursing the survivors back to health.

For Derek Bech, just getting out of his clothes – soaked and stiffened by the salt water – was a task in itself: 'When we got on board they took us down to the locker rooms where they used to dry out their oilskins. We had to have our lifejackets physically cut off us because they had shrunk onto our necks. Then we went below and I was given a hot bath by my mother. The sailors gave us a lot of their tropical clothes to wear – whites, they call them. Then Sonia and myself were put in the captain's bed, wonderful bed, and we thought we were in absolute luxury. We kept on hearing the ship stopping and starting as more people were being rescued.

'My mother had gone to help look after the children. She was reassuring them, but she told me many of them were very far gone. They were almost unconscious and she was slapping them to try and bring some life back to them. She rubbed their limbs to get their muscles to move but sadly, even after being rescued, I think some of them actually died on the destroyer, which was tragic. By this time Sonia and I had been moved out of the captain's bed because there were more needy people. Some of the children were just barely surviving and they'd been injured and needed medical care. And of course, Barbara still hadn't turned up, so my mother was anxious about Barbara. There was a pattern of rescuing little groups of survivors and bringing them back in. And my mother kept asking the sailors as they came in, "Is Barbara there? Is Barbara there?" and they kept saying, "No, no Barbara, no Barbara."

'Obviously, the captain on the bridge could see the various upturned boats and rafts and work out which people were in more desperate need. What we didn't know was that Barbara's boat was one of the few lifeboats that hadn't capsized and was more or less in a seaworthy condition. So my mother was beside herself. Then, with the very last boat of all, they came down and said, "Oh, here's Barbara," and my mother was reunited with her. It was funny because as she came in, Barbara said, "Oh, I was expecting to see you here. I couldn't believe that when I saw the ship go down I wouldn't see you again." So she had been the same as us – the whole night through, even though we were separated, none of us thought we would not see each other again.

'We all felt so privileged to have survived, because none of us even had a scratch on us really. Oh, we'd lost our belongings and everything we had was on the ship when it went down, but we were in one piece when so many other people confronted death that night – particularly amongst the evacuees. The torpedo had struck in their section of the ship and many of them were injured in their cabins before they even got on the lifeboats. Then those who did get into a lifeboat suffered because the lifeboats were so badly launched. The children were literally pitched into the sea, or they hit the sea and the boats immediately capsized. So there was a lot of loss of life in abandoning the ship the *City of Benares*. But we were so lucky, all of our family came through. By nighttime Sonia and I ended up in sort of sleeping bags on the floor of the officers' mess. They had a little black kitten. I always remember the black kitten they had as a mascot and very soon I got friendly with this cat. He came and curled up in my sleeping bag.

'They looked after us very well, the Naval chaps, because they hadn't ever had to rescue children before. We settled in quite well. Of course it was another adventure, another big excitement for us being on a warship. The next day we went up on deck and we were sitting there and crew used to say, "Look out for periscopes, if you see a periscope tell us." So we would have our eyes peeled. And we used to play ludo and all these games, and they allowed us to play in the gun turrets, where all the revolving guns were mounted.'

Derek's sister Sonia has equally happy memories of the wonderful moments of actually being rescued: 'The ship had been picking other people up first, but then she came to us, and put netting down the side. The sailors made two lines with their legs entwined in the netting and pulled us up hand over hand from one to the other, and they were all smiling and cheerful. When we got to the top and onto the deck, they said, "Can you walk?" and I said, "Of course," and I immediately fell down. I'd been in that raft and everything, and I was a bit – well, my hands were terribly swollen because I'd held onto this raft for ten hours or more. Those horrible buoyancy cylinders had been cutting in and making my hands bleed. But it was so lovely to be on the *Hurricane* and we were given baked beans and bacon. And they had a ship's mascot, a little black cat, and of course I'm so animal minded that cheered me up immediately. And I was so pleased to be going back home. We were told we were going to Scotland, we weren't going to America, so I'd be able to see my little Scottie dog again, Mackie.

'But Mummy had a rather gruelling evening because she stayed in the captain's quarters the whole evening where there was a big bath, and everybody had a hot bath with Mummy bathing them and sometimes she'd smack their faces to sort of bring them back to life. We weren't told about it until long after, but three children did perish that night from exposure and exhaustion, even though they'd been rescued. But we didn't know about that, we were thinking about baked beans and the kitten. What was particularly awful for my mother was that Barbara hadn't been seen, and all the time people were coming with these terrible stories: oh, ten children died in my boat, five children died in my boat, no children came out of our boat, they drowned on the lifeboats. People were telling her how they were up to their necks in water. They were waterlogged because it was such rough seas and they had lowered the boats badly. So Mummy was hearing all these stories and she kept on asking, "Has anybody seen a little girl called Barbara?"

'But Barbara was in the very last lifeboat to be picked up. I wasn't there when they took Barbara in to my mother, but when they came out they were dressed in the sailors' uniforms. Barbara was all dressed up beautifully. They looked so lovely with these lovely white trousers and a white top. I had one too, miles too big for me, but I just managed to roll up the sleeves. We were so thrilled. And we had our own little story to tell, my brother and I. But the other people had suffered the most terrible things and it was only afterwards that we realised how lucky we were. We hadn't really understood, we were so involved in our own little lives and keeping alive that we didn't think about everything. We didn't hear about the other children, you see it was kept from us about them, and we certainly didn't know about the waterlogged lifeboats. We didn't know about it until afterwards.'

As Sonia gradually discovered, for every story like hers of a happy reunion, there were many more tales of devastating losses. For John Baker, being rescued brought the realisation that his brother was still missing. John had been in one of the waterlogged lifeboats and was in poor shape when the *Hurricane* arrived. He explains: 'I have very little memory at all of being in the lifeboat.

I know I was wrapped in sacking and tied to one of the thwarts, but from then on I don't really remember any more until the sighting of HMS *Hurricane*. I don't know what happened in that intervening time. I have no memory even of being wet, or anything. I suppose I was cold, we were all cold, but I don't remember thinking I was cold. The first thing I remember is when the boat was sighted, which turned out to be HMS *Hurricane*. We all got excited and I managed to get myself free of the sacking and they allowed me to sit up – I think they were looking after me, which I was very grateful for.

'I just have this fleeting picture of us clambering aboard HMS *Hurricane* and then the next thing I knew was being in bed in a sort of ward on board the ship and I was feeling warm, but I don't know the time span there at all. Then I was beginning to recover a bit and the first thing I wanted to know – I was asking everybody who came anywhere near to me – was where was Bobby? When they allowed me to get up and go about under my own steam I immediately began looking for Bobby, and Bobby was nowhere to be found. So I just hunted the ship – every nook and cranny of the boat that I was allowed to go in and some that I wasn't allowed to go in. I asked everybody where Bobby was. There was one point when I went up to this gentleman and said, "Excuse me, have you seen my brother Bobby?" Well, he turned out to be Commander Simms, the captain of the ship, so he put me right. He said, "It's have you seen my brother, *Sir*." So I said, "Have you seen my brother, Sir?" and I wasn't being cheeky. I needed to find Bobby.

'I was always looking for Bobby in places I wasn't meant to be. Once I was out on deck and I was playing with fire, risking another of my nine lives, because I remember slipping right onto the edge of the ship and catching hold of the rail. This sailor came and grabbed me and pulled me back. He took my to the top of a stairwell and sat me there and then he ticked me off and said stay there. But as soon as I could I started looking again. I was frantic to find Bobby. And the thing is, I don't remember ever actually giving up. I don't think I ever really did give up – because I was still trying to find out information about what had happened to him 40 years later. That's not giving up, is it?'

As John eventually discovered, his brother Bobby had been lost at sea during the failed launching of their lifeboat. He had never made it on board HMS *Hurricane*. And not even all the children who were successfully picked up by the *Hurricane* survived through the night. It was something that experienced seamen like Albert Gorman just had to learn to accept. He had been organising the children into their quarters: 'The next thing we heard was that two boys had been taken to the sick bay. The doctor was rushing up and down between the bridge and the sick bay, so we knew something was wrong. One died about four o'clock in the afternoon and the other at one in the morning. We buried them at sea. There is a naval service for burial at sea. The captain, or chaplain if there is one, reads from the service, and it ends up by saying, "And we therefore commit his body to to the deep, God rest his soul." And they release the body, and the body is weighted with an ammunition shell, and it slides down into the sea. On top is a white ensign and as the body goes down, they pull the white ensign up, and so another one is committed to the deep. There were three who died on the ship.

'I remember the women crying. The men were silent, and the sailors, they just watched, and on their faces – we've seen it before. You have to accept it. It was sad that those boys had got rescued and yet still died, but you couldn't do anything about it. We concentrated on the number of kids that survived, because what had happened was absolutely catastrophic. A lot of those children, they didn't know what hit them. When the torpedo came into the *City of Benares*, what was so shocking was that it exploded right under the children's dormitory. Some of those kids never knew a thing – they went to bed and they never knew any more.'

Like many seamen, Albert had learned to switch off his emotions during a crisis, but there was one moment where even he couldn't hold back. 'It was Beth and Bess,' he says. 'I had taken them back to the ship and left them with the doctor. I was thrilled to hear later that he had given them the all-clear, but the best moment of all came later on. The skipper took me to one side and he said, "Come with me, I've got a little story for you." So we went down into the aftercabin where Beth and Bess were in bed. We opened the door and there they were sat up in bed, and the captain said, "Bess, I've got a surprise for you. You thought you'd lost your little brother? Well, here he is, we found him in the boiler room. Charging all over the place." You should have seen Bess's face. It was as though you'd switched a light on. And the boy, he said, "What are you doing laying in bed there? Come on, get up." And then the skipper and I left. That's the memory to hold on to.'

For Bess, of course, it was exactly what the doctor ordered – just the thing she needed to complete her recovery from her Atlantic ordeal. After all, the thought of her brother Louis was precisely what had motivated her survival. She remembers how it happened: 'When we'd been rescued and brought on board the *Hurricane*, they took us to one of the crew cabins and laid us in the bunks. The ship's doctor came along and said, "You're a lucky girl. Now hurry up and get better. We'll look after you." He said the same to Beth. Beth cheered up enormously, but I was still very down. I'd got this hanging over me, what shall I say about my brother? The doctor came to see me the next day and said, "Come on, Bess, cheer up. You're doing quite well. What's the matter?" So I told him, and he said, "Well, all I can say to you is that you are very fortunate and that your parents will be pleased to get you back, because there are some parents who will never see their children again, so cheer up." Well, I realised I couldn't go on making a fuss about that for ever, so I tried to do what he said, but it was difficult.

'Next day there was a huge banging on the door of the cabin and a voice saying, "Sit up, miss," and who was it but the commander of the destroyer? So I sat up. When the commander says sit up, you sit up, don't you? The commander came in, quite awkwardly really, and he said, "I've got something of a surprise for you. Look what I've got here." And from behind his back he produced my brother. I looked at my brother and I just said, "Where *have* you been?" Just like a mum having a go at a child who's late home. And he said, "What are you doing lying there?" and then we both laughed and he came up to me and we had big hugs, and I was a happy girl.'

For Bess's friend Beth, the happiest moment of rescue was a much more simple pleasure, – but equally vivid: 'When we'd got on board the ship, the first thing I knew I found myself in a bathroom and then this figure came in and I must still have been feeling a bit funny because – and this is silly – I thought, ooh, blue eyes and blond hair, he must be an angel. Obviously it wasn't, it was the surgeon! All of a sudden I saw a stethoscope round his neck. I can remember that stethoscope now, it was brown with like a marble effect and he checked me over. Then he started to cut my clothes off, which were wringing wet. And then they put me in a hot bath, a lovely hot bath. Then the next thing I had the most wonderful white Turkish towel round me. I've never forgotten that. I've always thought about white Turkish towels since then. It was a gorgeous towel, a great long towel all round me, what a moment!

'I ended up in the first lieutenant's cabin, George Pound's cabin, and I was put to bed there. My hair was still soaking wet and I remember thinking my mother always told me never to go to bed with my hair wet. These are the silly things that you you remember. Then Dr Collinson came in to dress my ankle. I knew I'd injured my ankle and he bound it up. But even while he was doing that, a sailor came in and said, "Now, you mustn't worry. We think we've heard a U-boat and we're going to drop a few depth charges." I remember him saying this distinctly. He said, "Don't be frightened." Then he went out and the ship started shaking and I felt it shaking with the succeeding explosions. And I thought, "Oh, they're going to get me in the end, aren't they?" '

CHAPTER EIGHT

The
Twelfth Boat

H MS *Hurricane* never found lifeboat number 12. It had been the last lifeboat to be lowered from the port side of the *Benares*, and therefore scooped up all those unable to get into earlier boats. Three seavacuee boys who had arrived late at their muster station ended up in number 12. Fred Steels and Derek Capel had both been delayed by helping other children out of the cabins, while Kenneth Sparks had rushed back to pick up his overcoat. This turned out to be lucky for all three boys, because the launch of lifeboat number 12 went well, and by the time the *Benares* finally sank, their boat was probably in the best shape of any. Yet by the afternoon of Wednesday, 18 September 1940, it was the one boat the *Hurricane* couldn't rescue. When HMS *Hurricane* got back to Gourack on the Firth of Clyde, two days later, Fred and Derek and Kenneth were added to the list of those missing, presumed drowned. But the boys weren't by any means drowned. While the rescued were getting back on dry land on Friday 20th, lifeboat number 12 was still going strong far out to sea in the north Atlantic.

That first night at sea after the *Benares* sank had been as rough for the boys as for any of the other survivors. Fred Steels explains: 'The night was rather horrendous because we were in a good half gale then. Nothing was organised. Poor old Mary Cornish, who had been escorting the girls, was sat right in the middle, she couldn't move. The seamen, they were trying to get the things sorted out, but that first night was just a matter of make-do. We were all soaking wet through and the waves were lashing us and coming right into the boat.'

Kenneth Sparks remembers: 'It was falling down with rain and I was thinking, I wonder how long we're going to have to stay in this boat all cold and wet. We were concentrating on pulling far enough away from the ship to be safe as it sank. None of us was thinking we were going to die, we didn't intend to die. Once we had got away from the ship we started to try to make ourselves comfortable for the night. The poor Indians, the lascars, only had thin cotton clothing. It certainly wasn't comfortable, I mean it was quite a full boat one way and another. But by daylight of the next morning, at least we could see what we were doing, and we found a piece of canvas to cover the front end of the boat, so that was a help in keeping dry.'

This became a focal point for the boat's activities, as Fred explains: 'There was actually a little cupboard right up in the bows which had held the stores and they put this canvas awning up there and it got named the duck house. We had Mary Cornish, the girls' escort, with us and our own escort, Father O'Sullivan. But Father Rory was in a bad way – he'd been ill even before we were torpedoed, and he spent most of his time just lying in the bottom. So it was Mary Cornish who was doing her best to try and form a bit of order.'

At least they had all survived the night still alive and still afloat. Derek Capel describes what they saw when day broke: 'When first light arrived, it was so peculiar because of the waves. One moment you appeared to be sitting on top of a church tower looking down, and the next moment you were at the bottom looking up. That's how the movement of the waves was. It was that frightening, and there was foam or froth on top of the waves now and again. And it was so blooming cold. If you can imagine your hands and your feet, how they go if you lie in the bath for too long – your hands go, like, all crinkly and white. And your feet go the same. That's what our hands and feet were like by then, and we still had more of that to come. So we were absolutely freezing, we were cold and wet. But somehow we managed to get hold of two blankets, one of them may have been from the lascars – anyway, we ended up with two blankets between the six of us boys. During the day the storm went down and gradually we got organised. All the food and everything from the little store cupboard was taken aft by the officers and they rigged a little cover over the bows. It was just a piece of canvas and two metal hoops, which were clipped down, so we had a little bit of shelter. And that was what we called the duck hole and we boys went up there.

'Then, I think it was late morning or early afternoon, another lifeboat came along. We saw this lifeboat and we waved to it. We called over to each other and said, "Where are you from?" and they said, "We're from the *Marina*," which was funny really, because that had been the boat in the convoy meant to look out for us. So we knew what had happened to the boat what was gonna pick us up! Anyway, they said, "We're gonna make for Ireland." But they were a real seamen's crew and knew what they were doing. They had a good sail and they were off to Ireland. We carried on and we gradually got ourselves organised. There were handles for this gear that rowed the boat – Fleming gear – which is a series of handles going through a crank that turns a propeller. So we all started to take a turn on that, and that was good because the exercise kept you warm.'

This was the moment when everybody on board lifeboat number 12 began to realise they might be in for a long haul. They discovered that due to its greater buoyancy, the unwaterlogged boat had already drifted a good deal further during the night than any of the other boats. As Kenneth explains: 'If our boat had stayed near the other boats we would probably have been picked up a lot earlier, but there you are. There was nothing we could do about it, and after we met up with this other lifeboat, well, it ended up we were gonna row to Ireland. I don't know why we were, but that's how it happened!'

With this plan formulated, the next step was to get organised: Ireland was at least 500 miles away. Fred describes their first confused efforts: 'Well, nobody could find the sail to start with. All we had was the mast up and we were using the rowing gear to make headway. I think it was the next day we found the sail – it was all rolled up under the floorboards of the boat. We got that up, anyway. I think the first actual meal we ate was on the Wednesday, which would have been the 18th. It wasn't much, a ship's biscuit and a bit of sardine, and you got a beaker of water. The beakers they used were about eight inches long and about an inch in diameter, tube shaped, like a cigar case. You used to get water twice a day, once at dinnertime and once in the evening.'

Kenneth remembers: 'It was one ship's biscuit per person per day, and a ship's biscuit is quite thick, but it requires something to moisten it and we had very little water. You had only a very small amount of water, but there was usually either a slice of peach or a piece of a sardine, or something like that. They used to arrange all that down at the stern end of the boat. George Purvis, who'd been one of the stewards on the *Benares*, was responsible for the rations, and they got passed all the way up the boat to us children in the bows. I think we were all starving hungry – I know I was. We had very little food, just enough to keep you going, and that really was the idea of it. That's how they eked it out for so long, otherwise it would have all been gone in the first two or three days and there would have been nothing left at all. But with next to no food, and it being so very, very cold, it made it hard. I was the luckiest one of the lot, I'd still got me overcoat – that coat I went back for – but all the other lads had only got their pyjamas on. And it was September after all, not the best of times to go running around in the Atlantic. Not forgetting, we were going all the way to Ireland – though we found out later the direction we were going we were gonna miss Ireland anyway, we'd have ended up at Iceland. We were thirsty too, the whole time, because the water was limited to a small cupful per person per day, just a little dipper.'

Derek explains: 'Though we were hungry to begin with, gradually the hunger actually disappeared, but the thirst was there all the time, and it was a terrible thirst. All of us were strictly rationed in the water we had, including the lascars, everybody had exactly the same water ration. We were told to suck things to keep your saliva. Well, I had this little Lamb of God charm that Father O'Sullivan gave to us which I was wearing round my neck, and so I used to suck that all the time. By the time I'd finished it was well worn. And I still say to this day, looking at that poor Lamb of God, I was the only boy – man or boy – on that boat who had a leg of lamb to keep him going, because that was a three-legged lamb by the end!'

Fred Steels didn't have a lamb to suck: 'Harry Peard – he was the gunner on the *Benares* – he told us that if you had any buttons, to suck one to alleviate your thirst. Well, we tried, but I couldn't get on with it – they're not very digestible, aren't buttons. The thirst was much more of a problem than the hunger. After two or three days your throat seemed to be swelling up and your tongue would be sticking to your mouth.'

Far better though than lambs or buttons – and certainly better than ship's biscuits – it was actually their escort, Mary Cornish, who really kept the boys going and made sure that their spirits didn't fall. Fred has nothing but praise for her efforts: 'By rights Mary Cornish shouldn't have even ended up on the boat because her charges were 15 girls whose lifeboat was on the other side of the ship. After the torpedo hit, she was dashing over to the other side to try and find her girls, but this seaman just grabbed her and put her in our boat. To us it was a blessing, believe me, it really was. She was a music teacher – a good one, she'd trained in Vienna and spent a long time there. She used to massage our limbs and whatnot, tell us stories. The one we wanted most of all was Bulldog Drummond – we used to keep pestering her for more Bulldog Drummond. She knew some of the story of Bulldog Drummond, but the rest she couldn't remember, so she was making it up herself, elaborating as she went along She'd have him in situations that he would never have been in in the books. But every night it was, "Aunty, aunty, tell us more about Bulldog Drummond." It used to be our treat last thing before we tried to settle down for the night.

'All the lads called her aunty. She had a very hard time there, because she was the only female on board the boat and it was very embarrassing for her. There was just her and 45 blokes on a lifeboat only three foot longer than a London bus. So when it came to toiletries it was awkward for Mary. It would have meant sitting on the gunnel and that was too dangerous, so we reserved the bucket for her and just held a canvas round it if she wanted to pee. And as regards doing anything else, you had nothing in your stomach really to warrant anything else. She was so good to us, rubbing our circulation. The first place that goes is your toes, and you seem to lose all sense in your feet. So regularly Mary used to come round and massage every one of the lads' feet – you know, rub them, twist them, to get the circulation back into them. But Mary was suffering just as much and there was nobody to rub her feet. Still, she used to get us singing all the old wartime songs like 'Roll out the Barrel' and 'Run Rabbit Run' and things like that. It was all right for a while, but your throat was that dry, you weren't singing, you were croaking more or less, you know. It was those sea biscuits were so dry, you just couldn't touch them. I reckon you could have mended the boat with them if you'd got holed.'

Kenneth even has some nostalgia for the happy atmosphere that Mary managed to create, despite their desperate situation. He remembers: 'We had this little enclave where we were in the bows and we used to have these stories from Mary Cornish. Then we'd chat and talk, and as we all came from different areas of the country we would talk about that, and our schools and things like that. We talked about what we hoped to do when we got back home – and we all decided we were gonna go in the Navy! We must have been raving mad, but funny enough, we nearly all did. Those of us that could.'

Derek agrees with Fred that Mary's role was absolutely crucial in keeping up the morale of the boat. 'Because our official escort, Rory O'Sullivan, was so ill he couldn't do anything and so Mary Cornish took charge of us six boys. She was the most amazing woman I think I've ever met. She was Miss Cornish, a spinster. But she looked after us all the time. She rubbed our feet and checked up on us. She used to start us off talking about things – we had talks about what we were going to eat when we got back home and everything like that. Now, everyone had their own choices, but everybody – I don't know why this was – but it was always sarsaparilla we wanted to drink! I think maybe it was because we didn't have hardly anything to drink, so this sarsaparilla would be like imagining a nice cold Coca-Cola today. And to eat, it was usually something very basic like fish and chips. Everybody fancied fish and chips, and sarsaparilla. It was wonderful to think of. So we were looking forward to that, but we would actually be sitting down to our morning ration. It was about four tablespoonfuls of water and a ship's biscuit, which you couldn't eat because it was so hard and dry, and possibly half a sardine. There was some condensed milk, but it made you so thirsty you didn't want it. But thanks to Mary we'd be telling these lovely stories about what we would eat when we were rescued.

'And every night she told us a Bulldog Drummond story. How she knew about Bulldog Drummond I don't know, but her stories were blooming good. And every night there was one episode before we all settled down and tried to sleep. Even in the night she still rubbed our feet to keep us going, all the time, she just didn't sleep at all. Then came the day when they decided they wanted a flag up the mast to indicate where we were. And so Mary lent them her petticoat. I'll never forget that. For a spinster lady to lend something like that to fly up the mast and make a better signal must have taken some doing. She was just the most amazing woman, yet she must have been suffering more than any of us because, being the only woman on a boat like that, if she wanted to do anything like go to the toilet or anything like that, it was so much more difficult for her. In the early days we did all need to go from time to time and we had a bucket, and she would say she needed it, and they'd cry out, "Bucket for Memsahib, bucket for Memsahib." I remember the lascars doing this, and the bucket used to go up to her, and we boys and everybody all used to look at the back of the boat. That was the golden rule. We did that until the bucket had gone over the side, been flushed out and come back again. But then later on nobody felt like going to the toilet anyway.'

Despite all Mary's efforts, it seemed that fate was determined to play trick after trick on lifeboat number 12. First it was the rain, as Derek explains: 'We did have terrible luck with water. I think it was possibly the second day, we had a terrific squall come over and so we grabbed everything which would hold water – the condensed milk cans, the balers, the buckets which had been cleaned out with salt water. And everybody said we must catch the water, so what did they do? They got the sail out, unwrapped it quickly, and everybody held it up. And as the squalls came, they caught the rain in the sail and let it drain into containers, and we all thought, wonderful, all that lovely rainwater. But what happened? We tasted it. Brine. Everybody forgot that that sail had been soaked in salt water, salt water all that time. We'd have done much better just lifting our heads up to the rain. So we didn't get any water out of that trick. That was very much of a down, it left us very down.

'Even so, we were all convinced we were going to get rescued. Though I must admit the lascars were getting very, very lethargic. We were seeing these little icebergs which they call growlers, that's how cold it was. It was like when you have ice in your drink, these little growlers floating on the surface. But we got round them all right and the weather was picking up nicer. On a calm night it was marvellous to see the sea, because it was all shining phosphorescence. If you touched anything, or ran your fingers in the waves, your hands came up shimmering with all these beautiful colours. I think it's caused by the sea life. Then on the third day we saw a school of whales. It was a very cold day, we were all freezing. The lascars were getting very lethargic and they just kept in a huddle with all their blankets wrapped around them. But we looked out and there was a school of whales, or pod of whales I think they call it, the posh term. They were coming along merrily – but then someone remembered that whales enjoy coming up from underneath and scratching their backs on any small boat or such that they come upon. Well, you have never seen such a burst of activity in your life. There were people leaning over with oars and beating them up and down on the waves. There were people splashing in the water and everything like that. Well, at least it got the blood circulating again, and the whales, they just cruised on – so that was one little happy thing.

'But I think the worst bit of luck was on about the sixth day. We woke up in the morning. It was a lovely calm day, just a little bit of mist. And through the mist, not very far away, we could see a ship. We thought, wonderful. We pulled everything – we had people working the gear and two people pulling towards the ship merrily with the oars. We were close enough that you could even make out people walking around the stern of the ship. It had no smoke up or anything like that. It was just stationary there, or appeared to be. We were rowing like mad towards it, and that cover we'd rigged over the bows, we threw that overboard because we wanted to get moving as fast as we could. We just had the one smoke flare on board and we fired that off for them to see. Then suddenly, as we were coming out of the mist towards them, there was a puff of smoke out of the funnel and voomph, it moved away from us.

'That ship just disappeared into the distance. Now, that was probably one of the worst days in our lives, I should think. One moment we were ready to be rescued, we didn't care who it was. We just knew there was this ship, and it was so close. And then suddenly it disappeared. People have said it might have been a German supply ship for the submarines. It might have been a blockade runner. Or it might have been a foreign ship which suddenly saw the lifeboat and knew that U-boats had a habit of sometimes sitting by a lifeboat and having a go when a ship came to rescue people. We didn't know what the reason was, but that really dragged us down. By the seventh day I know we were dead unhappy, and on that day it was announced that we'd have to halve our water ration because we were going down so low. Really that meant, well, we were beginning to be dying of thirst literally then.'

Fred also remembers the repeated disappointments, how it seemed as if each new trick of fate was testing them, sapping the morale of the boat as the days wore on. Even the whales gave them false hopes initially. Fred explains: 'I'm not sure what day it was, the Thursday I think, when we saw this blasted great black shape coming up in front of us like it was a ship. But then we thought it can't be a ship, "Oh Christ, no, it's a U-boat surfacing." As it happened it was a whale sounding, and he wasn't that far at all from us, only about the length of your living room. Then it went down again, and the next thing we knew it had come up astern of us, and we realised there was a whole pod of them around – just spread round us in the ocean. Then they all disappeared, but at least it was a bit of excitement, something you don't get to see.

'Then on Sunday, the sea was actually reasonably calm, and one of the lads, I can't remember who it was, shouted out, "There's a ship." We'd had so many false hopes before, with cloud banks and the whales and that sort of thing, imagining there was land or a ship. So nobody believed him to start with. Then we started looking and we could see there actually was a ship, and it got closer and closer. Of course, everybody started cheering and waving and whatnot. Somebody said, "Oh, we won't need this any more," and so that canopy we had, he took the hoops out and threw them over the side. Anyway, the ship got gradually nearer and nearer, and then she suddenly turned broadside onto us. We could see her distinctly, you could even see the crew on board her. I suppose she was, what, 50, 60 yards, something like that away from us, maybe a bit more, and we were waving and started pumping the rowing gear to get towards her. Then all of a sudden her propellers started up. She started turning and just disappeared and left us. That really did knock our morale, because we had been thinking it's the end of this little voyage. But it wasn't to be, I'm afraid. They just left us and we had to carry on again. Plus the fact that those hoops had been thrown over the side, so now we had no canopy to sit under.

'I think the ship may have been influenced by these reports that the German U-boats were following lifeboats and if a ship stopped to pick up survivors, the U-boat would either surface and gun them or else torpedo them. The Germans were thought actually to be using any lifeboat as a decoy. Another report we'd heard was that the Germans would rig up a dummy lifeboat on the conning tower, put two or three of their crew in it, and disguise the periscope as a mast. If anybody stopped to see what was going on, same thing again, they'd either surface and gun them or else torpedo them. So that was the only reason we could think of, that the ship's skipper was frightened we might have been trailing a U-boat with us. In one respect I suppose you couldn't blame him, because it's not much fun being torpedoed, and I don't think he wanted any of it.'

Kenneth admits that he found it hard to pick himself up again after the incident with the ship: 'I think our biggest disappointment was the ship. We had been going for five days at least when we saw it, and we were within hailing distance. But it pulled away. Nobody ever found out what ship it was. There were rumours afterwards that it was actually a German ship that was enticing British destroyers to come and rescue it, and there were submarines hidden underneath. But we will never know. It hit us all very hard, everybody, not just me personally. We were all really disappointed. We never got quite close enough to see what the name was, and I suppose there were no lookouts at the stern end. Anyway, as we got quite close, all of a sudden the propeller started. That really was a bad day. But you just had to tell yourself, if we've seen one ship we'll see some more. We couldn't at any time let ourselves get really downhearted, no. We all just kept hold of the thought that we were gonna either get to Ireland or be rescued. None of us thought we were gonna die, in fact – everybody on the boat I think was in the same boat – we all thought we were gonna get somewhere. Or we were gonna be rescued by a ship, because we'd seen one ship now, so if we'd seen one we must be in the shipping lanes.

'Those were our thoughts. Mind you, we didn't know at the time that we weren't actually in the shipping lanes after all. Seeing the ship was a far worse experience than dealing with the whales, because at least we hadn't got our hopes up. It was so sudden, we were surrounded by this school of whales, where they had come from or why, we had no idea. But we worried their tails would smash the boat to pieces, so we had to frighten them away. We had to slap the water and make a lot of noise to make them move away. But you know, maybe they were gonna shove us away home or something – we hadn't got a clue what they were about. It was one of those lovely days again, a glorious Indian summer day, and all of a sudden they turned up. It's something I shall never forget, that.'

But lifeboat number 12's need for rescue was becoming more urgent every day. The problems of exhaustion and exposure, and the shortage of water and food, were all combining to worsen the boys' situation. On top of all this, Fred Steels had a pressing new problem to cope with: 'Yeah, I had frostbite in my toes. It wasn't severe at that stage, but it was beginning to bloat up. Aunty Mary used to grab hold of my toes and wiggle them and rub them underneath, just to get the circulation back into them. Anything she could find, she would wrap my feet up with to try and keep the warmth in. All the lads got it, but there was one particular lad, Paul Shearing, and he seemed to suffer more than anybody. Paul's was really bad, and he got to the stage where if Mary even touched his toes he used to start crying. In fact, at one stage later on in the voyage we got the impression that he was going mad with the pain, but we eventually got him calmed down.

'By now we were hardly sleeping at all, you could forget that idea, it was just catnapping all the way. And we were soaking all the time – you are trying to doze and you get half a ton of water come hurtling in the boat on top of you, and there was no place we could get out of it. The only chance we had to try and dry anything was one day, and I think that was a Sunday – sometime round then. We had quite a bit of sunshine and we tried drying our pyjamas on the rigging of the mast. Not that it seemed to do much good, because they were still damp when you put them on again. And then when the squalls came over – heavy rain and hailstones and sleet – it drove in and it didn't matter where you went, you couldn't get out of it. I was feeling very damn depressed, believe me. All that time the rations that we had on board were just gradually going down and things were getting bad. It got to the stage that they used to give us the ship's biscuit with a bit of corned beef or a bit of sardine or maybe a bit of peach or something on it and we just couldn't eat the biscuits. Those biscuits are blasted thick and we couldn't swallow them, so we used to give them to Aunty Mary to look after for us! Not that anybody ever asked for 'em back!

'At night the steward, George Purvis, would give us little tins of condensed milk. He punched a hole in them and we used to suck on them during the night when we woke up – if we'd been to sleep in the first place, that was. So things just went on day after day like that. Gunner Peard, Harry Peard, he was a proper screwball he was, but one of the nicest chaps you could meet. And everyday if the sea was calm he'd go over the side, swim round the boat, two or three laps, and then get back on board again.'

Gunner Harry Peard, like Mary Cornish, played a vital role in the lifeboat's survival. Not only was his madcap humour helpful in maintaining morale, he was the only European on the boat who had the linguistic skills truly to communicate with the 32 lascars. Fred explains: 'Towards the end of the voyage you could feel a tension in the air. The problem was, I think, that the lascars were beginning to feel it most of all of us. They started getting very agitated towards the end. We had just the two barrels of water and they only carried about 20 gallons between them. So with 46 people that's not gonna go very far. At the end we were down to about half a beaker of water a day. But somehow Harry Peard always managed to calm the lascars down. I think they respected him. It was difficult for the lascars with such a different climate. They were used to a hot country and the cold North Atlantic isn't anybody's fun, especially for them I should think. Most of them were wearing just their thin cotton clothes.'

Lifeboat number 12 had now been at sea for a full week. On the seventh day the already meagre water ration was halved. The eighth day of their ordeal dawned fair – another cruel irony when what the boys really needed was rainwater to drink. Derek remembers: 'We thought we were done for because the water ration had been cut in half on the seventh day and we knew the water we were getting wasn't enough to keep us alive, and so we thought that's it, you know. We began for the first time to have thoughts of "Are we going to make it?" Instead of "We are going to make it," which it had been up until then, it was "Will we make it? Can we make it?' The eighth day, we woke up to brilliant sunshine, but nobody could enjoy the sunshine. It was a lovely day, but nobody could really enjoy it. We just sat around. We were actually losing interest by then, we were absolutely lethargic. There were no stories forthcoming or anything. Everybody was the same. I was thinking about my brother, Alan, and wondering what had happened to him. I was trying to imagine where he was, and everything like that, had he been rescued? I was feeling really down, and poor Billy Short, he was the same. He was thinking about what might have happened to his brother. He and I used to sit down there and talk about our brothers and things like that. None of us knew what might have happened to them.

'So this eighth day came along and in the morning we sat there in the bows, and it was a lovely sky – it was the first really good day we had. But that was no good anyway because we didn't want hot days, we wanted rainy days if possible. It was a lovely warm day. The sea was quite calm; it was beautiful. And then suddenly somebody said, "There's a plane." So what to do then? It was the same as when we had seen the whales earlier on. Everybody sprung to life, but I think we were just using the last little bit of energy we had. We ran the well-known petticoat up the mast as a flag and somebody said, "How can we signal it?" So we grabbed all the condensed milk tins – whether they were full or empty – tore off the labels, and held them up to the sun and kept on moving them around to try to make a flash.'

Fred agrees with Derek that by the eighth day, hopes of survival were really much thinner than anyone cared to admit: 'The food had almost gone. We had a drop of fruit juice that the steward had sent along for us, just a matter of a sip. We used to pour it into the empty cans of the tinned milk and shake it around in there to sip the last drops out. I suppose it must have been somewhere around dinnertime, when Ken Sparks I believe it was shouted out, "There's an aeroplane." And of course, we'd been that used to seeing seagulls and whatnot around that people had thought were aeroplanes, you know, we didn't take a lot of notice of it to start with. But gradually, as it got closer, we could see it was a Sunderland. It was captained by an Australian, we found out afterwards, and he came in and everybody realised that we had been found. He just circled us and they flashed us with their Aldis lamp that he was going for help.'

It was indeed Kenneth Sparks who was the first to see the aeroplane. He remembers: 'Time was getting on by then, for rescue I mean – it was about the eighth day, it was a lovely day as far as I can remember. But we found that we were all getting quite lethargic. I suppose we were beginning to suffer with malnutrition probably and certainly with hypothermia by then. So we weren't doing much, we weren't pushing the rowing gear, we just weren't up to it. We were just laying in the bows under a piece of canvas and I thought to meself, I can hear something buzzing. It was a sort of a droning noise and I thought I dunno what that might be, so I clambered out from under the canvas as best I could and looked up and, lo and behold, it was a plane, a seaplane. I didn't know what sort it was, but I waved me arms. The lascars were in just as poorly a state as we were, but the four crew at the other end of the boat realised that the plane was one of ours. Johnny Mayhew, who had been a signalman on board the *Benares*, started to semaphore to the plane. It turns out the plane had an engineer on board who said that he'd seen this object in the sea, and he thought that it could have been a boat. So they came and had another look. But they were on their last drop of fuel, so all they could do was fly over and drop some food, and then they went away. The aircrew signalled to Johnny to say they couldn't stop any longer, they were running out of fuel.

'I'm told that I semaphored the plane, but I couldn't really have done because I was only a cub scout and I hadn't learnt semaphore, but I did wave like mad. And Johnny Mayhew understood when they signalled they were sending another plane up, so at least we knew were gonna be all right from then on. It was terrific that, to see another plane. And that plane semaphored and of course it went through the boat like wildfire, "They're sending a ship for us." Well, that woke us up a bit, although we were very weak by then.'

Fred admits he didn't really believe Ken when he first spotted the plane: 'We'd seen so many things that we thought were ships or planes and none of them ever were. It always turned out we were just seeing things, but eventually this thing got closer and closer and we did realise it was a plane, a Sunderland. Of course everybody went wild, waving everything they could think. Mary gave her slip up to put up as a flag on the mast. I think the signalman even managed to get a couple of the turbans off the lascars and used them as flags to signal the flying boat. He flashed back to us with his Aldis lamp, telling us that we had been spotted and he was going back to get another plane to bring supplies. That arrived in an hour, more or less, and he dropped this float with everything to keep us going – tinned fruit, corned beef, everything you could want, as well as smoke flares. He signalled that the ship was 40 miles away and heading at top speed towards us. Sure enough, about an hour and a half later, HMS *Anthony* pulled up alongside us.

'And course, we were all in a bit of a blessed state there, we had cramp, frostbite, everything. So they lowered these big scrambling nets down over the side, and two or three of the sailors off the *Anthony* came down in the boat and lifted us kids up into it. Then they were helping Mary Cornish and Father O'Sullivan, and any of those that couldn't manage the nets. Mary Cornish said she was a bit worried at the time, because Father O'Sullivan was still laying in the bottom of the boat. She was frightened that when they took us up they'd missed him and the boat had drifted off with him in it. But she turned round and saw that he'd been carried on board on a stretcher. So they got us all on board and then we set sail for Scotland. We didn't know where we were at that stage. Originally we were trying to make Ireland, because we thought that was the nearest point of call, and then we thought we would end up by the north of Scotland, and then somebody thought maybe the Shetlands. With the ocean tides and whatnot, you never know where you are, and half the time the sky was covered in cloud, so that you couldn't work off the stars. By the time we were picked up we were way off – we discovered we were still well over 300 miles from the Scottish coast. Maybe it was even a bit more than that, because we never did get a true reckoning of where we were.'

Derek remembers that even once they had been seen, the rescue was still far from straightforward: 'The plane that saw us was a Sunderland, which was coming off convoy duty, so it was low on fuel. They threw out a little floating raft with what food they had on it, and it dropped about 50 yards from us. We tried to get to it, but we couldn't even get that far. We couldn't row that far, and this raft slowly drifted away with all it had on it. It wasn't until an hour later that the relief plane came and they dropped their raft with a long cord attached to it, and the cord fell over the boat so luckily we managed to haul it slowly over. I think then we had coffee and sandwiches and things like that, and there was water. Everything they had on board that aircraft they sent down to us. We had a lovely little tea party for a little while then. And there was a nice little note came with the supplies saying, "Boat on way". We were sitting there waiting for the boat. And they had given us a big red flare to fire when we saw smoke on the horizon. But before we even saw that, the Sunderland come up again and kept circling round us because they were so worried that the ship wouldn't spot us in time that they wanted to mark our position for it.'

Kenneth takes up the story: 'When the boat did arrive they had to lift us out, because they had put this kind of netting down the side of the destroyer, but we couldn't climb it. We were just too weak, so they had to climb down and pick us all out and put us in. A sailor lifted me up and put me over his shoulder and then the other sailors on the ship leaned over, grabbed me and pulled me into the destroyer. Oh, that really was something. Everybody was saved. Out of all that crew and boys and the escorts, only one person died in the end. He was one of the lascar seamen. When you think how long we'd been there, that was pretty good going.

'The people on HMS *Anthony* couldn't have been kinder. When we first got on board the medical officer examined us and said, "No food, very little food." But we had to have plenty of liquid, of course. And they took our wet clothes away and dried them off. In the meanwhile they gave us their own clothing to keep us warm until ours was all dry, because were all soaking wet from the rain and the seawater. They kept rubbing us down with towels and things like that and soon brought us back to a reasonable condition. The next day we were allowed to eat. Well, once we were able to eat, we couldn't get enough food down! They were making us sandwiches of a whole tin of salmon with two slices of bread slapped round it. We were soon well enough to start getting about round the ship. And a Royal Navy ship to a young boy was terrific. They used to take us round the engine room, the gun deck and everything. It really was a thrill for all of us, except for poor old Paul who was in the sick bay all the time. I'm afraid Paul couldn't walk at all, his legs had really gone.

'But it was ever so exciting to see the guns, and the speed the boat was going back towards Gourack, which is the port for the Clyde, was actually sending the whole ship throbbing. After rowing through the waves, it was a terrific experience in comparison. The crew couldn't have been nicer to us, they really couldn't. I think actually that helped us to make our minds up that we were gonna go in the Navy. I'm sure it did, definitely for me anyway. I went in the Navy at just over 15. That rescue and the voyage back made a terrific impression. I think most of us ended up trying to get in the Navy. Mind you, I think what made the biggest impression was all that lovely food, but there you are! But even by the time we got to Scotland we were still quite poorly. In some ways we were never really better – we were all suffering with trench foot, because our feet had been immersed in seawater for so long.'

Fred too remembers how much their legs and feet had suffered during the ordeal: 'When we got on board the ship our feet were that bad it was a job to walk. In fact you couldn't walk, you hobbled sort of thing, hanging on to anything that was available. But the sailors were very good, because they mostly carried us down to the cabins. The ship's surgeon went to see Mary, Father O'Sullivan and Paul first because Paul and Father O'Sullivan were in a bad way. Mary was also a bit delusional at that time, I think, because she told me she couldn't even remember how to undress herself. She'd got to the stage of thinking, now how do I get this skirt off, how do these buttons work, that sort of thing. I think she'd got to the end of her tether, she really had. Then the doctor came down to see us and massaged our feet and we had warm baths and showers to try and relieve the pain. And after a few hours it did ease off a bit, but it never really went away, not for quite a while. Even when I eventually got back home, I had to go everywhere by taxi or something because I couldn't walk very far.

'They took all our wet gear off us, and I think they ended up having to throw most of it over the side, it was good for nothing. We all wound up wearing bits of sailors' uniforms. I had a sailor's jumper, it used to come down to here, and sea socks which used to come up over your knees with a blessed great heel hanging out like a spur on a cockerel! I think the first thing they did was get us something to eat and drink, but they had to be careful with the eating. It was more drink than anything because we still couldn't swallow. We got really spoilt – we got soft fruit, peaches, pears all mashed up. And then the *Anthony* turned round and set sail and the captain told us he was heading back home to Gourack. It was great then, we had the run of the ship all the way back to Scotland.'

Like all the boys, Derek found just getting aboard the *Anthony* one of the hardest moments of all. He explains: 'The *Anthony* turned up and put its nets over and they said, "Right, up you come," and nobody could move. We were all sat there and nobody could move! I could hardly do anything. My joints were so wasted and so tired. Nobody could scramble up onto the ship, so they had to lift us. We hadn't realised at all that we had got into such a state. We all got put into the officers' cabins, and it was lovely. We were given one seaman each to look after us and start bringing us back up to scratch. There was a doctor on board and he fed us little quarter of a glass of water and some gruel – it was horrible white stuff that we had to have because we hadn't had anything for so long. So on the first day we had this – it was horrible, that stuff – but we had to eat it at each mealtime. It was getting horrible because our stomachs hadn't been working for so long. The doctor was expecting trouble, I think. But then the seamen decided to take us round to their own mess, and I'll never forget it. They carried us all round the ship, up and down everywhere, and we finished up in their mess. And they got an old tin bowl, a washing bowl of some sort, and put it on the table. They'd just come from America so they had tinned apricots, peaches, everything, and they opened all these tins of fruit, emptied them into the bowl, poured a tin of cream on top and said, "Dig in."

'They were breaking all the rules, but that doctor must have thought he had an amazing cure, because you'd be surprised how quickly we were all nipping and going to the toilet again after that. It was so wonderful to start feeling a bit better, and they were so lovely, the crew, and they really looked after us. But they couldn't tell us anything about my brother. I asked about my brother, and no one knew anything.'

The boys had done it. They had survived eight days on the north Atlantic in an open boat. Now at last, a full week after the other survivors from the *Benares*, they could turn and head for the Scottish port of Gourack, and eventually for home.

CHAPTER NINE

Homecomings

W hile the boys from lifeboat number 12 were still on board HMS *Anthony*, steaming towards Gourack, the reception port that sits at the opening of the Firth of Clyde, news had spread everywhere of their amazing survival story. By the time they reached Glasgow, a few miles further up the Clyde, they were already famous. Fred Steels had never seen anything like it. He says: 'Even as we got into Gourack, everybody was going wild. There were blessed photographers, reporters, you know, civilians come to wave. We were seeing things we'd never seen before, like being given blasted bananas and all that sort of thing, you know. Then we went on to Glasgow.'

HMS *Anthony* had finally managed to pick the boys up by mid-afternoon on Wednesday, 25 September, a week and a day after the sinking of the *Benares*. Steaming at full speed, the *Anthony* then plunged off towards Scotland, finally getting the boys back to land at seven o'clock in the evening of the following day, Thursday 26th. Fred remembers the excitement of that rush back to safety: 'The captain told us he was heading for Gourack and then he turned the *Anthony* and went full steam ahead. It was already pretty late by then, so we went to sleep. When we woke up the following morning and went out on deck, there was all these ships around us. It was a convoy coming back from the States to the UK and we had got mixed in with them. The *Anthony* stayed with them for a while, acting as an escort. But then the captain decided he'd had enough of that, so he pulled away and headed straight for Gourack. We were doing about 24 knots. We were standing in the stern and looking over the rails, down at the wake behind us, and thinking what we'd been through for eight days.'

It was hardly surprising that after their traumatic week the boys found their reception in Glasgow rather overwhelming. Fred explains: 'It was a bit confusing really, suddenly having a camera stuck in your face and everyone wanted to know what was happening, how you got on – all this, that and the other. I don't think any of us felt like talking about it then. I think all we wanted to do was just get away. But they took us into Glasgow and we were the guests of the Lord Provost and the City of Glasgow. They told us we could have had anything we wanted. The Provost even invited us to stay at his fishing lodge on one of the lochs. So we spent two or three days up there and then we went back to Glasgow. They took us into this big room and we were told that we could have the pick of anything we wanted in there, you know, books and that sort of thing. I think the two I chose were *Westward Ho!*, which seemed rather appropriate, and *Ben's Wonderful Fighting Forces*.

'We were each given a gold badge with a crest of the arms of Glasgow on it. And the Lord Provost told us that if ever we were in Glasgow, we were entitled to a free meal with the council of Glasgow – any time you went in there and you showed the badge, you were meant to get a meal, but in the end I never got back there. But there was a funny little thing that annoyed me, was that all the other lads had been presented with a kilt, sporran, Glengarry and what have you, and for some reason I never did get one. But you don't have time to worry about things like that, because the next thing was my Dad came up to Glasgow to pick me up and take me home.

'That was quite a reunion. I'm sure he was close to tears and I think I was, because it had at one point got to the stage where we thought we'd never see one another again. He gave me a big hug, but neither of us was the sentimental type, so it was just the fact that he was there and I was there that meant a lot to us. My father decided that we'd get the next train heading south, so we left Glasgow Central. I said goodbye to everybody and gave Aunty

Mary – Mary Cornish – a big hug, and off we went. But by the time we got down just north of London, it was being plastered with bombing. We must have been two or three miles outside when they had to stop the train. They got it backed up again and took us onto another line to skirt London. Eventually we got back home again and there was this reception committee: friends, schoolteachers and everybody.

'So Dad arrived at our door with me, and this entourage of different people, and Mum came to the door, and how do you all react? Well, my Mum was like all mothers, you know – damn near killed me! She opened the door and she just stood there for a minute and burst out crying, which started me off, and she hugged me, damn near broke me ribs. For at least a couple of days after that she just wouldn't leave me alone. I think at the time she was frightened that it might have been some kind of hallucination and I was gonna disappear again. In fact, the day the news came we had been picked up, my Mum and Dad were in an air-raid shelter under our local factory and the air-raid warden, he came down the shelter and woke my Mum. He said "Peg," which was my mum's name, he said "Fred's been saved." And she turned round to him and said, "Yes I know, I've seen him."

'It was wonderful, really, to come home. They couldn't do enough for me in Eastleigh. I had free cinema tickets, restaurants, cafés, anything I wanted. Mind you, my Mum confessed to me that when she thought I'd gone down with the ship, she gave all my toys away – so that rather peeved me a bit. But I was in such a state physically when I got home, I couldn't walk very far. It was either pushchair or taxi until my feet started to ease up. For a while after, I used to wake up at night literally screaming. It was with the pain and I suppose the remembering was coming back to me in my sleep. And I couldn't even bear anything heavy on my feet at all. It took a good couple of months really for my feet to get back to anywhere near normal.

'Even when I got home I think the Germans still had a bug about me, because they sent a raiding party over one day – three Heinkel 111s. They followed a Hudson that had been damaged coming back from Europe and decided to bomb the airport, machine-gun the park, the streets and anything that was available. I happened to be in one of the streets at the time, and I saw this German plane hammering down the road and it was that low you could actually see the pilot and the gunner. So we dived in the doorway and waited for them to pass.

'One of the funny things that happened afterwards was about our spending money that we had been given for Canada. All we kids were saying we'd lost everything that had been given us. One of the lads was saying that he had four and eight pence in money, and one of the others had had thirteen shillings because his uncle had given him some extra. We didn't think we'd get it back. But on our lifeboat with us was a Mr Nagorski, who was president of one of the big shipping lines, and he said whatever we'd lost, he would double. And he was good to his word. He not only doubled it, but he rounded it up to the next pound as well, so I came back with more than I went.'

But for Kenneth Sparks getting back to shore wasn't quite the same whole-hearted joy as for Fred. Given his troubled family situation – with his rather hostile stepmother and rarely present father – Kenneth wasn't sure what kind of reunion to look forward to. Even as a young boy he realised his wasn't a particularly loving family. His fears about the kind of welcome he might get were not totally unfounded, as he later found out that his stepmother had been trying to let out his room. She eventually succeeded not very much later when Kenneth enlisted as a boy sailor.

He describes the situation as he and the other boys reached Gourack: 'When we landed in Scotland we were taken to this hotel and they said, "You'd better write home to your parents because we don't know how long it will be before you can get home." I thought I better had because I didn't suppose they would get up to meet me – that was a certainty, knowing them – so I wrote to them saying that I'd survived and was looking forward to being home. What had happened was that this man from the Children's Overseas Reception Board, the CORB – I think his name was Mr Shakespeare – he'd actually gone round all the children's houses and told the parents that the boat had sunk, and then he didn't get round to tell them they hadn't all died. So I thought my parents ought to know at least that I'd survived, because I wasn't sure whether they had been told or not that a certain number of children had survived the actual sinking of the boat.

'So I wrote them this letter:

Dear Mum and Dad,

I hope you are all well, and happy as you know that I am now safe. We had a dreadful time on the lifeboat as we had very little water and only a small piece of salmon or sardine on a ship's biscuit. We saw a huge whale and we were ready to drive it away in case it broke the boat up. One day we saw a boat which stopped for us, but before we were picked up, it went away and we were disappointed. Three days we floated around when we saw an aeroplane which dropped us food and then went away. Soon afterwards two planes came along with a destroyer which picked us up and we had good food and water at last.'

As Kenneth had suspected, his parents did not come rushing up to Scotland to collect him. But there were plenty of people in Glasgow who did want to make a fuss of the boy survivor. Kenneth remembers: 'We were fêted by the Provost of Glasgow. The Glaswegians really took us under their wing. We had the tour of Glasgow, and they took us to see the Rangers and Celtic play football. Somewhere I've got footballers' signatures, in my autograph book somewhere. They treated us like lords. After all, I suppose when you consider, it was something unusual. There weren't many children survived eight days in a boat and it really was very nice indeed to be so well looked after.

'Immediately we had landed we were taken to this hotel and I think there were three of us in one bed and two in the other. But the first night I must admit we couldn't get to sleep, none of us. It was so comfortable we couldn't sleep! We hadn't been used to sleeping in comfort, we'd been sleeping on boards all wet and cold. So we had a terrible night the first night, it was most peculiar really. Eventually they decided that we were fit enough to be sent home, so I came back with Derek and Fred and their parents as far as Euston station. My mother met me there and I went off home. But when I got home there were the flags out in the street, and all the neighbours were there cheering and such forth. I looked at all and I'm thinking, 'Hey, I've only survived, you know, what's happening?' I've got pictures of it with all the flags stuck round the street and everything. To me in a way it was a fuss about nothing. I'd managed to live, but what I was thinking about was all the poor other children who didn't, especially me best friend, he hadn't managed to live. But that was one of those things that happened in the war, war did strange things at different times.

'I was quite surprised there were all those people. It seemed to me a lot of fuss for me when a lot of our friends – none of the people that were with me had managed to come home – and it didn't seem right somehow. But everyone was all so excited that I'd managed to live. I don't know why I lived, only God knows that. Nobody else from down Southampton did. And I wasn't used to being fêted like this, I was a very shy boy in those days, still am. My Mum and Dad – well, they hadn't got any choice but to make a fuss of me had they, with all the other neighbours there. But even though they had to be, I think they were pleased to see me at the time. I think the fact that I'd survived was something to celebrate, and of course all the neighbours were there. But I can't remember very well what it was like when I was at home. For one thing, I hadn't been home very long before I was having trouble with walking. They diagnosed trench foot and I ended up in Winchester General Hospital being treated. I think I was in there for about two to three months. But poor Paul Shearing, he was so bad that when he tried to go in the services, like the rest of us, they turned him down completely. His legs were too far gone.'

For quite different reasons from Kenneth, Derek Capel didn't really feel like celebrating his homecoming too much either. Reaching Scotland brought Derek the news that he'd been dreading, that his younger brother, 5-year-old Alan, hadn't made it. Derek remembers: 'As soon as I was rescued I was asking about my brother, but nobody could tell me anything. Nobody seemed to know anything, and that was so worrying. We came into Gourack and they put us to bed in a nice room there, all lovely and comfy, and we didn't think any more of it. But the next day they picked us up and we were going on to Glasgow.

'There were crowds of people outside. We thought what do they want, and then we realised that we were headline news and we didn't know anything about it. I still asked about me brother, but still nothing. And we went up to Glasgow. In Glasgow we met the Lord Provost, Sir Patrick Donlan. He was a lovely fellow, a real nice fatherly figure. And all the council members were really lovely. They looked after us and took us to the Glasgow Charity Cup football match, Rangers versus Celtic. We had the royal box there, the posh box we did, and there was so many people rapping on the windows, smiling and waving to us all the way down. We wondered what had happened. Then it hit us that we were the last to come back. It was as if we were dead and just come back to life. I still asked about my brother, but nothing happened.

'Then one day Sir Patrick Donlan, he took me to one side and said, "Your brother hasn't been found." He did it when nobody else would, none of these experts or anything, we couldn't get it off of them, because everybody knew except us. I think he told Billy Short the same, very nicely and quietly. He did it gently, and just said, "Your brother is still missing and I don't think there's much chance." That's the first I heard of it. We finished up in a place called Hillfoot Holiday Home, which had been changed to a hospital after Dunkirk. It was a small military hospital and they had nurses still in there, but any Dunkirk people were gone by then.

'Then Sir Patrick Donlan came up one day and said, "Your father's coming up to pick you up today." My father came up by rail and picked me up and I told him about Alan. I told him about my brother and he said, "Well, at least we've got one of you." Sir Patrick took us into the city chambers and we had a nice lunch there, chicken for lunch. And we were preparing to go home then, and just before we went, on behalf of Glasgow, he presented us with a little badge of honour. The badge is given to Glaswegians who do something brave or heroic so that they will never be short of a meal, because they can show this small medallion up to the city chambers, and they will always get a meal there and also they will try to find them a job or anything like that to help them on their way. And the provost said, "Only one person not a Glaswegian has ever had that before." And that was Franklin D. Roosevelt, the American President.

'And we set off home on a sleeper train to London. But when we got to Waterloo, we found out the line to Feltham had been bombed, so we had to go by tube to Hounslow East. But trying to get out of the station, I'll never forget that my father was having to piggyback me, a 12-year-old, and he was having to piggyback me because I couldn't walk. So we got to the road and there were about four little shops just down on the road and one of them, a greengrocer's, was open. My father popped in and said, "You can't tell me where I can get a taxi this time of the day, can you?" The grocer said, "No, you don't get any taxis up this way." But then he looked up and said, "You're one of the boys." I didn't know what he meant really, but I thought yeah, I suppose I am one of the boys. He said, "Hang on a minute" and he came back with an old van full up with all greengrocery. So I arrived with the greens I did – and that's the way I arrived home, in the back of a greengrocer's van.'

As the boys all point out, they were already headline news by the time they got to Glasgow. The actual sinking of the *Benares* had happened over a week earlier and the news of it had spread all over Britain long before the survivors of the twelfth boat had made it home. But the picture was rather different for the first group of survivors to arrive in Scotland, those picked up by HMS *Hurricane* near the scene the day after the *Benares* had been torpedoed. When these survivors got to Gourock, very little was known about what had happened, and the public had not yet been informed that the *Benares* had sunk. There had not even been time to tell the parents of the fate of their children. In fact, some of the parents were under the impression that their children had by now arrived safely in Nova Scotia, Canada. So rather than a hero's welcome, the children met with confusion and disorganisation, which Colin Ryder Richardson found rather comical.

'They actually asked to see a passport! The people at the customs just assumed that I would have my passport with me and they said, "Well, we can't let you in without a passport, where have you come from?" So we had to explain that we had in fact come from Liverpool – but via the Atlantic, we happened to have been torpedoed. They were just not in the right frame of mind to understand exactly what had happened. I said, "We are survivors." We were all sort of saying, we're survivors. Finally of course, somebody in authority suddenly realised what the situation was and we were taken into a Women's Voluntary Service place where they had spare clothes. It meant I could give back the crew's clothes. There's even a picture of me and my fellow survivors examining shoes that would fit. Then we were taken by bus from Gourack into Glasgow. My pyjamas were now dry. So I was wearing my pyjamas and carrying a package that the WVS had given us, walking into the Central Hotel in Glasgow thinking, well, this must be a first. And not a person batted an eyelid. They were so used by then to seeing unusual things happening it didn't upset anybody. I found that the clothes I'd got were really not very practical – I think they were girls' shoes, for starters. But I ended up dressed like that until my mother came up to pick me up.

'We were taken to a small hotel on Loch Lomond, which was where my mother came to pick me up. But to see my mother was so unexpected, because at that time contacting people was very difficult – you couldn't just get on a telephone unless you had a priority for use. And we used it so little that I didn't even know the telephone number of the house in Wales where my mother was living. So it was difficult for my mother to appreciate what had happened and then to find out where I was. The other problem for her was that she was diabetic and I think by the time she had travelled up all the way from London she was feeling quite low and unwell. She told me that she had to be helped across the road from the bus into the hotel. But then she just sort of saw me, and I saw her, and she realised that she had to say something that was totally fatuous. So she had one look at me and said, "What have you done with your clothes?" We let out a roar of laughter,

which broke the ice, and I mean after that, I mean we were just ...
we couldn't do anything else but hold each other until we'd both
cried our eyes out. It was a really wonderful reunion.

'Luckily my mother had Scottish relatives living in Glasgow
and one of the chaps offered us accommodation so that I could
get better kitted out. What I had been given I just couldn't wear,
the shoes wouldn't fit or anything. So to my mother's surprise,
when she got to this chap's flat he offered us bed and breakfast
and everything else. Then he asked me what I wanted to do in
Glasgow and I said, well, let's go for a swim. After everything I'd
been through, that caused my mother enormous amusement, but it
somehow felt the right thing to do at the time.

'One of the people in my lifeboat was Professor Day from
Canada. He wrote to the authorities to commend me for a medal.
Apparently there was a big discussion between my parents and
Professor Day, and eventually a letter came from St James's
Palace sending me a certificate of recognition of gallantry whilst
serving in the Merchant Navy in the North Atlantic. I thought it
was all rather strange. It was accompanied with a horrible plastic
badge which said 'for brave conduct'. Later on I found that these
were emergency medals given out in wartime. And then the proper
little oak leaf came after the war and I was told that the other
one was now discontinued. But I always felt totally embarrassed
to be receiving this thing. After all, when was I ever going to
wear it? Even if there had been a suitable occasion, people would
have asked about what it was and what it was all about, which
meant that I would then have to repeat the story. And I was
actually very reluctant to do that, because it was such a distressing
story. So I kept on trying to hide the medal from my parents. They
kept on saying, "Why aren't you wearing your medal?" and I would
say I'd mislaid it upstairs or something like that. I suppose I felt this
was the best way of dealing with a problem, not to say anything.'

Barbara Bech also remembers the comic irony of the fuss over
getting passports stamped. She says: 'I think there was a sort of
reception committee for us, but what amused me was that my
mother's passport actually had to be stamped to say that she had

returned to Gourack with her three children. It wasn't a place where you would normally land, but all the same they went through the formalities. Then we were taken to some big hall where I think the dear old WVS were being busy – as they always were – with clothes and drinks and anything else we needed. Then they sorted out those who were really did need a bit of checking over in hospital. But they took one look at us and decided we were all right. So we were taken up to Glasgow to the Grand Central Hotel during the afternoon and by then all the press were there. There was lots of talking, which I was rather fed up with by then. But the next morning the press were still there at breakfast. Then my mother decided we all needed some clothes. She still had the £10 allowance for each of us, which came to £40 – not an awful lot by modern standards, but probably the equivalent of £400 now if not more. We went to one of the big department stores in Glasgow and fitted ourselves out with raincoats and skirts and jumpers and underwear and shoes and pyjamas.

'I think the next stage was that we were being supplied with free rail passes to go home. Colin Ryder Richardson had tagged on with us, because he and Sonia were the same age and were getting on rather well. Then it had emerged that they couldn't get hold of Colin's parents at the address they'd been given and they were really rather at their wits' ends as to how to look after Colin. My mother offered to look after him, but it was decided we would have a couple of days' break first and they very kindly fixed us all up to go to a little hotel on Loch Lomond. It was a lovely old-fashioned hotel to relax in. Then my father turned up from London to take us all back at pretty much the same time as Mrs Ryder Richardson eventually arrived, and we all went off home. The adventure was over, and really life went back more or less to normal. Back we went to school. Our bicycles were still there to cycle off to school. Our house was still there – including our grandmother, who'd thought she was going to have it all to herself until the end of the war. And so life went on just the same.'

Typical of the confusion surrounding the whole story of the *Benares* was the garbled story received by the Bechs' father. Sonia

Bech explains: 'It's my fault in a way, because I was a terrible show-off when I was a child. There were all these gorgeous men – the reporters – all saying can we hear your story. So of course I got comfortable and did I tell them – I was a little so-and-so. But then, I don't remember which newspaper it was, possibly the *News Chronicle*, got hold of my story. The thing was that for some reason I had told my address in London, 15E Hyde Park Mansions, but I had never mentioned anything about my sister, my brother or my mother. So the *News Chronicle* took it upon themselves to get in touch with my father. He was woken up and told that the *News Chronicle* had interviewed me and that I was all right. But he'd had no idea that we'd even been torpedoed. So when he was told that I was very well and what a lovely daughter he had, he was aghast, and asked, "But what about my wife and my other two children?" Naturally they didn't know anything about them, because I had only been talking about myself, which was very bad of me.

'My father immediately phoned up my mother's sister, Aunty Lily, and said, "This is the most terrible thing, they've been torpedoed and Sonia has survived, but I don't think the others have." My Aunty immediately said, "Oh, well don't worry, don't worry, I will look after Sonia." So I was practically adopted, we always had a special affection for that aunt afterwards. Fortunately, by the morning the next of kin were informed, and off my father went to Loch Lomond to come and fetch us. He had a long train journey to come to us, and we were all reunited. But strangely, I don't remember it being very emotional, it just all seemed to fit in – it's funny, funny how things are. What I do remember is very near the end of the story but it always makes me want to cry. At the railway station at Bognor we all got in a taxi to go back home. We didn't have very many clothes, just the few things we'd bought in Glasgow, but we looked quite smart because we'd had bought these beautiful woollen skirts. When we got to the house, the taxi driver looked at my mother and said, "Madam, I do not want a fare, this has been an honour." I thought that was wonderful, and I still do.'

So for the Bech family the story had the happiest of all endings. The whole family, mother and three children, survived to be reunited with all the rest of the family down in Sussex. Things were very different for the little seavacuee child John Baker. When he arrived back on dry land he was in many ways just at the beginning of a story that even now he is not quite sure is ended. His actual landing in Scotland and eventual homecoming are today just a blur in his memories, so strongly was he preoccupied with what had happened to his older brother, Bobby. At the time, 7-year-old John Baker was clearly suffering from what would be called post-traumatic shock syndrome nowadays. John tries to recall how he felt: 'That period is so vague, but I think we had quite a reasonable time, and they treated us very well in Glasgow. They did their best for us. All the children that survived, their parents came to take them back home again. And of course, my Mum and Dad were no different. They came. I expect they were pleased to see me, I was pleased to see them – but I don't know quite how pleased they were, it's difficult to say, I can't remember. But I suppose they were concerned enough to come and fetch me and take me home, which I was very pleased about really.

'I'm not even sure how long it took to get to Glasgow after we were rescued. I just wasn't really aware of time or anything. But I knew I was there in Glasgow and I knew that Bobby wasn't. When we arrived on land we were just wearing what we had, pyjamas and big plimsolls – mine were probably about five or six sizes too big for me, and stuffed with newspapers. We boys stayed with some kind people, and we went and saw the Provost of Glasgow, who gave me a book. *The Red Axe* it was called, I don't know by whom. It was very sophisticated, I thought my father might like to read it. I don't suppose he ever did. I have a vague memory of staying in this lovely place with a little summer house in the grounds and we made that the captain's cabin. And of course, being the youngest of the group, I was allowed to be the captain. There are a lot of time lapses, but what I really remember, when we got home, was that it took me a full six months to realise that Bobby wasn't gonna come home.'

Like most of the survivors picked up by the *Hurricane*, Beth Cummings also had a sense of dislocation and confusion to begin with. She says: 'It wasn't until we arrived in Gourack that I saw Bess again for the first time since we'd been rescued. It was so strange really, I was taken to see her and Eleanor Wright, the other girl survivor. Because we were the only three girls rescued, apparently. Then the port medical officer came aboard and I thought that was rather odd. It would have been normal procedure, but I always remember thinking it didn't seem appropriate. Anyway, they found us clothes. I wore a pair of corduroy trousers belonging to Dr Collinson, the ship's doctor. We were then taken ashore and went by ambulance to a hospital in Greenock.

'They put us into this long ward – Eleanor Wright, Bess and myself, and Thomas Mann's daughter, Monika Lanyi, who lost her husband on the ship, and also Lillian Towns from New Zealand, who I think was one of the assistant escorts, and one other lady. Bess and I were bruised from head to foot, absolutely bruised, our ankles weren't at all that good either. And the medical officer of the hospital, he was so thrilled with our bruises he brought all his doctors to see them! We were black and blue from head to foot, absolutely black and blue. We were all given a jug of milk and a siphon full of soda water, and we were told to drink as much milk and soda water as we could – presumably something to do with the seawater.

'I think we had been there for ten days and then my mother came. But for her, what had actually happened was that she thought we'd already arrived in Halifax, Nova Scotia. Because on the Thursday night before we landed in Gourack, my uncle had rung her up and said, "Beth'll be all right, she'll be in Halifax now." Which obviously would have been the case. So she was feeling better, and then that night the doorbell went, and there stood two men in bowler hats and black overcoats. They came in and said, "Your daughter Elizabeth," using my full name, "has had an accident and she's in a hospital in Scotland, would you like to go and see her?" But my mother still didn't really have a clue what was the matter. They promised her a travel warrant and they left. Little did she know, those men had a lot more difficult jobs to do that night, because I was the only Liverpool survivor of 12 children. They were having to go to Joan Irving's mother and father, and Betty Unwin's mother and father, and Aylsa's, and the three brothers that were killed, and the parents of the two little Spencer children. But my mother didn't know that. She was only thinking that I'd had an accident, I was in hospital, she must go and see me. And so she went.

'She got the midnight train from Lime Street Station in the middle of Liverpool. She told me she was ages in Lime Street because there was an air raid on and they locked the gates, so she was sitting in a darkened train for an hour before it went. And she was obviously thinking about my father because of him being killed in a train, so all these things would be going through her mind. She arrived in Glasgow early morning and got the other train to the hospital, but when she got there she didn't know where the hospital was. She asked this great big, tall Scottish policeman and he took her to a café first, so she must have looked in a bit of a state. He said, "Now, you sit here," and went and got her a cup of tea with a lot of sugar in it. He said, "Now, you drink that tea. When you've finished it, come and see me and I'll show you where the hospital is."

'My mother was the first one to arrive at the hospital, and she was absolutely overjoyed. But she kept saying, "There's only three of them left." Mum was so overcome eventually that the nurses took her to a private ward and let her go to sleep in there for some hours. But she really was overjoyed, she couldn't believe it. Then she decided to come stay in Greenock to be with us in the hospital and one of the nurses put her up in her own home. She came every day to see us. She was absolutely overjoyed, she couldn't believe it, she absolutely couldn't believe it. And when I saw how happy it made my mother, my thing was that I was thrilled, absolutely. It was the fact that I'd managed to survive for her benefit, because that was really what it was all about. So I was thrilled. I felt relieved, I was happy to think that she was happy too. We were a very wonderful pair, my mother and I. We were great chums and I felt, oh I'm glad I didn't go to Canada. That's strange that, but that was really what I felt, I'm glad I didn't go to Canada. I'm glad I didn't get there, I'm glad to be home. That was the way I felt.

'My mother did cry when she saw us. She was so upset. But when she came back to the hospital next time, she had with her this cross, and she said, "This was given to me by a neighbour, for you." A neighbour she hardly knew. She'd come across to my mother and said, "Give this to Beth, it'll be a help to her." And I've had this cross all these years and I wear it every day. And the effect of this little gift on my mother was amazing. She decided she would go out and buy two more crosses, one for Bess and one for Eleanor. She had an awful job in Glasgow, they were very few and far between then, but she managed to buy the two gold crosses.

'At first, I remember I was actually a bit overcome at seeing my Mum, but she was there, and it was such a relief. It was like a shining light to me to see my mother, because she was the one person ... I was just overcome actually, but she was overcome too, of course. She cried a bit, but she was very, sensitive too. My mother always was actually, and she just hugged me. We kissed each other and that was how it went. We were thrilled, thrilled to be with each other again. I think all I said, was "Oh Mum," I think that was it, "Oh Mum, I love you." I think it was that sort of thing and she hugged me. She said, "Oh, thank goodness," she said, "Thank God you're home." And that was the way it was.'

CHAPTER TEN

The Aftermath

Very, very few people survived the torpedoing and sinking of the SS *City of Benares*. There were a total of 406 passengers and crew aboard the ship when it set sail from Liverpool on Friday, 13 September 1940. Only 148 came back. The chilling statistic is that nearly 90 percent of all the seavacuee children died in the tragedy. The initial figure was even worse. Only seven out of the original ninety seavacuees were rescued by HMS *Hurricane*. When the six boys from lifeboat number 12 turned up a week later, that made a total of thirteen children from the Children's Overseas Reception Board scheme still alive. On Monday, 23 September the *Daily Mirror*'s front-page story was headlined: '83 Children Die as Huns Sink Liner in Storm.' What possible reaction was there, in the face of such terrible news? It was only natural to concentrate on the positive, celebrating the arrival home of the survivors, rather than dwelling on the appalling deaths of so many very young children. So the survivors were treated like heroes. Derek Bech and his sisters, and Beth and Bess, and later Fred and Kenneth and their pals, were all treated to massive welcome celebrations and huge press attention.

At first the survivors were rather dazed by all this sudden, intense activity, coming at a time when they were still shocked by their experience. Derek Bech explains: 'Having survived it all, I think we were stunned really by the whole thing. I don't think we had an instant feeling of relief. For me certainly, the awfulness of it hit later when we heard about all the terrible stories. At first, coming back on the destroyer after being rescued, it was again an exciting time for me. After all, I was a 9-year-old boy, and it couldn't help but be yet another adventure which I was going through. But then, when we got back, then we began to realise we had been through a terrible ordeal. Partly it was when we arrived at Gourack, where we were met by a whole contingent of newspaper reporters, and it began to sink in that this was something really out of the ordinary that we had survived.

'We were taken to a reception centre at the Grand Hotel in Glasgow and everybody was buzzing around us asking, "Oh, what was your story and what happened to you?" The whole time I would be telling the same story over and over to all these reporters and people. Somebody would come along and it was "What happened then?" There was a lot of excitement. And of course, not only were you telling your own story but you were also beginning to hear the stories of the other people – it was through that really that we realised that it had been a terrific event. In later years it became obvious that this was the greatest loss of life of children at one time during the war. Of those 90 children on the Government scheme, 77 drowned that night. HMS *Hurricane* managed to rescue seven at the same time as it picked up my mother and sisters and me. There were another six rescued a week later by HMS *Anthony* – but on the first count we all thought only seven seavacuee children had survived out of the 90. That's a terrible loss, and of course it was after our experience that the evacuation scheme was stopped completely. They couldn't risk the lives of other children and so the *City of Benares* was the last evacuee ship sent out by the Government. Other people did sail later, but not on a Government scheme.'

The children may have been treated like returning heroes, but was this how they felt? The nation may have been looking for something positive to cling on to amidst so great a tragedy, but was that the truth for the children themselves? Colin Ryder Richardson's feelings in the wake of the tragedy are very revealing. He was ill at ease with the adulation right from the beginning: 'I was thinking of it only recently, because a lady wrote to me to remind me that she had been sent to see me as a 9-year-old girl immediately after the sinking, to get me to talk to her about my experiences. She had been asked by her parents to come to see me and go to the cinema together and things like that. They wanted to see whether I would, sort of, disgorge information about it all and how I felt – my distress or otherwise about the whole affair. But it was all rather strange really, and in the kind of situation like that, you just don't want to talk about it. I fear it takes you, well, 65 years later to be able to really talk about the situation, and even now I find it difficult.

'I think for me one of the difficulties was that it came at a particular time in my life, because I was aged 11. Before I went on board the ship, girls were really not in my life at all. I was at a single-sex boys' school and things like that. But in the ship you were landed with girls, and I was suddenly aware about Sonia and her sister and meeting them, and it was probably about the first time I'd really met a girl of my own age. There was an attraction, there was no doubt. Sonia has said it about me and certainly I was attracted. It was, if you like, the time of puberty, and I think having all that going on made it a lot more complicated. I feel in a way that had I been younger, I would not have been so aware of the experience. Again, if I had been older, I might have been able to rationalise some of it. There was an American lady, with whom I've been in contact since, who was in the same lifeboat as me. But she was 21 at the time and her resulting feelings are not the same as mine. I think maybe when you go through a trauma like that at the age of puberty, it gains a special significance. I have felt that I've been carrying a very big cross on my back for the rest of my 65 years after the experience.

'I still have constant nightmares, it's very difficult. These days people go into various forms of therapy, but in 1940 these kind of things weren't thought of. The attitude was: it's tough luck, now get on with your life. And probably at the time it seemed right and reasonable, but many people who suffered these experiences clearly needed more. I've read quite a lot about this since, and found that other people in these sort of situations take it in a similar way. They may be a hero at the time, but afterwards they find they're very reluctant to talk about it. When you are through it, the distress of the whole event becomes just too much. I have nightmares when I wake up screaming and I'm just back in the lifeboat or back on the ship, back into some part of the story. They have that saying, "Lest we forget" – well, you don't forget, you never forget. War veterans from all over, when they start talking about their experiences in the trenches and battles and things like that, they know what it means, they remember, and they're reduced to tears. It's not unique to me, it's general to those people who've gone through those experiences. The people who don't understand are those who've never been in these experiences. They have never truly understood the terror that is instilled in war and battle. You can't rationalise it. It's just terrifying and that's it.

'There are things like whenever I'm confronted with height, if I go towards Beachy Head or if I were going up Blackpool Tower or anything else like that, I really get nervous. I have a fear of heights and every time I have the fear of heights it takes me back to standing on the liner, on the main deck, waiting to get into the lifeboat. Seeing the high seas and everything else, and the distress, and the orders, and everything else happening. It just brings it back as if it was yesterday, it's as serious as that. It never really leaves you. It's with me now. Talking about it, I find it very difficult not to burst into tears ... very difficult.'

Another feeling commonly reported among those who have survived disasters is guilt – mainly at being left alive when so many have died. For Barbara Bech this has been a particular issue, because she actually felt guilty about the whole trip, even before the tragedy happened. Her feelings of doubt began right from the time she was saying goodbye to friends and family: 'It was before we were leaving to go up to Liverpool to catch the ship, we went to say goodbye to my mother's sister and her husband and my younger cousin – they lived not very far away. Their elder son was home on leave from the Air Force, and so naturally we said goodbye to him as well. But – and I always remember, I remembered afterwards – he looked at us and said, 'You're going all the way to Canada, I think you're rats.' I suppose you would laugh, but I thought, "Oh dear, yes, rats leaving a sinking ship."

I was thinking of Britain, of course. At that stage I had no idea our ship was literally going to sink.

'And then, after we got back and it was all over, this all came back to me. Everybody was saying what a dramatic thing it had been, how terrible and all the rest of it. But what I was thinking was that it was really our own fault. We didn't have to go in the first place, and we shouldn't have gone. I didn't want to talk much about any of it, not about being brave or what a great adventure or anything – because I actually thought the whole thing was something rather to be ashamed of. I felt it had fundamentally been running away. It was something we weren't supposed to be doing. I had listened to Churchill's speeches and seen all the preparations that were frantically being made with sandbags. I'd seen quite a bit of the Battle of Britain. So I knew how hard we were trying, how hard we were fighting.

'I remember the last day we were allowed down to the beach before it was closed, our bathing huts – that we'd all used all summer – already had soldiers in them who'd come back from Dunkirk. So I knew everybody else was getting ready to fight to their last gasp. I walked back up to our house, and when I got back I suddenly thought, we've been running away. I still think now it's rather a shaming thing to have done. So I rather clammed up, because I genuinely felt we'd been brought up as a family to be very proud of being British. This was partly because we weren't completely British, but we were British born and we were very privileged to live in Britain and be able to say we were British – so I was very proud of this fact. And then to hear dear old Churchill with nothing to offer but blood, toil, tears and sweat. And then that we were going to fight on the beaches and on the landing grounds. I began to put all this together and thought, what would Churchill say to us? What my cousin said – rats!

'So I think that was why I really didn't want to remember it very much. I didn't want to dwell on the voyage and the sinking and being rescued, because it was just one of the endless awful things that happened in those times. I hadn't done anything particularly heroic as far as I was concerned. I'd just sat in the lifeboat hoping to be rescued. I hadn't saved anybody, I hadn't done anything. So it was just one of those things. Everyone wanted to hear because, yes, it was a good story, but I didn't really want to make a big thing out of it. It was just one episode in a great war. Every day the headlines in the newspapers were full of one dreadful story after another. We'd only been back a month when one of the boys in my form at school and his mother were killed when a bomber got engine trouble and unloaded its bombs. It was just unlucky, it wasn't an air raid, and they were killed outright just like that. Then we heard all about Coventry being bombed and hundreds of people being killed in their beds. And airmen were being killed every day in dog fights and there was everybody else who was being bombed in London. So our little adventure didn't really seem any more important than any other – in fact rather less important, because speaking for myself I'd never really felt in great danger.

'I really didn't like the idea of having tried to get out of something that everyone else was putting up with and then trying to make out that I'd been so wonderful because things had gone wrong. I wasn't fighting on the beaches and on the airfields and all the rest of it with Churchill. I was running away, and that was not good. I think I've felt that ever since. Personally speaking, for myself it had not been a horrendous experience. But for those poor children, that was absolutely terrible. Compared with those little children who lost their lives in conditions that were ghastly, my story was not really very important.'

So in the days, months and eventually years following the sinking of the *Benares*, the young child survivors had any number of difficult emotions to cope with. Initially they experienced relief and elation at having survived and being reunited with their parents, but those very feelings quickly gave rise to half-formed anxieties and guilt. To be rejoicing when so many are grieving is in itself a difficult situation. Their public treatment as heroes by the press and public – encouraged by the Government – didn't help at all in the process of coming to terms with their confused thoughts. And there was the long-term legacy of deep-seated fears and recurring bad memories.

Kenneth Sparks, from lifeboat number 12, stresses that the huge fuss really didn't help matters at all. He points out: 'There was another boat picked up the day after us and they had all died. Everyone in that boat had died of starvation or thirst – presumably whoever was looking after their rations hadn't organised it properly. So when they presented me with this watch for my heroism, well, as far as I'm concerned, I was surviving. It was nothing to do with heroics at all. We were making the best of it. We were gonna live and that was the end of it – and long gone since, I'm glad to say.

'I didn't think I was a hero. I hadn't done anything heroic, I just survived, like a lot of people did in the war. In fact George Purvis, who was running our boat, he got torpedoed at least twice more. Now that was heroic, to go back and do it again. So no, I didn't feel a hero, and basically I was quite a shy boy. I wasn't able to go straight back to school because I had to go into hospital with trench feet, and it was some little while before I went back to school. In those days they had an assembly in the school first thing and the day I went in, I was cheered and clapped. But I thought, oh my gawd, what have I done wrong! I think I only did about three more months at school before I finished up altogether because I left school at 14, but for that time I was treated as a hero, even though I didn't feel like one.

'After school I was put into work initially in the GEC factory. I was making small parts for Spitfires on a milling machine. But at 15 you could sit an exam and depending on the results you became either a clerk, or you can go in the Navy. I passed the exam, but I decided I would rather go in the Navy, and before I knew what happened, my father had me down for the medical and he put me in the Navy for boy service, so I did the hostilities in the Navy. I think my father and my stepmother did want me out of the way, but also my Dad's brother had been in the Navy all his life, so he thought that it would be a good life for me. But I suppose my parents had been through it as well. My stepmother told me afterwards that Mr Shakespeare who ran the CORB scheme actually came round to the houses in London to tell them that the children had not survived the sinking of the *City of Benares*. I've still got the paper where it says I'm dead, funnily enough. Or missing, presumed killed. It makes you think.

'I was the only Wembley child that actually lived, out of all those that went, and there were an awful lot of them that didn't survive. I can't remember how many of us there were on the scheme exactly, but it was quite a lot – maybe 25, 30 of us. The only child to survive who lived anywhere near me was Derek Capel; he lived in Middlesex, but not in Wembley. Out of all the Wembley children, I was the only boy to survive. There was one lad, Terry Holmes, who was actually picked up still alive by HMS *Hurricane*, but I gather he didn't make it through the night. Terry was one of my best friends – he only lived just up the road from where I lived and we used to play together quite a lot. But I was the only boy that survived from the Wembley area.

'It was the war. Wartime, these things happened, you were fatalistic about it, I think. I'm pretty certain that's how I was about it. If your number was on it, you went, and that was how you looked at it in those days. I remember there was an air-raid shelter closer into the centre of London that got smashed with everybody in it, and it was nearly every single child from one particular school that died.'

Kenneth had lost his best friend, Terence Holmes, but another to die on board the *Hurricane* that first night after the rescue was Alan Capel, Derek's younger brother. The news was broken gently to Derek, who was simply told that his brother hadn't been found, rather than that he had actually died on board the *Hurricane*. Derek remembers: 'It was done in the best possible way, but for me the feeling was just pure shock. Because I was certain he was safe. And you literally lapse into shock, it was terrible. They took us to this hospital place – it had been a military hospital after Dunkirk but had been closed down. I can remember our treatment now for shock, or whatever they call it these days, stress or something, but then it was all just shell shock. They called us together into one ward. We dragged ourselves over there – we had found that, like all military places, they had terrifically highly polished floors and so by getting a pillow we could slide ourselves along on the floors, because of course, we still couldn't really walk.

'So we were there, and they moved all the beds together, and up came a very high-ranking officer, with a lovely big, shiny Sam Browne belt on and red bits on his shoulders. He stood there in front of us and he said, "You lads have had a very rough experience, now you must pull yourselves together," and with that he left. That was the treatment you got in those days. It was! I'll never forget that, because we nearly burst out laughing, because it was so crazy. I don't know if that was the treatment for everyone then – I feel sorry for the poor old troops who got shot if they were just told to pull themselves together after being blown up. But the thing was, I felt guilty. And I felt guilty nearly all my life.

'It was only when we had our first big reunion that I found out that my brother had been picked up alive by HMS *Hurricane* on the first day, but had died of exposure on the ship and been buried at sea. I didn't find that out for 50 years I suppose, over 50 years. Even then it was only because one of the people at the reunion was a crew member on the *Hurricane* and he told me about it. He said most of the crew and the surviving seavacuee escorts and other survivors were at the funeral – the burial at sea. He described everyone crying to see such a waste, and that really hit me, that did. After that I realised that I couldn't have done anything anyway. It wasn't until later that we found the diaries of Father Rory O'Sullivan and discovered more of my brother's story. Father O'Sullivan had been holding my brother while we were still on the *Benares* when a sailor said, "I'll put the little one on one of the bigger lifeboats up forward." He took Alan away with him. I didn't realise that, I thought Rory was still holding him. But he wasn't. I'm afraid Rory O'Sullivan had a breakdown afterwards, he had been having blackouts. So it wasn't until many, many years after the sinking that I found out about what had really happened to my brother.

'Only then could I began to come to terms with it and realised that, probably, even if he had been on the lifeboat with me, as a youngster of only 5 he was unlikely to have lived anyway. So maybe it was meant to be that way. And that's the way it went then. I only wish my parents had known. One of the most difficult parts of it all was getting home and finding that my parents had been notified that both I and my brother were dead. My parents had a long letter from the Children's Overseas Reception Board, stating that both my brother and myself had been torpedoed and were lost at sea and were considered dead. My parents had given me up long before I was rescued. So when I was in the lifeboat they thought I was already dead. I had been sitting there in the lifeboat, and being rescued, it was wonderful – but I didn't realise that my parents had already passed me off as dead. There had actually already been a service in the local church, praising both my brother and myself. So I really was back from the dead, I think.

'But when I first saw my mother and everything, she was so good about it all. She cuddled me, made me comfortable – I was unable to walk – and then that's when the problems started, I think. I don't know what happened exactly, I can't remember anything after that for a long while. I'm told I was in Ashford General Hospital for several months, still unable to walk, but I can't remember it at all. All I remember is coming out of the hospital and my mother having a thing like a glorified pushchair to wheel me around in. Then one of the patrons of the hospital offered us a cottage down in Cornwall to get over everything. My father couldn't come because he was a railwayman, so my mother and I and my baby sister all went off down to Cornwall and that was part of the cure, to see that part of the country. By this time it was early the following year, about February I suppose. And it did help a lot, because it was so quiet and peaceful. There was no rat race, no neighbours running in and out all the time, which was happening up in London. In London in the suburbs during the war you'd have neighbours in the house all the time. My mother was a good needlewoman and she spent half her time making siren suits and things like that. People would bring old coats and blankets and she'd make siren suits for them, and she would get out any old fur coats that came along and use the fur to trim the suits for the girls.

'So by comparison, Cornwall was so peaceful. It was so nice and the people were so lovely. They were very quiet people, kept very much to themselves. But you'd wake up in the morning, you'd open the front door, and there would be a rabbit hanging on it or a cabbage down by the front door and a few potatoes, something like that. You never knew who gave them to you, but there they were. But even then, I always had that feeling that it was my fault I didn't hang onto Alan. For years after, all that time I had been thinking if only I had hung onto him, I didn't realise that he'd been rescued until then.'

The fact that Derek was misinformed about his brother Alan's fate was typical of the various official mix-ups and mistakes surrounding the voyage of the *Benares*. In the aftermath of the sinking there was a great deal of criticism about the *Benares* and the CORB scheme in general, voiced not only by the press but also by the adult survivors and by their rescuers aboard the *Hurricane* and the *Anthony*. Lt-Cdr Richard Deane, the Royal Navy reservist who had offered his help to Admiral Mackinnon, was foremost among the adult survivors to write a detailed report of his criticisms. Among the CORB escorts, Marjorie Day raised her concerns about the way the voyage had been handled. Members of the *Benares* crew, including the purser John Anderson, pointed out that if other tactics had been employed the disaster could have been avoided.

The main issues raised centred on three stages of the tragedy. First there was the handling of the convoy itself, and here the criticisms were that the Commander-in-Chief of the Western Approaches had not been informed that the *Benares* was carrying seavacuee children; that the ship was not treated as a 'mercy ship' (i.e. it was neither protected within the convoy nor carried identifying markings); that the escort left the convoy too early; that the convoy did not scatter at the time stated in its orders; that there was confusion between the Admiralty and CORB organisers; and that no ships had been instructed to stand by for rescues by the Admiralty, despite the fact that CORB was convinced this had been done. The second area of concern was the actual abandonment process. It was noted that only one full drill of both crew and passengers had ever taken place; that the lifeboats appeared poorly maintained; and that the launching of the lifeboats had been erratic and inefficient, causing great loss of life. The third stage at which problems occurred was in the rescue itself. Officials at CORB wanted to know why it had taken 16 hours for a ship to arrive at the scene.

By October the momentum of criticism had reached the level where the Ministry of Shipping had to begin an internal inquiry. Among the questions it had to answer were those raised by Lt-Cdr Deane in his report to the Admiralty. He wrote, 'When did our escort leave us and why did they not return to pick us up?' He queried, 'Sixteen hours seems to have been an excessive time before rescue ships could come to the scene.' Another point stressed in his report was, 'Surely if a ship is carrying evacuee children it should be put in the centre of the convoy, masked by the other 17 or 18 ships in proper formation.'

Geoffrey Shakespeare MP, then the Under-Secretary of State for Dominions Affairs, was the man who organised the CORB scheme. The question he wanted answering was, 'I understood from the Admiralty, that in a convoy, one or two ships were told to act as rescue ships and were charged with the duty of stopping to rescue survivors of any ship that was torpedoed.'

As the inquiry progressed, it became clear that communication – both between CORB and the Admiralty, and within the Admiralty itself – had been poor. The Commander-in-Chief of the Western Approaches, Admiral Nasmith, had not been informed by the Admiralty that the *Benares* was carrying children, and on 5 October 1940 he demanded to be kept informed in future. But the big question that nobody seemed able to answer, was why Admiral Mackinnon, the commander of the convoy, had acted as he did – especially in holding the convoy together at slow speed for so long after it had lost the protection of its escort. Replying to insistent questioning on this from the Ministry of Shipping, the Admiralty could only say, 'We have in fact tried to find out from survivors including both the chief officer and the fourth officer, why the commodore disregarded his instructions to disperse at noon on the 17 September, but no information could be obtained on this point.'

Admiral Mackinnon did not survive the sinking, and to this day the reasons for his actions remain a mystery. The files for the period, from the Admiralty Office and the Dominion Office especially, are now available for all to study at the Public Record Office, but tantalisingly they give no glimpse into the thinking of Admiral Mackinnon or of Captain Nicolls, the captain of the *Benares* itself. Did the two men have a clash of personalities, as the crew hinted to Derek Capel at the time? Even in October 1940 that question was already unanswerable, and since it was really at the heart of the whole tragedy, it was perhaps inevitable that it was decided not to hold a public inquiry.

Yet there was one more official investigation into the sinking of the *Benares*. After the war Kapitanleutnant Bleichrodt, the commander of U-boat U48, was tried for war crimes – specifically torpedoeing the *Benares*. Rolf Hilse remembers: 'Yes, he was tried for war crimes but the whole trial only lasted two days and he was acquitted. It was ruled that he hadn't made a mistake, but that the English Government made the mistake.' Rolf believes very strongly that if his commander had known the *Benares* was a seavacuee ship he would not have engaged it, even though rules of engagement came to be flouted later in the war. He says: 'I remember when we found out what had really happened. It was 1941. I got a coded message for the captain, and he said, "What the bloody hell do they want now?" So I handed it to him and he went off and he put on the decoder. Then he come back and said, "Hey Rolf, I think you should read this." So I read it and that's when I found out that there were these children on board. I turned to Bleichrodt and said, "What have we done, Heini?" He said, "It's the British government which forgot to register them under the Red Cross and the Geneva Convention. It should never be where it was." After he found out what happened it must have played on his mind, because he got nervous and started to shake sometimes. Eventually they sent him to Innsbruck for a while, convalescing.

'But Bleichrodt was an officer and a gentleman – one of the old ones, in the Navy long before Hitler came. He was a fair, straight man and I was proud to serve with him. I respected him as an officer, and when he said something you could trust him. When he said, "That ship shouldn't have been there with children on board, they should run on their own, they weren't even registered under the Geneva Convention," I agreed with him. They should have had the flags on, Red Cross flags. All the lights should have been on, which nothing was done, and it definitely shouldn't have been in a cargo convoy.'

Rolf may well be right in his assessment of his commander's character. Of all the U-boat commanders operating during the war, only one was convicted of war crimes. Doenitz, the overall commander of the German Navy, was tried at Nuremberg and given the comparatively light sentence of ten years, largely because it was felt that the U-boats and ships under his command had behaved little differently from those of the Allied forces. And we know from the British records relating to the *Benares* that those involved, including, for example, Lt-Cdr Deane, felt that the ship should have been marked or treated differently in some way to make it stand out as a mercy ship, just as Rolf and Commander Bleichrodt himself had pointed out.

Rolf Hilse sums up his memories of the whole tragedy with the simple words, 'We were all in the wrong place at the wrong time.' It is probably the best epitaph there could be for the *Benares*. As the Admiralty note to the Ministry of Shipping said in 1940, 'It appears to us that the balance of advantage would probably lie in saying nothing.' So no public inquiry followed. It was so much easier to blame it all on the war – in the words of officialdom: 'the loss of 256 lives on the *City of Benares* was a war casualty resulting from Germany's unrestricted warfare at sea.'

Essentially, this is true. After all, two previous seavacuation attempts – on the *Arandora Star* and the *Volendam* – had both ended with the ships being torpedoed, though without the terrible loss of life on the *Benares*. Under the CORB scheme overall 2662 children were evacuated to Canada, Australia, New Zealand and

South Africa, with another 838 going to America under a separate scheme. However, by far the majority of these were successfully evacuated during the 'phoney war' before hostilities really escalated. In September 1940, when the *Benares* set out, the circumstances of the war were changing so rapidly that even Churchill found it hard to react and keep pace with events. After the *Benares* sank the seavacuation scheme was quietly abandoned, leaving those parents who still wished to evacuate their children overseas to do so privately. One positive lesson was put into practice, though. All future convoys of any type from that time onwards contained one or two specialist 'rescue ships' whose sole purpose was to rescue survivors if the convoy was attacked, and these saved many lives during the war.

From the stories the survivors tell, it seems that the lack of a Government inquiry into the facts of the sinking of the *Benares* was less of a problem than the lack of opportunity for the child survivors to understand their feelings about it. Among the hard truths for the young children coming home from the *Benares* was that wartime Britain offered very little scope to explore their ongoing emotional turmoil. Perhaps, given the way the Second World War operated on the population of Britain, this was inevitable. Britain really only survived the dark days of 1940 through a national effort of willpower, whipped up by Churchill's stirring oratory. That extraordinary phase of the war was won by a national act of collective denial of personal fears and needs.

So it was that the child survivors of the *Benares* – clearly suffering from what today would be called post-traumatic stress syndrome – were told to cheer up and get on with it. They succeeded to a greater or lesser degree. Fred Steels was one who pulled himself together as instructed, and it is still hard for him now to articulate feelings about the experience: 'Well, I mean, what do you expect from a kid who's come back from the dead – everyone thought he was dead – and then seeing his mother again? For a time it was just something you couldn't cope with – it was just out of this world as far as I was concerned. I think that applied to every one of us. And it's not the sort of thing I'd like to relive though, believe me. No, I certainly wouldn't.

'I think of all the poor kids that went down in the damn things, those lifeboats. There was nearly a 100 kids on that ship, and there was only 13 of us saved – six in our lifeboat that drifted away and seven that were actually picked up by HMS Hurricane, the destroyer that found them 20 hours after the ship had been torpedoed. Well, it's hard to describe – you can't really put a finger on anything and say you felt this or you felt that. For me, it's just the fact that you knew you were alive. I can't think of anything else to say on it.'

Perhaps this was the true price of survival. Certainly, a consistent feature of all the survivors' descriptions of their experiences is the degree of stoicism they display. Most of the stories show how the children were able to put their feelings to one side and concentrate purely on survival. But they weren't unique in this. Britain at war had set the stage for their survival feat. At one level the children, along with the rest of the nation, had already spent months preparing themselves for exactly these acts of endurance. Beth Cummings explains the background attitude that set the context for her own heroism: 'At the time we were convinced we would be invaded anyway. All of us: the nation. And as children, well, we knew about the Germans of course, and we'd heard lots of stories about them, and I think it was a question of wait and see. We were prepared for invasion, or for anything. We would wait and see and accept whatever happens in the right spirit, as British subjects. And it was really important that Winston Churchill was doing an awful lot to help us accept all those things and to fight back. So we didn't really fear. I remember thinking "I wonder which way they'll come?" At the back of my mind I did wonder, "Now will they come?"'

'But that's the way you were, and it was a hit-and-miss business. It was one of those things, and that feeling applied to all of us. I think there were a good crowd of people in this country at the time. I think we accepted a lot. I honestly believe that the way we were helped tremendously, not only by Churchill, but also by circumstances which contributed to the fact that we didn't get invaded, was really quite remarkable. I think we all looked upon it as a bit of a miracle, actually. And as a British girl there was always this feeling that we were British and we were fighters. Even if they invaded, we thought we'd be all right. We considered we'd always been fighters, all down the years. So I don't think we were that frightened of an invasion. I believed we would cope with it in our own way, in our own British way. I was sure of that. Quite sure. It was a definite thing that we would fight them. There's no two ways about that. In our own way, whoever you were, you would fight somehow. And it was just a question of seeing what would happen when they came. Even today, I feel that we would have coped very, very well if they had actually arrived. I'm quite sure about that.'

Another factor in her favour was that she was physically very strong and healthy. She remembers: 'Very shortly after my mother made the application for me to go on the CORB scheme, she was asked to take me for a medical. It was very extensive – heart, lungs and all of this, height, weight and all the usual things. I seemed to be there for an awful long time, but I must have passed it because they accepted me. But with hindsight that was obviously part of the whole thing, that we would have to be physically fit, both for the journey and to live in Canada. This was really the point of the whole medical, that we had to be fit to cross the Atlantic. The idea wasn't to live in Canada permanently, of course, but to come back, and if the war was still on, then to join one of the services and fight for the country.'

But even though she was physically strong, Beth's 19 hours clinging to the side of a lifeboat left her with lifelong health problems: 'For years and years afterwards I had nodules, quite big ones, down at the base of my fingers on both hands. I can still feel it where they were, very peculiar little knobs on each hand right across the palms, which didn't go for years, and then gave rise to arthritis. And I started going deaf quite young, only in my late 30s, which I think may have been something to do with it – possibly the seawater and the exposure.

'For me personally as a 13-year-old girl at the time, I was just waiting to join the Wrens or one of the other services. This was the way you were, and at 13 we were quite grown up in a way. We had a lot of common sense. We were prepared to fight in our own way. And I would soon be 14, so that made me feel a bit older and more confident. Yes, I'm quite sure that we girls would have been very good, we would have coped.'

So when it came down to it and Beth faced her own personal part of the war, she was well equipped, both physically and mentally, for survival. And as she knew she would, Beth coped. Her own health and resilience were her two greatest allies. But the context for her survival was set by the speeches of Churchill, with their extraordinary rhetoric, at once rousing and fatalistic. This she has in common with all the survivors of the *Benares*. Their ability to accept what was happening to them, without wasting mental energy on questioning and self-doubt, was a key part of their survival. But it was probably less helpful when it came to coping with the aftermath of their traumatic experience. At this stage, the lack of any meaningful counselling made it difficult for the survivors to come to terms with what had happened. Some, like Beth and her friend Bess Walder, had friends and family they could talk it through with – and retelling the story in later years was to become therapeutic in itself. But for those who had lost siblings, and for the boys especially, the whole episode came to be buried in a way that was not beneficial in the long term. Probably more than any of the children, John Baker would have benefited from the kind of counselling that would be available as a matter of course nowadays.

He admits: 'I was a pain after I got back from the *Benares*. I was evacuated again for a while, but it wasn't a happy experience. I didn't want to be away from home and so I rebelled, I'm afraid. I played with matches. I didn't light any fires or anything like that, but I knew where they kept the matches and so I used to go and find them and light them. That was naughty. Then I fell out with one or two kids, had one or two little scraps. But I wasn't happy. Bobby wasn't there, and I didn't want to be there. I wanted to be at home. I was just an unhappy chappy.

'When Mum and Dad had picked me up and we came home, it was quite a long period of time before I realised that Bobby was never gonna come home. It was about six months, when it suddenly hit me. I was walking down Uxbridge Road actually, in Southall, when wham, it suddenly came home to me. So it was pretty bad at that time. But I don't think we ever talked about it as a family, not really. It's hard to remember how we discussed it, or whether we really did. Because Mum was just as sad as I was, of course, and her memories were shattered as well as mine were. So I think we just sort of sort of compartmented it to shut it off. I suppose I was difficult – difficult for other people to live with me as I was trying to cope with the situation.

'At the time, 65 years ago when I was a little boy of 7, I didn't know how I felt emotionally. My emotions were totally tied up with trying to find my brother, because he was my big brother and where was he? I couldn't find him and there was no indication to me that he wouldn't be around somewhere. It wasn't until that moment on the Uxbridge Road down in Southall ... you know, of all the children that went from Southall in Middlesex – and there were nine of them, with a guardian – I was the only one that got back.

'It was a sadness. It must always have been there, but with the happenings of the time, in order to survive as a human being you had to put all those bad memories behind you. I spent 40 years forgetting and putting it into a little box in my mind. It wasn't until there was a reunion that the box was opened slightly. Really what I wanted to know was if anybody else knew what had happened to Bobby. I wanted to know, I wanted the door to be closed finally. I used to have these funny, wild ideas that he had been picked up and had gone somewhere else. Maybe he had been picked up by the Germans and taken to Germany, I don't know. You don't know these things. I used to have these little fancy ideas. This is why I suppose I put it into a box and shut the door.

'It's only at moments – like the reunions – that I open the door, and open the box, and ... and I don't always like what I see inside. I don't know how I'm gonna get this out, but this is something I haven't faced, can't come to terms with, that whatever has happened in my life in the intervening period – my life since the *Benares* – I'm here because of what Bobby did for me. He possibly gave me his lifejacket, and he saved me from going down and getting lost. And I've had many happy years. I mean now, after all these years have passed by, Bobby gave a great gift to me and I shall forever be grateful. Because he gave me, possibly gave me, did give me, his lifejacket and he has given me 65 years of life which he didn't have. So I'm grateful.'

And in this John speaks for all the living survivors of the sinking of the *Benares*. Of the 13 seavacuee children to be brought back home, more than half are still alive 65 years later, enjoying happy retirement all over the country. Beth Cummings and Bess Walder remain the greatest of friends – in fact they are now sisters-in-law, as Bess eventually married Beth's older brother. Bess went on to become a primary schoolteacher, and she still retells the story of her amazing survival to each new generation of children. Despite the long-term physical and emotional effects of their ordeal, it is a case of once a survivor, always a survivor. The tremendous resilience and spirit of those *Benares* seavacuees burns just as bright now as it did when they were children setting out on their great adventure, 65 years ago, at the height of the Second World War.

Acknowledgements

John Farren, editor of Timewatch for commissioning the television programme; Assistant Producer, Mary Parsons for her excellent research work; Dan de Waal for his editing skills; Mike Pharey for his sensitivity when filming the interviewees; special thanks to Bess Cummings for introducing us to all the survivors; and our sincere thanks to all the survivors for telling their stories.